Arabia Besieged
A Muslim Insider Looks at Islam's Deepening Crisis

Anwer Sher

Copyright © 2010 Anwer Sher
All rights reserved.

ISBN 1463698178
ISBN-13: 978-1463698171

Printed in the United States of America.

Dedication

To the loving memory of my mother Amita Sher.
To the continued love of Eileen Verdieck, my wife.
To the hope my children Aadil and Ali will see a peaceful world.

Acknowledgements

Writing a book such as this has to be an engaging effort, both within oneself and most certainly with people around you. As much as I can take credit for the words and the thoughts in this book the truth is that a great deal of time and effort was spent in exchanging ideas and thoughts on the subject matter. Thoughts and feelings, especially in politically charged moments like those that face the Middle East, the Arabs and Muslims, are usually the results of a shaping of ideas that are the result of healthy exchanges with people.

I would like to thank my father, Brig Abdul Qayum Sher for always encouraging me to examine and explore and not jump to conclusions. My late mother, Amita Sher, for making me write and to enjoy the passion of writing and reading, and I learned from her enormous energy of writing as she churned out over half a dozen books.

When I started out this book yet again, and as the dust of the US invasion of Iraq was clearing to show a more horrifying image emerge I once again was losing my zest for writing. I recall talking to Eileen, then my life partner and later to be my wife, and she said 'Just write it.' I am deeply indebted to her for the encouragement and space she gave me through her understanding and patience to let me write this book. Her love has carried me through the pages of this book and life.

I am deeply grateful to my dearest friend Gunta Mackars for reading and commenting on the first draft, to Alison Magrath

BOOK TITLE

my friend, confidante and lawyer for her early read and advice on the manuscript and for the discussions on the subject, to Clare Woodcraft and Nicholas Labuschagne for the heated discussions on Palestine and Arab Society.

Most of all I am deeply indebted to Mr. Pranay Gupte, an accomplished author and writer, who spent days editing the manuscript and offering be invaluable advice. He opened a new vista for me in terms of his advice, suggestions, comments and introductions without which I would not have had the courage or the inclination to finish this book. Thank you Pranay, those mangoes were not wasted after all.

I want to thank the following HE Shaikh Nayahan bin Mabarak al Nahayan, HE Mohammed al Gergawi, HE Shaikh Tahnoon bin Saeed al Nahayan, HE Mehdi al Tajir, Mr. William Eagleton and his son Richard Eagleton, the author Michael Fields, Edmund O Sullivan, Linda Route, Professor Lenny Hausman, Tamar Millar, Lesley Gregory, Anthony Harris, Hassan Jarrar, Hassan al Hammadi, Vivian Salama and many others, for their support and wittingly or unwittingly provided me through their discussions a deep insight to the subject matter of this book.

Most of all I acknowledge the many people who I cannot name for their contribution to the book but were instrumental in providing me an inner eye to see this region and its turmoil. It was these people who spoke at length to me about the Arab world and as Muslims how they perceived their world in a rapidly changing environment. I am sure that they will be pleased that I have honored my word in the discretion that was offered to them.

Thank you all.

Anwer Sher
July 2011.

Contents

I	My Muslim Crisis and Yours.	1
II	A World Torn By Mistrust	16
III	Fractured History	75
IV	Understanding The Divisions	122
V	The Arab Nation-State	164
VI	Arab Societal Relations with the West	199
VII	Muslims in A Unipolar World	233
VIII	Looking Ahead	264
IX	Epilogue	295

1

MY MUSLIM CRISIS AND YOURS.

I decided to write this book because, as a Muslim-born man who has spent much of his life in Islamic societies – Pakistan and the United Arab Emirates – I am increasingly alarmed by the deepening crisis of my people and those around them. Some parts of my world have already slid into irreparable chaos, and some other sections are slipping toward a point beyond which societies may implode.

In the wake of 9/11 and the war in Iraq, and the killing of Osama bin Laden, much of the world outside of the Middle East and Muslim societies is feeling the impact of the social, cultural and political crises in which Islam finds itself. That's why I'm calling this book "Arabia Besieged." By "Arabia" I don't mean only the Arabian littoral states of the Gulf. For me – as for tens of thousands of like-minded Muslims – "Arabia" is a metaphor for Islamic societies that are under siege on account of the impositions of the outside world and the exigencies of their own domestic conditions.

Arabia Besieged

I first thought of writing this book in September 1990, a month after Saddam Hussein invaded Kuwait and created a crisis that changed the Arab world as few other events have in contemporary times. I recall discussing the idea of the book with a member of a royal family from the region. He warned me that the region was destined to witness a great deal of change within a short piece of time and "keeping up with the wind" would always be an issue. Like some soothsayer from Arabia's past this Sheikh was so right, even though at that time it was felt that the Gulf War would, in one sweep, bring peace and tranquility to the Arab world.

To put it another way, the prince was saying that any contemporaneous book about the Middle East was doomed to be overtaken by events. He was far too polite to say that, just as many a diplomatic career had sunk in the quicksand of the region, I risked authorial irrelevance if I advanced my notion of putting together a book examining the short-term consequences of Saddam's ill-advised action. The prince suggested that, of course, there was a story to be told by newspapers and magazines, and by the broadcast media – the Internet was still in its infancy then – but that it would be premature to compose a book about "Arabia Besieged."

The prince was prescient. I eventually gave up the idea of the book altogether – although, if truth be told, I made a few feeble attempts to start one, even as I held on to my day job as chief executive of one of the most prominent banks in the United Arab Emirates. Few, if any, of the books written by outsiders about the 1991 Gulf War withstood the test of time, and fewer still achieved the status of being memorable, if only for their prose. Then came the Iraq war of 2003, and, predictably enough, there was a plethora of books on the Middle East, the Arab world, Islam and terrorism. Few, if any, of those books captured what it was like within the entrails and hearts of Arab societies to be subjected to a massive outside military invasion, and the subsequent disruption of everyday life in a region where, arguably, history was born.

And because the central player in the Iraq war was the United States, the only superpower in a unipolar world, most of these books predictably focused on America's role in trying to inject democracy in a region accustomed to other systems of governance. I felt that an insider's account would be useful for a global audience to understand the region's political and social perspectives. I felt there were pressures that had emerged from within these Muslim societies that needed to be addressed – pressures and fissures that had created a siege mentality among Arabs. I often thought of an analogy: an animal that's backed into a corner will act irrationally. I'm certainly not calling my fellow Muslims "animals," but my fear and anxiety remains that the Arab and Muslim world has been backed into a corner for some years from which its actions or reactions may not always be rational. We are already witnessing jihad in various guises, and not only in the attitudes and attire of suicide bombers.

Hence this book finds a place in explaining an insider's view that might shed some light on why the Arab and Muslim world in the situation it finds itself today. Rather than concentrate on the Iraq war, I examine the competing pressures – whether political, social or religious – that are shaping the Middle East and the Muslim world (which extends in an arc from Morocco in the west to Indonesia in the east), and are likely to continue influencing Muslims well into the present century. These are fragile times, because unlike the pressures from the Arab-Israeli conflicts in the post World War Two era – pressures that mostly centered around Jews and Palestinians – Arab societies risk imploding from within because of the rapidly changing politics, sociology and political demography of the entire region. If that happens – and it may well happen – then the resulting chaos and anarchy will be irreversible.

Arabia Besieged

As a veteran high-level executive in the corporate world, it is my business to monitor chaos. It is my business to monitor market trends, which means that the politics and anthropology of societies fall within my purview. But I am not an outsider to the Middle East. My background as a banker and as a CEO in the real estate development industry, my decades-long experience within the region, and my exposure to its people, enable me to understand "Arabia" as an insider. In fact, there's something else that qualifies me to term myself as an "insider" more than most self styled insiders: I possess a "third eye."

You see, I am also a photographer by vocation. When I'm not crunching numbers in my office, or addressing company directors in lushly appointed board rooms, or donning hard hats and visiting construction sites, I traipse around the region taking pictures of everyone from royalty to everyday people, and I take pictures of the animals they adopt – like horses – and I take pictures of children. Through this third eye of mine – the camera lens – I can see for myself the range of emotions of my subjects. I am able to capture the anxieties, aspirations, ambitions, and apprehensions of my subjects. When people open up themselves to you in such a manner, when they allow you to imprint them pictorially, you automatically become an insider.

I am also a columnist for local newspapers in the Gulf, and the author of two previous books, one of them a collection of children's stories. That's why I feel emboldened to say to my readers that you will see perspectives in "Arabia Besieged" that you're unlikely to obtain anywhere else. I am being a storyteller in the bazaar, and this book is a blend of narrative, anecdote, analysis and insight.

The problems that I write about in this book of "Arabia Besieged" will not simply go away through some peace initiative or pact between Washington and, say, Iran, or various factions in Iraq. While the problems of the region predate me, and most likely will outlive me too, what is important never to forget is that the region is extremely fragile, despite its natural resources of oil and gas. And precisely because the region sits at the crossroads of the world, there is a need for a broad based understanding of how the region works and what is in store for us.

I do not claim to be the "Oracle of Dubai," although I am fortunate that I live in Dubai, a place that is as cosmopolitan, tolerant, and engaging as they come. But less than a couple of hours by plane, you will see hatred, destruction, war and religious intolerance. It makes one wonder why one country can achieve peace and prosperity while others are caught in a turmoil that doesn't seem to end. I feel, in speaking to my friends from the West, that their understanding of the region needs to be fine-tuned to see the milestones differently. While the clash of civilizations is a much-touted argument the truth is, as a high-ranking cabinet minister in the United Arab Emirates government said in a recent conversation to me, "It's a clash of ignorance."

In "Arabia Besieged," I am not setting forth to rid the world outside Arabia of its ignorance of this region. But my objective in writing this book is to enhance readers' understanding of local societies and the sensibilities that shape those societies. I feel strongly that it's time that moderate – and, yes, thoughtful – voices such as mine must speak out. Our region has allowed itself for too long to go voiceless, or to let shrill, strident demagogues serve as representatives of the masses when, in truth, these hate mongers act in their own self interest. Who elected them, anyway?

I count myself as a moderate Muslim, even a liberal one, and many of my friends are of the same persuasion. That doesn't make us any less Islamic than those of our brethren who foreswear the ways of the West. But I like to think that, liberals, moderates and conservatives alike, we all share a common concern for our collective future in a world of globalization, a world in which Muslims – as much as Hindus and Catholics and Protestants and Jews and Buddhists and animists – are going to have to work even more relentlessly to improve the economic and social lot of their societies as the expectations of their increasingly young populations keep rising. The reference points and exhortations of earlier centuries simply may not provide adequate solutions for the daily problems of a world of 6.6 billion people, of whom 1.3 billion are Muslims.

Of those Muslims, at least 75 percent are below the age of 30. N. Janardhan of the Gulf Research Center in Dubai points out that the oil-rich region is also very socially backward. The only other region in the world with an income level lower than the Arab world is Sub-Saharan Africa. Arab countries have the world's largest proportion of young people – 38 percent under the age of 14. Janardhan notes that even more alarming is the fact that more than 25 percent of the world's unemployed youth between 15 and 24 years are in this region.

Consider these statistics: Between 2002 and 2025, Saudi Arabia's population is expected to double to 48.5 million, Egypt's likely to grow from 73 to 103 million, and Iraq's, from 24 to more than 40 million. Thus, unemployment and its impact on local economies will be stupendous.

Some leaders in the region recognize the gathering problem. Sheikh Mohammad bin Rashid Al Maktoum, UAE Vice-President, Prime Minister and Ruler of Dubai, in announcing recently that he was setting up a $10 billion fund to help develop a knowledge economy, said that "there is a wide knowledge gap between us and the developed world in the West and in Asia." He added: "Our only choice is to bridge this gap as quickly as possible, because our age is defined by knowledge." However, as Janardhan points out, the most difficult part of the process lies in drawing up a strategy and implementing it.

Janardhan, whose work I respect, points out that the neo-classical economics model recognized only two factors of production -- labor and capital -- for over two centuries. Now "New Growth" theorists emphasize a third dynamic – technology, where knowledge is seen as increasing the return on investment. Taking a cue from this and realizing the need to diversify their oil-reliant revenues, some Gulf Cooperation Council (GCC) countries are attempting to tread the "knowledge economy" route – "one in which the generation and exploitation of knowledge play the predominant part in the creation of wealth," where human capital is the chief source of economic value, and education and training the main tools, Janardhan says.

That's why the Gulf sheikhdoms are investing more than $1 trillion in infrastructure and real estate projects, translating into one of the largest construction booms in the world. The Saudi
Government, for example, is planning to privatize 20 state-owned corporations and institutions. The new economic cities in Rabigh, Hail, Madinah and Jizan, as well as the new industrial city in Jubail, are expected to attract more than $100 billion in investments and create about a million new jobs, according to Janardhan's research.

Dubai is a good example of what scholars such as Janardhan call the "post-oil age" in the Gulf. Crude oil contributes to only about four per cent of the emirate's gross domestic product, down from 50 percent in 1975 – which suggests why Dubai is rapidly transforming itself into a financial, transportation and tourism hub for the region. In Abu Dhabi – the biggest of the UAE's seven emirates and its wealthiest – new development projects will involve expenditures of more than $500 billion over the next 15 years. The emirate is positioning itself as a manufacturing hub, with plans under way for aluminum smelters, as well as aerospace components and shipbuilding ventures. Neighboring Qatar has allocated $130 billion for investments in the next six years, with about 50 percent of it going into the non-oil sectors. Such expenditures, of course, are made possible by the enormous annual revenues from the sale of crude oil and natural gas – so much so that the Gulf countries are building up huge foreign-exchange reserves. For example, Saudi Arabia's foreign assets are conservatively put at $250 billion; Kuwait's reserves overseas have grown from $60 billion in 1995 to more than $200 billion; and the UAE has a nice stockpile of more than $500 billion – and growing.

What is striking is that the oil-rich sheikhdoms have learned important lessons from the 1970s, when many of them squandered their wealth. Now, keeping in mind the rising expectations of increasingly young populations, their leaders are emphasizing economic diversification. As Janardhan puts it, economic reform is also encouraging private sector growth, which in turn is providing competitive and underprivileged nationals with opportunities to take up challenging jobs, rather than rely just on the public sector.

But the demand for education far exceeds supply, says Robert W. Richards, chief executive officer of the Center of Excellence for Applied Research and Training, which was established in 1996 by the Abu Dhabi government. He says that the Gulf countries suffer from a deficient educational system, particularly lacking in providing an adequate foundation for human resource development. "As a consequence, this strategic and wealthy region has failed to generate a capable indigenous workforce that can keep pace with the advanced skills and technological capabilities required. Instead, the region is dependent on foreign technologies and labor," Richards, a Canadian who received his doctorate at Brigham Young University in Utah, says.

Since the academic-industry linkage is a major force in the knowledge economy, the newfound understanding in the region

– in researcher Janardhan's words – is that the learning community will facilitate a rich environment of ideas, creativity and expertise that will stimulate strategic growth for companies. Adds Richards: "The notion behind this is that there is a body of knowledge and a set of business skills that will enhance the likelihood of success of a potential entrepreneur. Exposure to thought leaders from around the world is part of that learning process." Richards' organization – which was the brainchild of UAE's minister for higher education, Sheikh Nayahan Bin Mabarak Al Nayahan – provides specialized student training, promotes entrepreneurship and creativity, and facilitates technological advances. It is part of an ambition master plan to groom today's young people to become leaders of tomorrow. Clearly, the expectation is that by expanding Western and Asian styled universities in the UAE, Qatar and Kuwait, these countries will do what Stanford University did for Silicon Valley -- provide the right human resources. "Perhaps the attempt is also to draw a leaf out of Japan's modern history, which shows the benefits of investing heavily in people," says Janardhan. "However, the Gulf countries must hasten the process of exploring the interaction between technological change and human capital if diversification has to be sustained. At the same time, the next phase of development in the region must focus on bridging the gap between research and application. The youth must be empowered with tools required to face the challenges of the new economy. Crucial factors that could help meet these requirements are e-learning and e-education."

Sheikh Nayahan has stressed that the medium of education in UAE must be in the language of globalization, English. I recall what the architect of modern Singapore once told a group of young Arab and Asian leaders: "What we did was to switch the education from native languages to English and keep native languages as a second language. It was a very difficult thing to do, emotionally. If it were done by legislation, we would have had riots. Instead we let the market decide who got the better jobs.

Parents then began to shift their children into English language schools with the mother tongue as the second language. Forty years later, we are connected with the world because the modern world is in English."

I know a thing or two about the modern world, and I know a thing or two about education. I also know a thing or two about young Muslims, being the father of two sons barely past their teens. I know about their impatience with the speed of change, even though the place where we live – Dubai – is a host of warp speed economic and social change. They are, of course, sons of privilege – I am the chief executive officer of one of the biggest construction projects in the Middle East, and a former banker to royalty in the Arab world – and so their impatience has perhaps more to do with the accouterments of their everyday life – better gadgets, faster cars, flashier clothes. But I also know about the impatience of a vaster cohort of young Muslims specifically in the Arab world, where more than 70 percent of 325 million people are under the age of 25. Many, if not most, of these young Muslims have no access to the privileges that my sons and their friends enjoy; worse, they cannot even aspire to lives of privilege in an Arabia where unemployment rates easily soar beyond 50 percent for young people. You can just imagine the frustrations of these young men and women, and you can begin to understand the inexorable build-up of their resentments of the ruling classes.

Perhaps nowhere in the Muslim world are such frustrations and resentments more evident than in my native country. I was born the youngest son of a Muslim Pakistani army general (who had the temerity – as he sometimes joked – to marry a Hindu woman, Amita Chandra; she bore him two other sons, and two daughters). My father, Brigadier Abdul Qayum Sher – a widower who now lives in Lahore, a splendid 15th century garden city developed by the Mughals – served in the Indian army during the last days of the British Raj, and then, after India was partitioned into India and Pakistan in 1947, served in the Pakistan army with great distinction. All sorts of nice privileges came with life in army cantonments, and my earliest memories are of a retinue of servants whose eagerness to please was only matched by their occasional incompetence.

Although my mother had been a highborn Bengali Hindu who converted to Islam after her marriage to my father, he forbade her from changing her name to a more orthodox Muslim one. He was a man of great tolerance; perhaps the fact that some of his early years were spent in Europe may have accounted for that. Indeed, on their very first visit together in 1946 to my father's ancestral village in the Pathan tribal areas of northwestern Pakistan – where to this day women are covered in the "burkha," a black shroud that falls from head to toe – he told her that he would never countenance it if she donned the burkha. It was a revolutionary gesture on his part – in more contemporary times, it would surely have been labeled as un-Islamic in certain quarters; but all of us in the family were taught that tolerance was more important than labels and symbols. We were taught that forcing someone to be somebody that they were not, never quite worked.

My parents taught me those lessons the hard way – which is to say, they had to shout in order to be heard. Being the youngest of five children, I usually had to assert myself to be heard above the incessant chatter of my siblings. This resulted in a propensity to be very talkative, and inquisitive. My parents tolerated the talkativeness, for the most part. But the inquisitiveness elicited a curious response. "Go look it up," my parents would say. That encouraged me to read from an early age; my eldest sister still maintains that I was reading books before I was five. I was inquisitive about life, people and beliefs; I was never deterred from exploring other cultures beyond Islam and Hinduism.

Arabia Besieged

When in my early youth I had to be imparted religious education, as was normal and expected, my mother insisted that I am not taught to read the Koran in Arabic, but in English (the language we spoke at home), as she insisted I must know what I am reading and understand it. My mother – who wrote books herself – did not want my understanding of my own religion to be screened through a language I did not understand and set the tone for the rest of my life so as to ensure that my understanding of faith was clear and unadulterated and not burdened with the obstacles of language.

When I reflect on those early years of my life, it occurs to me that the very tolerance that our parents fostered in their children enabled us to take different philosophical and theological routes in later years. One of my sisters turned to Shia orthodoxy; other siblings retained their father's Sunni Islam in varying degrees of intensity and observance. My own personal journeys took me from existentialism to Buddhism and made me appreciate the essence of my own religion Islam. None of these travels of the spirit and the mind truly bothered the family in the aggregate, of course – so long as we never forgot our mother's oft-repeated admonition to be "good people."

Being among the "good people" meant tolerance. It meant patience. It meant attempting to understand what it was that explained the underpinnings of other societies and culture. To be sure, my siblings and I grew up in a time of the least radicalism. There was no continuing clash of civilizations. And while Muslims and Hindus were still reeling from the horrific "Partition" by the British colonial rulers that created India and Pakistan from the same cultural womb, and displaced more than 12 million people from their homes in the greatest cross-border movement in history, people of both countries were by and large reconciled to each other's existence. After all, neither nation was about to be dismantled, or returned to the Raj.

My Muslim Crisis and yours

The absence of religious radicalism notwithstanding, the raw feelings left over from the Partition were perhaps slow in the healing. It seemed only natural, therefore, that I pursue studies in international relations. A product of elite private schools in Pakistan – and a victim of frequent canings that were administered to me in recognition of my endless capacity to be a mischief maker in class – I went on to receive a master's degree from Quaid-e-Azam University in Islamabad, one of my country's most prestigious universities. I was only 21 then, and was hired by the Institute of Strategic Studies in Islamabad. As a researcher, I published numerous articles on issues ranging from nuclear proliferation to the strategic balance in the Middle East in the 1970's – and on pretty much anything that caught my fancy. Yet working for a government-run think tank in a country where the definitions of free thought and unhindered research were blurry, I was intrigued when an opportunity unexpectedly arrived to join an international bank. I pounced on it. While politics may have been an alternate career at some point – in view of the fact that my family enjoyed political connections, and I'd also spent five years at a boarding school, Cadet College Petaro, with Asif Zardari, who was to later marry Prime Minister Benazir Bhutto and go on to become the President of Pakistan– I relished being on the outside, especially being part of the international financial community.

In 1981, my bank transferred me from Pakistan to Abu Dhabi, one of the seven entities that constitute the United Arab Emirates, and the wealthiest one because it has most of the federation's oil and natural gas. With the transfer came an immediate interest in the history and peoples of the Middle East – and the fascination with the region continues to this day. Having been fortunate to meet personalities like Wilfred Thesiger, perhaps the most engaging personality who traveled, lived and loved the Arab world, the understanding of the region became more engrained into my thought processes. My banking career brought me in touch with the royalty of the region, most of all with the Al Nahayan ruling family from Abu Dhabi. While my involvement was mainly with the financial work of the family, the access also allowed me to grasp first-hand the unique perspective of the Arab world as the significance of the region in world affairs increased through the 1980s and 1990s. I got to know people of consequence all over the world, from diplomats to financiers to the Palestinian leadership to internationally renowned political commentators who passed through the region. The discussions one held with them and the economic leaders whom I met through banking – especially during my years as the chief executive of a large local bank – set the stage for me to explore more deeply into this fascinating society, all the more because it seemed that the view from the outside seemed disjointed, judgmental and, in a dismaying sense, always incomplete.

On the other hand, the voices from within the region clearly seemed to me that of angry Arabs who spent endless hours narrating the injustices through history; but I heard little by way of solutions for these perceived inequities. For the Arab, irrespective of his standing and background, history and the world had not only been unkind and unjust but had also created a siege around the Arab man's world, where without the acquiescence of the Western powers any change in the political landscape was impossible. Even everyday people – and not just the educated elite – would cite the division of spoils in the Middle East by Britain and France after the Ottoman Empire collapsed in the wake of World War One.

In those years, the emotionally freighted discussions about historical injustices notwithstanding, I heard little about radicalism and fundamentalism within the same Arab societies. These phenomena rose only much later, but I was already starting to sense that the everyday frustrations I'd hear contained the possibility of evolving into more ferocious forms of expression. While my discussions with the youth of the region, and in some cases with disgruntled elements within these Arab societies, did not reveal the extent of the problem that would explode within months of the beginning of the new millennium, new century, it was evident that there was a growing air of discontent within the educated youth of the Arab world. Was the explosive anger of 9/11 visible at that moment? I am not sure; some signals were clear, others too muddled to make sense at the time. I wish now that I'd truly been the "Oracle of Abu Dhabi" at the time.

I still don't qualify to be any sort of oracle, of Abu Dhabi or of Dubai. I do not have an agenda to pursue for Arabia beyond the wider one of wishing for peace, security and prosperity. I want to share my extensive experiences with readers in the hope that they will develop an objective view of the region. If this goal is accomplished, then, the story of 'Arabia Besieged" will be better – and perhaps more kindly – understood around the world.

I've also written this book because I believe that understanding "Arabia Besieged" is as important to the Western mindset as it is to the Arab within the realm of this siege, some of it of his own making. I have learned that hatred has worked across many different platforms within the Arab and Muslim worlds. We may not get universal peace and prosperity within our lifetimes, but it's certainly not too much to ask of ourselves to work to lessen our hatreds. After all, we inhabit, all of us, only one planet. And each one of us has only one lifetime in which to do something so that when our time comes to depart our planet's precincts, it can be said that, well, each one of us made some difference in enhancing the well-being of our fellow human beings. Arabia, which is besieged, isn't a bad place to start.

A WORLD TORN BY MISTRUST.

I was once invited to participate in a symposium organized by the Middle East Center at Harvard University. The title was timely: "Doing Business in the Middle East." But, as these things go, it was about more than making money in the 21 countries ranging from Morocco on the Atlantic Ocean to Iran in the east that constitute the contemporary Middle East.i The subtext of the proceedings was the fate of the foundering peace process between Israelis and Palestinians.

Harvard had organized that conference at a time – during the mid 1990s – when there was some hope that the long festering Arab-Israeli crisis would be dealt with by international diplomats with renewed vigor. As various Israeli and Palestinian business and political figures were being introduced at the Harvard seminar, I began to sense some anticipation building up in the audience. This was certainly not a "peace conference" in the conventional sense, but who knew what would happen in the corridors when delegates mingled and exchanged thoughts?

After the Palestinian educator and parliamentarian Hannan Ashrawi delivered a keynote speech at breakfast, reminding people of the imperatives of history and the need to engage in a dialogue, there seemed to be even more anticipation. An Israeli businessman from Haifa leaned toward a Palestinian political figure sitting next to me and asked, "Can we really trust you and your people?"

I wondered what the Palestinian's response would be.

He looked at the Israeli, smiled and said, "Do you think sitting here in Cambridge we have an option to think otherwise?"

The peace process concerning the Middle East has always been all about options relating to the same piece of land claimed by both Arabs and Jews – Palestine. Yasser Arafat always stuck to the maximalist approach: all or nothing; the Israelis, unwilling at first to yield even a hectare of land they obtained through the intervention of the United Nations in 1948 that established their independent nation, subsequently see-sawed between an option to give up part of the seized territories, as a result of the 1967 war, in exchange for an Arab commitment to peace and security, or agree to the creation of a full-fledged Palestinian state on their porous borders.

Whether there are real options or not, the reality is that mistrust has been written in every page of the tumultuous history between the Palestinians and the Israelis. This mutual mistrust isn't confined to Arab and Jews. I often hear prominent Arab business and political leaders express mistrust for other Arabs. The deep mistrust between Syria's late strongman Hafez al Assad and Iraq's Saddam Hussein was legendary. Moroccan leaders often display contempt for their counterparts in neighboring Algeria, which they accuse of fomenting rebellion in the Western Sahara territory held by Morocco but claimed by the Polisario guerrillas.

But of course, if there's one thing that seems to unite most Arabs when it comes to distrust, it's the West. That's when few Arabs display reservation in expressing venom and political bite.

From the political perspective of Arabs and Muslims, distrust of the West – and of its wards, the Israelis – is to be expected. After all, for Arabs the entire history of the region after the collapse of the Ottoman Empire suggests continuous betrayal by Western leaders. The division of the spoils of war between the British and the French still isn't viewed kindly. The gifting of Palestine to Jews is viewed to this day as a particularly insidious bit of treachery. No wonder the prospects of peace are less than ever before. While the notion of nation-states at war with one other is a historical fact of life, the contemporary intrusive nature of world politics and the velocity of traumatic change that it generates causes serious concerns at a non-nation state level. Just look at how civilian society in Iraq has been utterly shattered in the wake of the Iraq war.

The mistrust that has emerged into the political and social fabric of the Arab world, while directed towards the Western powers, is essentially set into their psyche. This is so even though decades have passed since the first 'wounds' of this mistrust were inflicted on the Arab mind. For the Arabs the seeds of mistrust have not only been steeped in the history how they were dealt with but more importantly how they were taken for granted. However, given the tribal nature of the Arab society there was a natural propensity to be suspicious; the manner in which the Western powers initiated their dealings with the Arab political entities did not ally the natural suspiciousness of the Arab leaders.

Arabia under 300 odd years of Ottoman rule still retained alarming independence in terms of local administration. Even in Egypt while a 'Pasha' was appointed by the Turkish Caliphs, his presence was not obtrusive unless the wishes of the Ottoman rulers were not met. As it was becoming evident that the Ottoman Empire would be at the losing end of the First World War, British and French administrators drew up the Sykes-Picot agreement in 1915 under which Arabia and its hinterlands were divided into direct French and British administered zones and other zones where each other powers would have a predominate area of influence. While various permutations of this agreement were implemented in the post World War I environment the reality is that from an Arab perspective these agreements were a let down.

For the Arabs the agreements were against the grain of previous understandings between McMahon and Hussein, the Sherif of Mecca. For the Arabs the understanding was clear that in a post Ottoman Arab world they themselves would guide the region into the future. The Skyes-Picot agreement, which received endorsements from the Americans and even the Russians, went entirely against the grain of the understanding and it has often been referred to by Arabs are evidence of the mistrust with the West. When a few years later the Balfour Declaration was announced, giving the Jews the right of abode and implied an homeland for them in Palestine, the Arab leadership of that time became suspicious of every move and suggestion made since then. It was no surprise when after World War II it took President Roosevelt three days on a warship to convince King Abdul Aziz of Saudi Arabia to join the United Nations. An encounter all the more uncomfortable as goats were brought on board the warship each day to be slaughtered for the meal for the King.

As the settlement of Israel was a major event, perhaps the most important for the region, in post World War II, Arab countries were being carved out of maps, and they were struggling with their own unique task of nation building. The 1956 Suez Canal crises between Britain and Egypt made it clear that there was an emerging divergence of interests between the influence holders, Britain, and the newly emerging countries. The 1956 crises also created a sense of Arab Nationalism and pride in many Arab countries because it was seen as a sign of independence from the colonial past. When a decade later the 1967 war with Israel burst onto the political landscape of the Middle East, it became clear for the Arabs that they had no support from the US and the British and left on their own, apart from licking their wounds after a week long of fighting they also had to contend with the sense of being alone. The crisis with Israel has moved from states at war to essentially an issue of peace between the Palestinians and the Israelis. Hence for over forty years the persuasive theme of international politics has been the issue of peace in the Middle East. No other human conflict has demanded so much attention for so long in modern history.

In an attempt to bring peace to the Middle East, and to address the perceived nature of terrorist threats, US policies have entered a phase of intrusive presence that's deeply resented within the Arab and Muslim worlds. Arabs don't view this intrusion as just another step for bringing peace to the world, nor as an occurrence that will not have far reaching consequences. Many Arabs see the American invasion of Iraq as neo-colonialism, a sign that the West is re-occupying the Middle East politically. On the other hand, the Arab and Muslim societies themselves have failed to deal with core issues within their own political and social fabric that makes reform and peace all the more difficult. While new initiatives for peace had emerged from Washington under President Clinton and the recent expectations of President Obama, the caution that Arab states show is dictated from five decades of let downs on such initiatives. On the other hand the frustration of not having put their own house in order makes some of the Arab nations open to criticism by the West as being the harbingers of international instability.

From my perspective I feel that Arab societies have to deal with the core issues of political and social reform. While this does not necessarily mean an overhaul of the system, it does imply an urgency to deal with inequalities, bring in administrative and legal and most importantly institute transparency and accountability into the process of governance. It is important that we do not equate mass scale democratic reforms to be instantly possible, as that may well be the desire, the reality is that there are essential building blocks to the process that have to be initiated first before we abandon the existing systems. It is naïve to think that grafting a Western style democracy across the Arab world will solve the issues, as some countries are perhaps more ready for such changes than others and a sweeping reform of such a nature in some countries will open social and political fissures that have not been reconciled.

While opponents of this view will argue that the events of Tunisia and Egypt show that change on the back of mass support are possible, they ignore the simple fact that the revolutions in both countries are simply not complete. The political gains from the protests at Taheri Square in Cairo were the removal of the Mubarak regime, but the fruits of democratic reform are controlled by the military and may well be rationed out to the population rather than be seen as one sweeping change. Elsewhere in the Arab world where the call for reform spilled over into protests, the resistance from the old order in Syria, Yemen and Libya was brutal and uncompromising. Elsewhere the idea of a monolithic sense of nationalism was put to test in the schism between the Shia majority and Sunni ruling family in Bahrain, signifying the weakness in our concept of a nation-state in the context of the Arab world.

The tensions within the world of Islam have culminated on the world scene with the sense of a prophetic mission fuelled by a radical form of Islamic theology. This theology is in continuous confrontation not only with the Western value system; it also threatens the core of Arab and Muslim societies the world over. In the most obvious way we see that a radical Islamic theology challenges the need for a reformed Arab and Muslim world. It implies that issues of education and political reform have to be subservient to the interpretations of the radical clergy that is not conscious of the challenges of modern society. Though the wish is not to create Western Muslim societies but more to create Modernized Muslim societies. Even though one has to acknowledge that both the Muslim and Islamic world are not monolithic in the sense that they can be considered to be unified for both opportunities and threats to the West.

Muslim societies have a sense of being besieged from the pressures of world politics on the one hand and by the radical form of Islamic movements from within. Arabs are hence besieged in a manner that they have not been used to. The sheer scale of the confrontation within and without is stunning. The social fabric of their society, while cohesive on the surface, has developed fissures of divided sentiment, some of it very radical at times. One look at the events within Iraq we see since the invasion of Iraq there has been a progressive eroding of the sense of oneness as an Iraqi society to a new set of challenges that have emerged and are tearing the society. While pre 2003 Iraqis prided themselves on the secular nature of their nationalism, today the divisions are tied to religious alliances that were never the focus of these societies. These fissures threaten to tear apart the order of things that has been taken for granted for the last 50 years or more. While Islamist radicals welcome the ensuing chaos as a means to expedite the conditions in which their struggle will acquire prominence and success, the established order of Arab societies see the present conditions as a threat to the economic and social pattern of their society. This can truly be the worst case scenario where society will be torn apart in a sea of radicalism, the impact of which is very difficult to reverse within society.

The US political presence and the pressures that accompany this presence do not help moderate Arabs desirous of stable and sustainable societies. In fact, the very association of Arab governments with Washington's regional aims – that of spreading democracy, opening up markets, and containing Islamic terrorism – erode some of the credibility of the governments of the region. In this sense governments of Jordan, Iraq and even Saudi Arabia have come under fire for their close alignment with the US. That's because relentless US pressure has forced many of these governments to acquiesce in the pursuit of US regional goals; such acquiescence is viewed by the Arab "street" as spinelessness, or worse. At times this support for the US policy objectives, not matter how subtle and tactful, are most of the times divorced from the reality of public opinion in these very countries.

The role of the local and international media in the current environment has been highly questionable, and, in a sense, has fuelled the current insecurity within the Arab world. The fact remains that in the wake of 9/11 both local and international media has been manufacturing fear based upon which we have actually lost the ability to see what is happening to our societies. While in the United States and to some extent in several European countries, anti-Establishment journalism has always been encouraged, the more investigative and aggressive forms of journalism seem to have been suppressed in the "manufacturing of consent" by the larger, perhaps better funded conservative press. Take, for instance, newspapers such as The Wall Street Journal and The New York Sun. Their editorial pages were unabashedly and unapologetically supportive of the Bush Administration's foreign-policy misadventures; any dissent was viewed by the editorial writers as nothing short of anti-patriotic. Do the Arabs have any friends on the editorial pages of American newspapers, for example? If they do, then their views are safely buried behind niceties. While some Arab figures like Prince Bandar bin Sultan, the former Saudi Ambassador to the US cultivated a great relationship with social figures and the media he had served in Washington and was more the exception rather than the rule. To make matters worse, both Arab governments and Arab business interests have not supported the creation of literary and journalistic collaborations between the West and the Arab world; this creates a vacuum at the grassroots level.

But at least it could be argued that in the West, moderate newspapers such as the New York Times and Le Monde balance the right-wing vitriol spewed by publications funded by conservatives. In the Muslim world, on the other hand, the tradition of a free press has been largely absent. Even in countries where the press has not been entirely muzzled, the tone and texture of the media has been more anti-American rather than questioning the basis of the inner conflicts between conservatism and the issues that confront modern Muslim societies. Thus for Arab media to raise issues of governance, accountability and transparency within their own societies is very rare. This is a trend that has been reversed in small measure in the past decade but not as a rule.

As a result, the orthodox religious elements in Muslim countries are assured of not being questioned as to their motives or means – in the same manner that the Republican right-wing leadership in the United States seems relatively immune from the wrath – or even inquisitiveness – of the free press. While the analogy may not be identical in all respects, there is some truth that the conservative media in the United States do have formidable influence on public opinion. It would therefore seem that just as the right wing press in the US has had moments of unquestioned acceptance, so too has the conservative Arab media always been able to maintain and support the status quo.

Tragically, there is no platform where the current – and growing – gap in perceptions and mistrust between the West and Islam can be meaningfully addressed, let alone bridged. The results of international forums like the World Economic Forum, the Arab Leaders Forum and others are short lived and the contact is not maintained consistently enough to remain effective. On the one hand, bilateral relations between the United States and the Muslim countries, while reasonably good on the surface (mainly on account of trade), are essentially one of an imposition of will; on the other hand, societal interaction has actually decreased to the point where there is hardly any significant contact between the cultures. American tourism in Arab countries has slowed down. As for Arabs or Muslims trying to get tourist visas to the United States – well, good luck! Even with my business credentials and record, it took me more than five months in 2006 to obtain a visa to visit my wife's family in Colorado.

It would be naïve to assume that the current problems concerning mutual tolerance and coexistence stem only from cultural differences and suspicions between the West and the Arabs. The reality is that there are fewer cultural and more political dimensions between Arabs and the Western world. This implies that even though political interaction between Western and Arab societies is infrequent the social interaction between people of the Arab world and the United States remains even less. How can two societies understand the compulsions they face unless they have more frequent contact?

The social dimensions that have framed the perceptions are born from as much as internal factors as the result of actions of each side. Thus both Western and Arab societies have dealt with their own inward processes and given a low level of interaction do not have the language that allows them to understand each other on a broader front. In this insular view of each other, the dimensions of understanding are subdued to the point that what little understanding has emerged it has always been fragile and prone to being overshadowed by political animosity and indeed socio-religious suspicions. Thus in moments of need for better understanding it is more common for the political leadership on each side to point to what is different between the two societies rather than mention what is common between them. This implies that as much as inter-societal dialogue is necessary so too is inter-faith communication becoming more urgent. The inter-faith dialogue, while an important dimension of understanding and creating trust has not been within the limelight of the media and society, resulting in fragmented and isolated success at best. The result has been that the more sensational differences are more important to the media, as they are news, rather than the quiet successes of inter-faith understanding and tolerance.

In short, the moderate voice of Islam that has been present through the crises we face have not really been heard, both by the West and neither within the Arab world, leaving some to suggest that there is no moderation within the Islamic and Arab world. Subsequent chapters will highlight that there is a very profoundly neutral voice of concern from within the Muslim clergy who feel that the radical Islamists have hijacked their faith as Muslims.

The emergence of the various dimensions of 'terrorism' on society is as much Western in complexion as they are common to Arab and Muslim societies. All that 9/11 has done is brought about a crystallization of radicalism in the context of actions by militant Islamic organizations that has prompted the now infamous "war on terror."

The result of this is that while America leads a war on terror it also expects the same vigor to be demonstrated by Yemen, Saudi Arabia, Afghanistan, Iraq and Pakistan. Indeed the hawks in the Pentagon would want to pursue such a war with frontline states such as these assisting them in the war on terror. However, having other countries be the frontline states in a war on terror implies that such countries regimes are either strong enough to withstand any backlash from within, or are representative of people within a country who really do want to pursue this 'war on terror'. This 'War on terror' is nothing more than what President George W Bush declared, in the aftermath of the 9/11 attacks, to an effort on the part of the US government to seek out any threat to the US which does not come from a conventional military threat and destroy it. However, it is unlikely that given the manner in which the initial framing of the 'war on terror' was commenced that any of the Arab or Muslim countries would have public support for the US governments position. Part of the problem may well be that the war on terror is being associated with 'Islamic terrorism' when some would argue that given all the participants of the 9/11 attacks were Arabs why is it not considered as Arab Terrorism?

What most observers fail to understand is that the compulsions for Arab governments to fight such a "war on terror" are totally different from what Washington would deem as important. Take the case of Algeria; a country that has been ravaged by terror attacks from the Islamic parties, resulting in some cases the decimation of entire villages by the Armed Islamic Group. During the period 1992 to 2002 over 160,000 people lost their lives to terror attacks in Algeria. Thus for the government in Algiers the urgency of dealing with armed insurrection on its own doorstep is far more urgent that dealing with what Washington may define as the urgent needs of the war on terror.

This is all the more because each side sees the reasons for such an Islamic radicalism as born from a different set of conditions. Washington, and especially President George W Bush, had us believe that this is a pointed war of Islamic radicals which emerged from a theological framework and can only be explained in the context of its own radical fervor. To the hardliners in Washington, the acts of terrorists seem solely designed against American interests, ignoring the complex face of terrorism within the Muslim world itself. The reality is that Muslims have faced more terrorism from within their own societies then what the US has faced from its perceived terrorist threats. The litany of attacks ranges from Egypt to Jordan, to Iraq to Pakistan and India, to Central Asia and indeed the history of Lebanon is littered with examples of extremism that has resulted in mass scale terror.

Terrorism has long afflicted Muslim societies – or at least in the last two or three decades. Sectarian violence within Pakistan, for example, which pitted Sunni and Shia radical groups against each other in the 1990's (the infamous Kalashnikov culture) saw many innocent Muslims from both sects get slaughtered in machine-gun and bombing raids that had all the characteristics of systemic organized terrorism. Similar sectarian violence has been seen in Lebanon during the civil war of 1975-1991; in Taliban-controlled Afghanistan; and more recently in Iraq. Among the worst of such recent attacks have been the Al Askari Mosque bombing on February 22, 2006, which resulted in the death of more a hundred people, and scores of injuries. The Shia mosque's destruction created the gravest danger to possible Shia-Sunni reconciliation, and while speculation continues as to who bombed the mosque there is no denying that radical elements would welcome further inter-sect terrorism within Iraq and elsewhere. In the current situation it suits the radical elements within Iraq to see further strife between the communities as it allows them to further destabilize the government in Baghdad, and for sure to not give it the chance to nurture a semblance of law and order within the country.

From an Arab and Muslim perspective, there are some social conditions in their society that have created the backdrop under which radicalism has grown over the past few decades. The widening gap between the rich and the poor, the failure of a number of Arab governments to adequately distribute wealth and create opportunities for the people has resulted in a growing dissatisfaction with the Arab and Muslim leadership. When one mentions the growth of this radicalism as being a recent phenomenon, we are not referring to the long history of radical

Islamic political thought and action through movements like the Muslim Brotherhood, and the Islamic Jihad, but more to the wider implications into society of such a radical theology as that preached by such party ideologues. The Muslim Brotherhood, which was founded in 1928 by a sufi schoolteacher Hassan Ali Bana, became one of the most powerful Islamist movements in the Arab world. While its creed remains non violent it has often been accused by the Egyptian government of violent means and has faced harsh crackdowns. Its ranks have boasted such intellectual heavyweights as Syed Qutb, whose influence on Islamic fundamentalism cannot be underestimated. The Islamic Jihad and many other militant Islamic organizations were the result of Muslim Brotherhood members leaving the brotherhood ranks to set up their own organizations which agreed with violent means to bring about change. The Islamic Jihad, perhaps was the first and most violent of the militant organizations and it is notorious for attacks against Egyptian officials including an attack on the Egyptian embassy in Pakistan in 1995. One essential difference that most people do not completely comprehend is that ideologues such as Dr. Ayman Zawahiri, Abdullah Azzam and earlier activists like Mohammed Qutb and his brother Syed Qutb all Egyptian activists were not preaching converts to their cause to win a political campaign in an election. This was never seen by them as merely a political process, but a deeply religious undertaking which would change not only society in its political aspects but in all aspects. Thus Islamic reform to them was to change Muslim societies at the base level by bringing in only Islamic laws, Islamic forms of governance and conducting the economic activities based on Shariah.

It is for this reason that the motivation of such radicalism is fundamentally different from that of a political party operative; in a fundamental sense, of course, the radical's motivation is more zealous, but it is also unrelenting and not amenable to contrarian persuasion. What these ideologues achieved was to not only spread Islam in the realm of its religious beliefs but also to use it as an effective means for political change but the focus being entirely on social change first. To them electoral victories are incidental to the process and not the key motivating factor and since 1991 assumed the "jihadist" fervor that the same ideologues preached in the earlier war in Afghanistan against the Russians. The reality of the Afghan conflict during the era of its Soviet occupation was very complex. The mujahiddin were seven fractured groups who with foreign, namely CIA and Pakistan military intelligence were waging a war against the Soviet troops, they were also involved in a power struggle of their own. Yet the ferocity of the fighting, which left 14,453 Soviet dead and 53,753 directly wounded from the fighting, shows the high cost that Soviets paid for this Afghan adventure. The Soviet General Pavel Grachev, who was later to be the Soviet Defense Minister, learned the hard way the lesson the British had learned in their Afghan wars of the 19th century that there is a massive price to pay to tame the Afghan.

What Dr. Zawahiri and Osama bin Laden are asking their followers is to embrace the same zeal with which they assisted in the defeat of the Soviet Union in their current fight against the "near enemy" -- the existing regimes of the Muslim world -- and the "far enemy" -- the United States and its allies. Osama bin Laden, born on March 10, 1957 into a rich business family of Saudi Arabia was the 17th son of Mohammed bin Awad bin Laden. There was nothing significant about his life till the late 1970's when he went the to King Abdul Aziz university in Jeddah and came in contact with Mohammed Qutb and Abdullah Azzam, who were then professors at the university. It was from this point onwards that the radicalism of Osama started and by 1981, when he graduated he had already been inducted into the mainstream of the movement, then led by Abudullah Azzam to encourage Arabs to help fight against the Soviet occupation of Afghanistan. Given that Ossama's family was extremely rich he could always rely on financial backing for his plans, even though there is no evidence to suggest that Osama's siblings might have known of his political motives.

The conditions of unsatisfied masses and poverty that Arab and Muslim societies have been faced have nurtured the very conditions that allow radicalism to be preached with ease. Though some of the richer countries in the Muslim world, like United Arab Emirates, Kuwait and even Saudi Arabia, have spent a lot of money on education, this has contributed to a large cadre, running into tens of millions of young people, who are educated and unemployed, or are working in jobs that are far below the educational background of these young people. In addition the governments of these countries have not created the economic conditions for this large, and growing, young educated labor force to be absorbed into the economy. On the other hand the values system for some of the rich within these societies has meant the lack of respect for the dignity of labor. In general, and especially in the case of Saudi Arabia, the liberalization of the economy and broadening of the job market has only occurred in the past five odd years, prior to which the rising tide of unemployed educated Saudi youth posed serious problems for the country.

The result has been an educated majority of the "unheard" that are perhaps readily convinced about the need for radical solutions. This is the situation most conspicuous in Saudi Arabia where strict orthodoxy on the one hand and the lack of economic progress for a growing educated population, on the other hand, is setting up young people for being won over by radicalism under the guise for change. The rise in Saudi unemployed youth has meant a growing number of trends of juvenile delinquency, loitering around the shopping malls, and in some cases also drug addiction. While it would be fair to say that these youth have not had a political format to be drawn to, some of the more disgruntled have been easy prey for the fundamentalist organizations in seeking more into their rank and file. In most Muslim countries, opposition in the form of political parties opposed to the governments in power do not exist, or where they exist they are too small and too closely watched by the state machinery to be considered as viable political threats to the existing political order to be even considered a threat. The result, then, is this educated majority of the unheard in their disgruntled state becomes the first to be impressed by the "underground" nature of the Islamist movements; it begins to see radicalism as the only possible instrument of change in their society. In addition the religious fervor and teachings within such organizations give the mission a religious authenticity that is powerfully imprinted in the minds of these young people, allowing the imparting of religious instruction as having a wider meaning for social change.

A highly educated Saudi, who had returned from the US and was well established in Jeddah, mentioned to me during a visit to Dubai that while many youth in Saudi Arabia look at Dubai's openness and progress with admiration, for them the issues of a decent job are more pressing. I cited to him the proposed reform program of King Abdullah, and he sighed and wondered if decades of neglect could be simply undone through one reform announcement. In his mind the issues confronting the Saudi youth are more urgent that most people realize; the promised change from both the government and the fundamentalists is confusing to some of the youth and neither seems to be "around the corner." To these youth the need for economic stability and opportunities is all that is important and this has not been happening. In some instances the need to have a say in the social structure either through a political voice or a social presence has also been felt.

In the post World War II environment, most of the Muslim and Arab societies have felt a sense of persecution that has never been addressed. A large measure of this persecution has come from foreign forces as large tracts of their land were under foreign control to the point in the post-1945 era that wide-scale and arbitrary state lines were drawn, rulers imposed and even countries like Israel implanted in their midst with no choice for the society itself but to accept.

There is a sense amongst many Muslims and Arabs to at least avenge, and if possible, to correct, the wrongs of history. The result has been a choosing of an enemy who is foreign to the domestic societal context -- Great Britain for the period till the 1960's, and thereafter the United States of America and Israel. This has led to a widespread tendency amongst Arabs and even non-Arab Muslim countries to blame both America and Zionism for the wrongs in the region, and it is not surprising that the conspiracy theories abound even in the minds of some of the most liberal Muslims.

In fairness to these Muslims and Arabs, the actions of Great Britain, the United States and Israel are not entirely innocent and have often shown a disdain towards the Arabs and Muslims, and in recent years the war on terror has added to the need for a larger section of the society to "avenge" the historical and current wrongs imposed on their society. Much of this need to avenge is largely emotional in nature, but for those who have crossed the line to embrace radicalism as a means of change, the means for avenging these wrongs is being created. It is from this mentality that the mentality of the suicide bomber is being shaped. The mind of the suicide bomber is also conditioned by the historical context of this struggle and creates, in his mind, the justification of correcting a wrong of history.

The social and economic impact of the huge population explosion occurring in Muslim and Arab societies is having a huge and perhaps irreversible impact on the resource management of these societies. A number of Arab countries have been witnessing phenomenal population growth rates; UAE 3.99%, Palestine 3.6% Kuwait 3.56% to name a few. It is estimated that in the next ten years close to 70 million jobs will have to be created in the Middle East for the young men and women entering into the work force. While on the one hand, massive urbanization has taken place in cities like Cairo, Tehran, Baghdad, and Karachi, it has also meant a radical change from rural societies to urban societies with a greater pressure on the resources available for the population. The need for arable land, water resources and basic necessities of life are so huge that the current system of governance in these countries and cities cannot cope with the building pressures. In these urban centers the seeds of discontent are the ideal ground for organizations to nourish their message of radicalism. As one sees the issues of urbanization become more acute the congestion, the teeming millions who are living at the edge of the poverty line all indicate that the urbanization of many of these countries has put a pressure on the already meager resources of water, hygiene systems and health care. Any study of Muslim Brotherhood and the Islamic Jihad will show that these movements have done best in recruiting people from the mass of dissatisfaction within the urban centers where there has been a greater degree of success in recruiting jihadists than from the rural areas.

The radicalism that this growing urban poverty can embrace is potentially very dangerous to the existing political order in these countries. The appeal of organizations like the Muslim Brotherhood and Hamas, or Harakat al-Muqawama al-Islamiyya as it is officially known, which has become a major political force in Palestine, have provided schools, and medical clinics in areas where the government has failed to even provide basic sanitation. Initially the resources for medical clinics came from donations and with sympathetic doctors putting in voluntary time into the cause. Today the membership of just the Muslim Brotherhood in Egypt is over half a million from whom donations and charity drives are organized for the funding of the activities. Such small benign acts of radical movements have actually not only underscored how ineffective the government apparatus is, but also highlighted the need for social change from within.

The social contract for governance in some of these societies, while totally imposed, is not even constitutionally fair in operation. These societies have had those who are above the realm of constitutional authority and hence a law onto themselves as was witnessed in Syria, Iraq and Libya to name a few governments where the ruling clique has always been above the law, while the multitude have had to obey laws which were never born from a social contract between the governed and the governors.

Even in those countries where a model of democracy was applied, such as Pakistan and Egypt, to name a few, the social contract has remain unaltered, resulting in governments in power through the ballot box but which have not been accountable to those they have governed. Thus it was common to see Nawaz Sharif and the late Benazir Bhutto in Pakistan, or Hosni Mubarak in Egypt being unaccountable in many respects to the very masses who elected them. These parliamentary dictatorships have managed to govern under a decorum of democracy; they are usually rife with corruption and intrigue, but have survived with remarkable stubbornness. The ruse has been so successful at times that such governments have been cheered by both Western governments and even their domestic press as champions of democracy, ignoring the track record of these governments on issues of human rights and corruption. The potential for change has been marred by the lack of a proper monitoring system and lack of accountability, resulting in an emotional embracing of change. In reality, practical changes for the betterment of society have been slow in coming to the very population that needs the benefits of social and economic change.

One of the crucial catalysts of change that needs to be embraced by these societies has to be education. By that I mean a synthesis of a liberal and modern education that respects the religious values of Islam, too. While a lot of noise has been made about the impact of the madrassa – or religious -- type education in countries like Pakistan – and this has been blamed for the radicalism of society, especially amongst the young -- the reality is that only about 1% of the school-going children attend the madrassa type schools according to a World Bank Group study. It is true that while education may not be progressive in the liberal context, it is clearly not also the hate provoking preaching that is often portrayed in the Western media. Yet the very existence of madrassas would prompt one to ask about the role of education in the shaping of these societies. Indeed the more enlightened leadership of the Muslim and Arab world does realize that education is perhaps the most important element for the future of these societies. Some countries like Bahrain, and particularly the United Arab Emirates have embarked upon very ambitious open-minded education programs, some of them even supported by Western universities. As one minister said to me, 'we need to build tolerant and dynamic societies and for this the importance of education is paramount.'

There is no denying that both Islamists of a modern mindset, and radical Islamists agree that education is pivotal in the shaping of society and, more importantly, the next generation. However, they disagree on the content, emphasis and thrust of this education. For the radical camp education that is not "purely" Islamic is not acceptable. While most radical Islamists do not adhere to the Taliban style of orthodoxy which seeks to impose only the Shariah law and system, there is little to cheer about their model for social change in terms of progressive thinking which while not as imposing as the Taliban does create restrictions such as those in Iran and Saudi Arabia, that do effect the human condition. .

Many modern thinking Muslims, who are anxious to see a modern Muslim society emerge, feel that their religion and faith is being hijacked by the fundamentalists, who have managed to create the sensationalism within the minds of the Muslims on the one hand and the West on the other. This sensationalism has been on the back of the events of 9/11 and further encouraged by the reaction from the West in their war on terror. However, given the emotion and fervor that has been generated by the Islamists, the ability of this forward thinking bloc of people within Muslim societies to bring about mass scale change is limited. Yet in some Islamic regimes while religious education was more firmly entrenched in the social fabric, it was not essentially at the expense of a modern education; examples of Iran and Pakistan do stand out to a degree. However, there is no denying that it is also a function of perspective as what education means. To a Western mind looking at some Arab or Muslim regimes, they appear to take their societies into the dark ages. On the other hand, liberal Muslims – even in deeply conservative societies – are relieved that their Islamic governments do not necessarily take a "Taliban approach" to education.

Prior to the 9/11 tragedy, I was having a conversation one afternoon with Sheikh Nahayan bin Mabarak Al Nayahan, the Minister of Higher Education of UAE, who was the chairman of the bank I was running. We were in his car coming back from a function, when a newsflash came that scores of people had been killed in Pakistan in an attack on a mosque as a result of sectarian conflict between two sects of Islam. The Minister's face fell.

"How can these people even call themselves Muslims?" he said. We then discussed the role of education in Muslim societies, and he was very clear that only education could change these "misguided" youth and make them realize that they were being exploited in the name of religion. He said that what we all need to do is preach tolerance.

Here was a western educated member of the royal family who since the late 1980's had reformed UAE's higher educational system. He had virtually single handedly brought in modern educational systems and replaced the rote type educational system with a forward thinking model. In this participative educational system he had brought tolerance and acceptance to the forefront insisting that a merit based system was the only way for the next generation to compete in the world they would face. A hard working man, who started his 13 hour work day with breakfast meetings, he set a pace for change that was highly motivating and encouraging. It was clear to me that afternoon in Abu Dhabi that I was listening to a responsible voice of reason within the Arab and Muslim world. I'm sure that there are many other such voices; we only need to find them.

In so far as issues of trust between governments of the West and the Muslim world are concerned, it is fair to say that there is a lack of parity in the dialogue between them. For many in the Muslim world, the presidency of George W Bush will be remembered as being devoid of a sense of compassion and genuine understanding of the world – even though, ironically, Bush campaigned in 2000 as a "compassionate conservative." American leadership in world affairs has been characterized by bullying and even at times enforced through the barrel of a gun. It's doubtful if these strategies are truly sustainable. Already, even staunch Republicans are back pedaling on American involvement in Iraq because of a growing realization that President Bush's engagements in Iraq and Afghanistan – however well meaning – were ill conceived and poorly executed. It is this sentiment that has favored the election of President Barrack Obama who has promised a pull out of Iraq, but curiously sought to engage more actively, and militarily, in Afghanistan.

The war in Iraq and to a lesser extent, the conflict in Afghanistan, have given the Jihadist movements, whether directly aligned to the Al Qaeda or not, the very battle they wish to wage. For them, the situation in these countries is a rallying call. While much has been made of US intelligence reports that the strife in Iraq is inspired and carried out by elements from the Al Qaeda who are non-Iraqis, the truth is that there are enough internal divisions within Iraq for the strife to continue for the foreseeable future. The militant foreign elements have exploited that situation in what is already a volatile mix of Shia and Sunni politics. In essence, the US presence has ignited and even stoked the fire of intolerance between the communities within Iraq; the foreign influence of Jihadist fighters happens to be an incidental element of the current strife.

What has emerged is an indigenous Iraq Jihad that is finding wider support than expected amongst the disgruntled population that has not seen the benefits of ridding the country of Saddam Hussein's tyrannical rule. While the ostensible reason for the invasion of Iraq was also to bring economic prosperity to the average Iraqi and to create a sense of good governance within Iraq, both aims have yet to be realized. My own feeling is that these laudable aims are not going to be achieved during our lifetime. Iraqi society has been irreparably torn asunder, and perhaps the national entity might work better as a federation of three or four separate states, each predicated on ethnic lines.

The war on terror has actually widened the gap between the two societies. However, the face of political Islam should not be confused with "fundamentalism," the former being more a state centered movement for change, while Fundamentalist Islam being more society-centered as a movement for change. While the agendas of a number of Islamic political parties have drawn heavily on fundamentalist thought and rhetoric, the essential nature of these parties remains political.

Barring a few exceptions within the context of a political system which seeks a political change as the means to achieve social change, most of the fundamentalist movements have preached social change and relied on the concepts of "Tableekh" – the propagation of religion through preaching. Until the 1990s, their role in politics was marginal; they seemed content to offer tacit support for like-minded Islamic political parties. The world of "Political Islam" which is where Islamist parties have emerged with largely political agendas rather than a purely religious appeal, has battled the larger framework of the cultural Islamic world; the struggle seems to be between those who believe the political process will embrace the cultural differences and schisms within Islam, and those who aver that revolutionary – and violent – changes are needed to elicit social and political transformation.

The world of Fundamentalist Islam contends through its preaching that societal change will bring about the conditions where the cultural dichotomies will become secondary to the unity that Islam will provide. Fundamentalists are thus not concerned with the reform of the current political and social system, relying instead on the belief that once a 'pure' Islamic system is brought it automatically means that the entire legal, economic and political system will have to change to the Islamic system. In this process the current dichotomies within society, which are ethnic, economic or social, will all be driven out by the force of the new purist system. To the fundamentalist participation in the current political system to bring about social and political change is meaningless, like a political Islamist will continue to participate in the current political system with the belief that upon wining elections the political Islamists will change the system, all the more since they are armed with the power of the popular vote.

The common error we make in our understanding of the Arab and Muslim worlds is that we assume all political parties with an Islamist agenda are also proponents of either political terror, or supporters of a militant movement. The error rests across the spectrum of some of the media, but more so within the mind of most in the Western audience to whom the use of the term "Islam" in the context of a political party assumes it must be a radical party. We have to be careful in such sweeping judgments as we will see that an Islamist party in secular Turkey or Bangladesh is more liberal than the even a self professed liberal political party in Pakistan or Indonesia.

At various times since 9/11, a number of political leaders from the world of Political Islam have either supported the acts of Osama bin Laden or have tried to justify the reasons for Al Qaeda being so militant. Therefore, it has been assumed that the faces of Political Islam and terrorism are synonymous. For the political leadership of most Islamist parties, the public condemnation of Al Qaeda's activities would clearly rid them of some of their moral support within society and is perhaps the main reason that the lack of condemnation is often seen as a tacit approval on their part of the acts of militancy. This inability to publically admonish the acts of Al Qaeda should not be seen as anything other than political expendiency on the part of these Islamist political parties.

On the one hand there has been Fundamentalist Islam, with its focus on social change and preaching, and on the other hand Political Islam seeks a political agenda of change in governance and political systems.

A new fundamentalist-cum-political movement has emerged which has differed from the rest in their manner of seeking change. This is the current phenomenon of change through violent means and enunciated in the radical militant philosophy of Osama bin Laden and Dr. Ayman Zawahiri. Some would argue that this departure from fundamentalist teachings to violence was the result of a number of factors which have jolted the Arab and Muslim worlds not only from within but also created conditions of conflict with the Western world at a level that is dangerous for all parties. This Jihadist movement has imbibed the need for political change through militant action steeped in fundamentalist and radical interpretations of the mission of Islam. As the Jihadist see the mission of Islam to be a 'war' for the purification of the soul and the preservation of Islamic values. For the more radical Jihadists the mission is the preservation and also the spread of Islam and to thwart possible threats to Islamic communities.

Perhaps the only common thread between the Jihadists and most Muslims is the sense of being colonized by the West. This is not a sort of political and territorial colonialism of past centuries, but cultural colonialism, which threatens to change the face of essentially Muslim societies under the guise of modernism and secularism.ii When President Bush talked of reforms within Arab and Muslim societies and nations he, perhaps unwittingly, played upon these very fears that exist amongst Muslims. A large body of evidence suggests that while modernism in terms of development has been embraced by the Arab and the Muslim worlds, the social side of modernism has been only marginally accepted; the upper and upper middle classes are the forbearers of this wave of modernism. The tensions that this process has created within these societies are not easy to reconcile, and often they have spilled over into a wide body of political and social debate that remains un-reconciled.

Western audiences frequently fail to recognize that there are a number of eminent scholars from the Muslim and Arab world who have spoken against terrorism and even suggested that Dr. Ayman Zawahiri and Osama bin Laden have hijacked the Islamic cause and taken it into the realm of hate and terror. This is partly because the Western media has not made an effort to speak to these voices of dissent with the Muslim world. In addition it would seem that because Arab and Muslim media is fragmented, disorganized and weak in it's spread of information the news of Muslim scholars disagreeing with face of radical Islamist actions. Take Tariq Ramadan, the grandson of Hassan Ali Banna, the founder of the Muslim Brotherhood in Egypt, and a scholar of emmense standing based on his work where he advocates that Muslims in Europe must adapt to European conditions. For example just four days after 9/11, he called on all

Muslims to condemn the attacks on the US, or that of Nasr Abu Zayd, a prominent Muslim scholar from Al Azhar University who seeks to present a humanistic view of Islam. Abu Zayd asks people to consider tolerance rather than anger. Nasr Abu Zayd's case is interesting that he is a man of learning who having achieved recognition also criticized the high handedness of the Muslim clergy resulting in a backlash that served as a test case for the lack of tolerance especially in his case as he fell from grace into a world of wrath. There are a growing number of Muslim intellectuals who do not agree with the way Islam is being portrayed by Muslims themselves? Nasr Abu Zayd was accused of being an apostate, tried in an Egyptian court on charges of apostasy and found guilty which mean that the court annulled his marriage on grounds that he was a heretic and could not be married to a Muslim woman. He continues to contest the case from exile in the Netherlands while being ostracized by the mainstream of Muslim theocracy on grounds of his controversial views.

Similarly the treatment of the late Sheikh Zaki Badawi shows how short sighted American policy makers can be on the issue of what they are calling "Homeland Security." Sheikh Badawi was perhaps the most illustrious Islamic scholar of modern times. He was made an honorary Knight Commander of the British Empire (KBE) in 2004, and was perhaps one of the most sensible voices of reason in the Muslim world. Soon after the London bombings in July 2005, Sheikh Badawi was refused entry into the United States even though he had a visa. It seems that an over cautious immigration official deemed him as inadmissible. Even though an apology did come from the US government, one would imagine that someone as well respected as him, who denounced terrorism should have been welcomed with open arms rather than being rejected. Shaikh Zaki Badawi who died in January 2006 of natural causes, was an Egyptian scholar who had made England his home was a voice of reason and perhaps one of the most prominent Muslim minds of the modern era. Sheikh Badawi was the first promienent muslim scholar to criticize Muslim imams of mosques in Great Britian who did not preach in English, thereby bringing a voice of modernism into the realm of Islamic societies at a time when more and more imams were trying to be fundamentalist in their approach.

Muslims do want to hear such voices of reason, and they do want more attention to be paid in the Western media to those voices from within Islam who condemn Osama bin Laden, and who condemn the use of force. Such voices are being heard through the Arab world in the newspapers and the moderate television stations do bring to the forefront a face of Islam that is not often expected in the West. To be sure, such voices will also call for an American withdrawal from Iraq and Afghanistan and will question US policy on the matter of detainees and human rights. Americans must be prepared for such divergence of views, and, perhaps more importantly, also be prepared to accept that not everyone in the Arab and Muslim worlds will wholeheartedly subscribe to America's world view. Policy makers in the United States supposedly want a rule of law to emerge in Muslim countries, and yet many of them often give the impression that America prefers to simply impose its will on Arabia. When Muslims get such an impression, can they be blamed for thinking that US policy makers have few clues about how to encourage a modern Muslim society that is based on human liberty, justice and the rule of law?

For many outside Arabia, understanding the progression of Islamic intellectual thought on the subject of state and society has been difficult to comprehend. If Hassan Banna, born in 1906 and died in 1949 and the political reformer in Egypt set the pace of social change through an revival of Islamic values through his Muslim Brotherhood in Egypt, then others who followed -- especially Islamic political thinkers -- set a different pace concerning the contemporary issues of Islamic society and the state.

Interestingly enough, a major influence on the theological approaches to state and society within the Islamic world came from outside Arabia, relying on developments that were happening in India, as it split into two countries, India and Pakistan after the British Raj ended in 1947. Even though mainstream Arab intellectuals might not readily accept this source of influence, the fact remains events in India were shaping, and in a way testing, the broader applications of Islamic thought in a framework of decolonization.

Early in the 20th century, three important figures appeared on the scene who shaped the way Muslim theology was to influence the interaction between society and state. Mohammed Iqbal, a philosopher and poet from Pakistan, is credited with the conceiving the idea of a Muslim homeland for the Muslims of India. Western philosophers, particularly Nietzsche, heavily influenced Iqbal; but as much as he admired them, he criticized them for advocating a separation of state and religion. Yet he did not conceive of a Muslim state ruled by the religious class but by the Ummah (Muslims in general).

The slogan of "Ummah and not Ulema (religious clergy)," was conspicuous in his pronouncements, but Iqbal sought an elected system, based on adult franchise and yet felt that secularism would not work in a Muslim state and that it would "erode the spiritualism of the Muslim state" Iqbal's thinking was unique in that he was the first Islamic thinker who conceived the idea of nationhood for the Muslims (he espoused the two-nation theory in the context of a pre-Partition India that had been ruled by the British for nearly 200 years), and in that sense provided the first political framework for Muslims to consider statehood under the influence of religion. While he was poetically inclined to speak of communal harmony between different religions and faiths, he was nevertheless staunch in his view that Islam alone provided a Muslim state the basis for its governance; yet he clashed with the orthodox clergy because Iqbal felt that they had no role to play within the political framework.

In contrast to Iqbal, the founder of the Pakistan nation, Mohammed Ali Jinnah, was a political figure who did not come from a religious background. An astute thinker with a legal background, he started his political career advocating Hindu-Muslim unity within the context of one nation; disillusioned with leaders of the Indian National Congress – such as Jawaharlal Nehru, who was to become the first prime minister of independent India in 1947 – Jinnah began to campaign for a separate homeland. He drew inspiration from Mohammed Iqbal's thoughts on the subject, but believed a secular Muslim Pakistan was not only possible but also desirable in the long run.

Jinnah represented the view of what Political Islam wished; his was indeed very modern thinking during that time period. Any particular Islamic ideology or theological school of thought did not inspire him, and he mainly concentrated on the concept of Muslims as a people that needed their own homeland. His appeal was emotional, economic and essentially religious in its political format but not steeped in any theological underpinning. Jinnah received tacit support from a wide section of society, including the feudal aristocracy and the business class of Muslims. He rode a wave of popular Muslim support; Jinnah ignored orthodox Muslims, who saw no merit in his Western lifestyle, stunted Urdu and British mannerisms, because he was indeed the classic "man of the people."

Jinnah was the political visionary for the Islamic movement without portraying the image of a die-hard radical.iii

About the same time in India, a Muslim revivalist scholar named Syed Abul Ala Maududi was preaching his unique message to the Muslim community. It was a message that influenced other scholars like Syed Qutb in Egypt, one of the forerunners of the Muslim Brotherhood movement there. The essential message from Maududi was that of "Iqamat-I-Deen" -- the establishment of religion -- whereby he preached that both society and the state must be guided by a higher law and that the law could only be traditional Islamic Law. He argued that for a Muslim society that would require total purging of sectarian views and principles. He opposed the formation of Pakistan, yet upon its creation in 1947 migrated to the Pakistan moving the headquarters of his political party Jamaat-I-Islami (which he had founded in 1941) to Pakistan.

Another concept that Maududi espoused was that Jihad was a permanent revolutionary strategy and not a condition of defensive measures to be taken during a state of war. His views deeply influenced both political Islamists and Fundamentalist Islamists. Maududi created a political party, the Jamaat-i-Islami.. Curiously, while a staunch Sunni Muslim, Maududi's theological writings – spread over 120 books -- preached a more broad based, yet conservative, view of Islam. By not letting his Sunni views effect his political work for the Ummah, this gave him more acceptance within the realm of sectarian politics of India and Pakistan. Moreover, because Maududi was a self taught scholar in many respects and his adherence was to the ritual of Islam rather than the theological foundations of Islam, he found support amongst the common people. Of course, Islamic scholars frowned upon what some characterized as his naïve views of the relationship of state and society. In addition, Maududi possessed an extremely dictatorial style of leadership of his political party resulting in both the Barelvi and Deobandi School of scholars to part ways with his Jamaat-I-Islami.

However, Maududi's message for social and state change by its subservience to Islamic Law was one of the key messages that Syed Qutb adopted. It became a cornerstone of theological discourse for the Muslim Brotherhood in Egypt. While Maududi sought -- through a permanent state of Jihad -- the supremacy of Islamic law, his failure to achieve power through a political democratic process was the one weakness of the synthesis that he tried to establish between Islam and politics. Even his son, Dr. Haider Maududi, was to break away from his father's teachings and political party; he accused his father of preaching extremism that had no place in an Islamic society.

But for Syed Qutb, the lessons of Maududi's struggle were critical. As a result, the Muslim Brotherhood shunned the political process and concentrated on social change as a means to eventually achieve a change in the Islamic state. Such a path was considered seditious in the Egypt of President Jamal Abdul Nasser and later President Anwer El-Sadat, resulting in confrontation with the Muslim Brotherhood with extremely bloody consequences. While Nasser died of a heart attack on September 28, 1970, the Egyptian Islamic Jihad assassinated Sadat as he reviewed a military parade in Cairo on October 6, 1981, a month after a brutal crackdown on Islamists, intellectuals and others. More than a generation later, Egyptian society remains riven by tensions between secularists and fundamentalists. This very tension will perhaps surface in Egypt on the back of the populist movement that ousted Hosni Mubarak, and will in a sense be the litmus test for the intent and depth of populist change in such societies.

One of the biggest mistakes Western commentators make in drawing a parallel between the thinking of the Al Qaeda leadership and Fundamentalist Islam is that they assume these two paths are synonymous in flavor and roots. While there are indeed strong connections in terms of some of the philosophical percepts and the focus of the religious sentiment, the political connection is very dissimilar. While each may at times sound and be sympathetic to each other, the reality is that the percepts of each are quite divorced.

It could well be that because the thinking of the Islamist reformers who are guided by fundamentalist principles but also wish to assert a political influence on Muslim societies, who went on to influence Osama bin Laden were people closely influenced by the thinking of Syed Qutb, his brother Mohammed Qutb, the common mistake is to assume that their radicalism comes from the same source. Indeed, this conduit was largely through people like Abdullah Azzam, who was considered a mentor for Osama bin Laden; some believe that Azzam, a radical political activist who fought alongside Osama against the Russians in Afghanistan, did not necessarily agree with militancy against the West or the "new enemy" – the United States. Azzam, prior to his assassination in 1989 had begun to fall out with Osama bin Laden; Azzam wished to take the successful Jihad model from Afghanistan to his native homeland "Palestine"; but Osama bin Laden and Dr. Ayman Zawahiri argued for a broadening of the battle against the West, focusing in particular on the United States.

These dissensions and diverse approaches toward change among Islamists point to the nature of the so-called "Islamic threat" emanating from Arabia. In some ways, for example, Saudi Arabia sees as much of a threat from the radical Islamists as it sees the threat from reform minded intellectuals and moderates; it also sees threats from reform oriented Islamists. On March 15, 2004, Saudi security forces killed Khalid al Hajj, the alleged leader of the Al Qaeda in Saudi Arabia and the mastermind of assorted attacks on foreigners and Saudi government apparatus. While the world press noted his demise, Saudi security forces rounded up and incarcerated 11 reformists -- including some moderate Islamists who had been campaigning for human rights organizations within Saudi Arabia. Thus the lines are often blurred between those political Islamists who are against their dictatorical regimes but not supporters of Osama bin Ladin and those political Islamists who believe that the politicalization of Islam including the use of force for political means is acceptable.

Arabia Besieged

It is not surprising that the media never really caught on to the strange twist that was going on within Saudi Arabia -- when in reality the "war on terror" was used yet again as an example of how threats broader than just the terrorists were being dealt with. It is not surprising to me that the perception of motives and actions emanating from this "war on terror" bring about a degree of mistrust within the minds of many Muslims. The rebuilding of the trust is not simply a matter of proclamations but more of concrete visible action to bring about a sense of confidence with Arab and Muslim societies that their regimes are to be trusted – and that, indeed, the motives of Western governments are for their good. These concrete steps will have to be at the grass root level, where a broad based contact between the media from both sides indulges in an objective interaction and sets the pace for both societies to appreciate that the way forward has to be in a better understanding of each other.

Given this growing chasm between Arabs and the West, it is important to examine how both parties deal with the issues of trust. There are complex issues that preoccupy Arabs in dealing with trust within their own society; while the family ties and tribal ethos suggests a strong bond of trust within the nucleus of this structure, on the broader front trust of state-established systems has been low. This may well be that the perception remains that such state established systems have always followed their own political agendas. The situation gets even more complex when we examine, say, Saudi Arabia, where strong tribal and religious alliances created a monarchy that is essentially tribal and feudal in essence and has been challenged by the Political Islamists and followers of Osama bin Laden. One explanation is that the way Saudi Arabia has transformed its society through the accumulation of wealth and political power. The country's annual revenues from the sale of crude oil exceed $100 billion. But critics like Osama had said that Saudi Arabia's ability to incorporate tribal affiliations into the texture of a modern state seem to have fallen short of expectations. Until the 1980s, the strong leadership of the Al Saud clan – which benefited from the legacy of King Faisal, who was very much an astute leader in touch with his subjects -- sustained the ethos of a tribal modern state where tribal allegiance was supported through the personality of King Faisal and his personal contacts with the major tribes. However, once wealth and its unbalanced distribution, coupled with surging population growth, began to impact Saudi society, the fissures of modern statehood began to emerge. It would seem that King Abdullah, the current king has made more efforts to restore tribal affiliations and be more traditional in his approach to Saudi society by not remaining as aloof as the monarchs did after King Faisal.

The view that Saudi Arabia was actually a diverse tribal society glued into one modern state began to become more apparent, more so with competing religious strains within society. The Political Islamists, who mainly came from Egypt, managed to upstage the Wahhabi clergy with their better education and worldly approach and, indeed, implicit approval from the House of Saud. Into this mix the political dimensions of militancy were born, brought to the front by the new religious clergy, and the politically militant message of Osama and his followers that was to emerge some years later. While indeed some of this militancy was infused with the experience of these Political Islamists from their experiences in fighting Soviet occupation of Afghanistan, they saw, given the view of the Muslim Ummah in their mind, that the battlefield for change, whether radical or not, was indeed Saudi Arabia itself too.

In other Arab countries, the story was different. Unquestioned obedience to central authority was prevalent, but in many cases the strong arm of government also demanded and got loyalty. Hafez al Assad in Syria relied on his Alawite community for support, and Saddam Hussein depended for political survival on his Tikriti clan. Meanwhile, the Lebanese leadership was having a much harder time pulling together ethnic and religious ties to gain political mileage. These are all examples of where the state apparatus was eventually controlled by political cliques who had strong tribal or clan links upon which they drew their sustainability. With the exception that in Lebanon ethnic and religious divisions were more prominent rather than any tribal association. Yet the long drawn Lebanese civil war also showed that the use of force while not necessarily resolving issues, as in Lebanon, provided a potent political chess piece to negotiate with.

In the other Gulf States, such as United Arab Emirates, Kuwait and Qatar, the traditional rulers proved wiser in transforming tribal societies into modern state structures. Of course, the massive revenues from oil and natural gas helped a great deal as these leaders sought to modernize their societies. But it's important to note that the leadership of these countries was careful to ensure that socially oriented expenditure programs were instituted. Oil revenues were distributed by providing free education, housing and medical care to all. To be sure, given their smaller populations the task of creating socially dynamic programs for the distribution of wealth was relatively easy to achieve. Little wonder, then, that in these countries the level of trust in the leadership has been visibly higher and social resentment is not expressed in terms of overt discontent or violence.

Where the social development model has failed the level of trust in the government has been proportionally low. This is true to a number of Arab countries, particularly in Saudi Arabia. This would explain why alternative systems or courses of action – be they political or religious (or a combination of them) -- have been embraced by disaffected Arabs. The rise of allegiance to both the Muslim Brotherhood in Egypt anxxxd Hamas in Palestine, clearly shows that loyalty has been shifting from state structures, where they have failed, to social and religious organizations. Some would agrue that such predominantly social driven agendas have meant that these organizations have had to assume political roles of greater prominence, as in the case of Hamas even leading to electoral victory.

In the case of both the Muslim Brotherhood and Hamas, the political platform in their formative years was subdued and even surreptitious. It was the emphasis on social work, community development, schools and clinics -- with dedicated volunteers giving a lot of their time to the cause of what they saw as social righteousness – that won the hearts and minds of the people. In the case of Hamas, even Israel actively supported the organization in its formative years, seeing it as a proactive social mechanism that might bring about the conditions for positive change within Palestinian society. While the Hamas was formally set up in 1987, from 1973 a 'mujamma' (office for relief) with affiliations to the Muslim Brotherhood in Egypt was set up in Gaza. This office and its key officials were, in 1987 to formally set up the Harakat al-Muqawama al-Islamiyya, (Hamas) under the guidance of Sheikh Yassin. Till 1987 and even for a few years on, Israeli authorities saw the Hamas as important in bringing social services to the people of Gaza and Palestine, with a majority of their US$70 million budget going into health care and education. Even though the flavor of the Hamas was radically anti-Israeli in its formative years it was seen more as rhetoric and only when in 1988-89 Hamas established its political agenda Israel realized the political ambitions of the Hamas were dangerous.

The political role that these organizations have since played was perhaps more a result of the political vacuum that exists in most Arab countries; that role also was reinforced by the trust and support that they received from the general public. In some cases, the ability of these organizations to deliver has been judged in the light of the governments having failed to deliver on a number of essential social issues, health, law and order, public services and education. The result has been that as mistrust of some governments increased it was inevitable that these organizations would assume a political platform for change. In some instances, the resulting electoral victories, like those of Hamas in Palestine, have translated into an inability to function as governmental apparatus effectively. Indeed during the phase of political movements and prior to achieving office, both the PLO and later the Hamas realized that the challenges and the ability to perform were quite another cup of tea. While the PLO was never really able to break the cult of key personalities within its leadership, from Arafat down, a factor that impeded the governments ability to perform. In contrast the Hamas are discovering that while they can propose to reduce corruption they still have the challenge to convert a political and emotional movement into solid measurable actions that improve the life of the people.

There has been a tendency amongst the politicians of Muslim and Arab countries to not face the scrouge of corruption. Even when confronted with issues of lack of accountability and rampant and often open corruption, they tend to deny it with almost sacred denounciations. There is usually deep denial of the existience of corruption to the point that they fail to understand that supporting accountability and a corruption free system is better for their own political longevity. I have often argued that this myopia is perhaps the single more noticeable aspect of the lack of maturity in the political leadership of these countries.

I recall a conversation with Benazir Bhutto, who came to visit my mother during my mother's terminal illness. Having met both Benazir Bhutto and Nawaz Sharif, her political opponent, I always found Benazir engaging, well read and eager to discuss and participate in a conversation. This has been different to the quieter, even withdrawn style of Nawaz Sharif, leading me to believe, perhaps rightly, that Benazir Bhutto would possess a worldly view which is broad, open minded and fair. We got around to talking about politics and I recall telling her that political parties have to also hold accountable its owns ministers for corruption. She sat in my sitting room with all her elegance and charm and refused to accept that any of her party members and especially her ministers could have been corrupt.

It is this lack of internalized accountability within the political system that forces some of the best political minds to shed their progressiveness and see themselves under some sort of political "siege" when out of power. The way political power comes with perks and a lifestyle that is so out of touch with the reality in some of these countries that when political power is lost, there is always a sense of desperation. The stakes for political power are high, being out of power usually also means financial loss and thus issues of good governance are not important.

On the flip side US policy towards the Middle East, while well debated, had not really been the focus of a deep debate within the US public. While the US public had become disenchanted with the position that the Bush Administration had taken in respect of what is being called the "Iraq Misadventure", it was only when the US Elections came up that the war in Iraq and Afghanistan became significant issues, allowing a surge of popularity towards Senator Barrack Obama, almost as if the was was not more being endorsed by the people of USA. If we track the initial stages of the pre war debate which appeared in the public media, we will find that there was little opposition to the war on Iraq. In the public domain too the impression was that the case for war on Iraq was a proven case. Prior to the events of 9/11, the US public in general saw the Middle East as a region of oil producers, and one where there was an intractable conflict between Israel and the Arabs. American's interest in Arabia and the Muslims was marginal; even lawmakers in Washington tended to view the Middle East in economic terms, and not terribly important to American geopolitical interests; the Middle East, if not much more than a marginal issue to US foreign policy, was certainly less consequential than, say, Russia, Europe, or China.

The events of 9/11 changed the perspective of Americans concerning the Middle East. The plane hijackings pushed Arabia and Muslims into their lives with a dramatic suddenness that few could have anticipated. Nevertheless, I would argue that even US politicians do not fully comprehend the enormity of the task ahead involving understanding "Arabia Besieged." US politicians will have to see the events from an Arab and Muslim perspective and for this there has to be more dialogue and more importantly to have them visit the region and understand the issues first hand. It is sad that the tragic events of people dying on each side of the divide have to be the only catalyst for the people to realize that there is a need to change.

My own view is that, in essence, the few voices that understand Islam and Arabia are marginalized from a policy planning or advisory role to the US government. The concept of "Orientalists," "or "Arabists," just does not exist within the decision making processes of the US government. There are experts on foreign policy and a fair number of academics, but it is debatable as to the weight of their voice within the echelons of power. An important Arab leader once told me that while with the British one still felt one was talking to a friend who did not necessarily agree with you, with the Americans "It's like talking to a friend who wants you to agree only with them."

Of course, American foreign policy has, at times, been directed and led by academics who have had a deep understanding of world affairs; some of the more recent Secretaries of State in this sense being Henry A. Kissinger, Madeline Albright, and recently Condoleezza Rice, all of whom were prominent professors and visionaries in their own right. However, it would seem that their engagement into policy for the region has been largely based on a preconceived model for US interests alone and not necessarily having a broad based dialogue within the academic and social fabric of the Muslim and Arab countries.

However, their worldview and their view of Arabia and Islam were never really tested except in the case of Ms. Rice, who, her critics allege, abandoned academic objectivity for political necessity. Dr Henry A Kissinger, while a well known academic was an exception in terms of his approach and engagement into the political process. His now famous 'shuttle diplomacy' set a fast pace for action and political solution which has not been repeated since, and stands to the credit of Dr. Kissinger's genius and political acumen. Whether or not Arabists and American academics have a say about US policy toward the region is not the only question; it's more the political compulsions of policy that create circumstances which prompt the Arab nations to harbor a mistrust of US policy in their region. The vision from the Arab point of view remains that the major US political compulsion is that it cannot abandon or see to be abandoning Israel and its interests. While pre 9/11 the mistrust was construed in the context of the Arab-Israeli conflict, in the post 9/11 environment the mistrust comes from the unilateral approach that has been taken by Washington to the region. For example, post 9/11 and close to the invasion of Iraq in 2003 it was common to see US forces in civilian dress patrolling sea ports in the Gulf with machine guns and sirens stopping any traffic for inspection as they chose to do so. The sea lanes of all the Gulf states and even as far as the Red Sea were controlled and patrolled by US forces, at times within the perimeter of the ports along the extended coast of the Arab world.

The view from Washington of friends and foes in the Arab world is murky and misleading. It assumes that there are two Arab worlds -- one that is moving toward "democracy and modernity," and hence an ally; and another an assortment of poor states who are poorly administered and therefore the breeding ground of terrorism. There seems to be little effort to understand the latter and to take for granted the former. Admittedly President Barrack Obama has shown a commitment to heal America's relationship with the Islamic world much of that healing will have to be the handiwork of his Secretary of State, Hillary Clinton, who is not an academic and comes with a perconcieved, albeit unjust, perception that she would be pro Israel in her approach. The first interactions on the unfolding US Foreign Policy under Obama seem to have the footprints of a differently course to his predecessors. However, one could argue that President Obama's pace of progress towards peace in the Middle East has been painfully slow.

This view, of America's apathy towards understanding the region, often ignores that the two countries where US military and foreign policy are most bogged down are Iraq and Iran, both of whom are actually very rich oil producers with combined resources more than those of Saudi Arabia and the Gulf States. Saudi Arabia's oil export quota as of first quarter of 2007 from the Organization of Oil Exporting Countries (OPEC) is 8.8 million barrels a day, while that of UAE is 2.5 million barrels of crude a day. At a price of US$ 60 per barrel that translates into a daily income from crude oil of US$528 million for Saudi Arabia and US$150 million for the UAE. Add to that figure the income from gas sales, which are not a part of the OPEC quota system and we are talking of serious money. Related to the population of 27 million for Saudi Arabia (2006 estimate) and 4.5 million for UAE (2005 estimate) the per capita income numbers are staggering.

Arab leaders find it hard to believe that in the case of Iraq the US administration had no viable game plan for the post-Saddam era, and that, on the other hand, a quarter of a century after the fall of the monarchy of the Shah and the ascendancy of the Islamic theocracy, still have not found a viable way to interact with Iran. Moderate elements within the Iranian government expected that with the attack on Afghanistan, for which Iranians are believed to have provided logistic support, there would be a rapprochement between Washington and Tehran. The fact that George W Bush imprudently labeled Iran as a part of the "axis of evil" immediately after the Taliban had been defeated shocked the moderates within Iran; after all, they had lobbied hard with domestic conservatives that it was in Iran's long term interest to welcome a healing with the United States. Was it that the United States did not correctly read the signals coming from Tehran? Did they not notice that Iran always refrained on commenting on issues where they agreed with foreign events where the US was supporting the Iranian view such as Bosnia, where the US intervened to prevent the continued persecution of Bosnian Muslims by the Serbian elements? Why did American policymakers miss the fact that by openly calling for an end to the Taliban, Iranians were offering Washington an olive branch?

It is now revealed by Flynt Leverett, the former senior director at the US National Security Council, that in Spring 2003 an overture was received from Iran for commencing discussions on a wide variety of issues ranging from Iran's nuclear program, to "efforts to bring stabilization to Iraq," and US concerns over Iranian support for terrorist organizations. While Leverett was denied publication of his book based on his "Dealing with Tehran" talking point 35 page memo which had been approved earlier for publication, it seemed that the sensitivity of dealing with Tehran was too much for the US Administration to handle. It was established at that time that the offer that came through the Swiss Ambassador Tim Guldimann and was cleared by the Iranian spiritual leader Ali Khamenei and the then President Mohammed Khatemi, and that it was a credible offer for negotiations in a neutral location such as Paris.

Secretary of State Condoleezza Rice, then President Bush's National Security Adviser, denied seeing the Iranian offer; she later changed her position, saying that she'd seen it but didn't consider it serious -- even though Colin Powell, then the Secretary of State, specifically wanted the White House to assess the Iranian offer. General Powell, never one to be particularly assertive with the White House, was pushed aside by the stronger views of then Secretary of Defense Donald Rumsfeld and Vice President Dick Cheney.

It would seem that a unique opportunity to bring Iran to the negotiating table was passed by due to a weakness of understanding the dynamics of the region and its political behavioral patterns. The State Department has since admitted such an offer was received through the Swiss official in question but did not consider the offer serious as "such offers and channels are not always credible"; this position seems to ignore Mr. Guldimann's standing as a serious and mature diplomat who would not merely have acted as a messenger had he not satisfied himself with the contents of and the authority behind the offer.

Could it be that US policy has not been cognizant of the subtle messages that have come from the Arab and Muslim worlds because within the US policy apparatus there isn't a coterie of experienced Middle East specialists?

While there may well be some specialists within the policy making group, one cannot be sure how effective their voice has been on the shaping of policy toward the region. In a sense too academics are typically avoided if their views are not in line with Administration policy on key issues. Richard Haas, the former Director of Policy Planning at the State Department and now heading the Council of Foreign Affairs, has perhaps summed up the situation for US policy very aptly:

'America's options are limited in such a context. Its thirst for the region's oil, vulnerability to terror and commitment to Israel and a moderate Arab future require it to stay engaged. But how? The U.S. experience in Iraq should serve as a caution about using

military force. It has not proved effective against loosely organized militias or terrorists who are well armed, accepted by the local population and prepared to die for their cause. And despite calls from some quarters to use force to keep Iran from getting the bomb, the case for not doing so has grown more, rather than less, compelling over time, for reasons ranging from the dangers of retaliation to the likely oil shock to the global economy.'
(Newsweek International January 8, 2007)

The result has been that the dialogue for bringing peace to the region has been fragmented. In large measure, it has not been strong enough to eliminate or alleviate the mutual mistrust that surrounds the parties involved. The fact that Saudi Arabia, through the Arab League, has actually begun to welcome a peace initiative with Israel within the context of the creation of a Palestinian state, is a major change in the Saudi position. Indeed, the Saudi leadership is aware that so long as the issue of Palestinian statehood is not resolved and a new Palestine is built with economic aid from all parties, the situation will spiral out of control and allow for radical elements like Hamas and others to take advantage of the uncertainty.

It is clear that the Saudis have sent messages through the Egyptians and Jordanians (both of whom have diplomatic relations with Israel) and to the United States that from 2002 they have had economic aid packages totaling $1 billion to commence the rebuilding of Palestine, subject to Israel taking a step forward.

When Israel suggested that the quid pro quo would be the recognition of Israel by the Arab League and recognition of its right to exist, an understanding was given that if Israel kept its part of the deal – that is, allowing the creation of a full-fledgd Palestinian state on its borers – then the Arabs would do the same on their side.

It is frustrating that in 2002 the Middle East was within a whisker of a settlement of the thorniest issue – the establishment of a Palestinian state -- and the Saudis had also deposited the first $250 million in the Islamic Development Bank toward the rebuilding of Palestine. The Israeli response was: "First we talk, then we recognize"; the Saudi position was "Simply recognize Palestine as was done at various peace parlays, with the US acting as broker allow them to achieve statehood as promised, and we will talk and formally recognize Israel."

The US preoccupation with the "war on terror" completely ignored this unique opportunity that emanated from Riyadh; it meant essentially missing the one opportunity that perhaps will take a long time in coming back to the region. For the Saudis, it would seem there was a consensus on their approach from amongst their Arab allies; when the Israelis did not take up the offer, they lobbied hard with Washington to convince Israel of the sincerity of the offer and the benefits that it would bring to the region. One has to wonder if the Saudi offer fell by the wayside because it was hard to believe that it came from Saudi Arabia and not the Palestinians -- or was it that the US policy toward Israel never had factored an initiative as comprehensive coming from an orthodox Muslim country such as Saudi Arabia?

In the event, US policy makers ensured that the United Nations never got to debate the offer made by Saudi Arabia, and this crucial episode did nothing more than to further the deepen the mistrust between the Arabs, the Israelis and the Americans. When the Americans joined Israelis in shunning the UN debate on the initiative by King Abdullah and the Arab League, it seemed that the desire for peace was being countered with emotional indifference toward peace and technicalities on the offer that were best debated rather than shunned. It is abundantly clear that this condition of statelessness for the Palestinians cannot continue for ever and longer it takes to even acknowledge proper statehood the deeper will the the mistrust of US and Israeli motives be.

Many Arab commentators and senior statesmen have been unequivocal in suggesting that for the Saudi leadership to have taken such a bold step in the post 9/11 political landscape could well have been political fodder for the followers of Osama bin Laden. While Israel might have sense a lack of sincerity in the Saudi offer, the reality is that in a perverse sense it created a foundation for a peace process that would undercut the radical Islamists in exploiting the Palestinian issue with the masses of the underprivileged within Arab and Muslim states.

What was frustrating for the Arab leadership was that while they expected Israel to perhaps not trust the offer being made, the fact that the United States leadership did not believe there was substance to the offer indicated a deep mistrust within the Bush Administration of Saudi intentions.

It would seem that all the "sounding out" that the former Saudi ambassador to Washington, Prince Bandar, a close friend of the Bush family, had done, amounted to nothing. On the broader front on interaction, it would seem that both sides have not built channels of communication they can trust, and thus both societies struggle to understand the true intent of what each has to say to the other. It would seem that between the Arabs and the West there is not enough dialogue across a broad platform, resulting in a weak understanding on the part of both sides. When it comes to inter-faith dialogue the interaction has been minimal and in fact almost absent.

Independent and knowledgeable observers on Arab and Middle Eastern affairs are at times shocked at the depth of the mistrust that exists between all parties. One is led to believe that a large measure of this mistrust flows from the lack of knowledge with the region and its nuances.

This is particularly so in the case of the United States where key decision makers often give the impression that they have not even an elementary knowledge of the region. A recent example is the appointment of US Congressman Silvestro Reyes, Democrat of Texas, as the chairman of the House Intelligence Committee. When asked if the Al Qaeda was a Shia or a Sunni group, said he thought Al Qaeda were Shia group. It is astonishing that a person in such a sensitive position – whose responsibilities include being part of the Congressional oversight of the activities of CIA and other US security agencies -- would have no clue about America's number one enemy.

One would imagine that an elected representative to the US Congress in such a role would have a more sophisticated and worldly view of the issues at hand. Indeed, the argument can work the other way, too: Not all Arab leaders are conversant with the nuances of Western societies. This leads one to believe that it could well be the lack of exposure and perhaps even the absence of a basic interest in matters of world affairs.

Interestingly, it would seem that some Israeli officials are also unaware of the Arab situation and a number of misconceptions emerge from their side, too. It would seem at various times key officials in the Israeli government were not sure of the differences between Hamas and the Lebanon-based Hezbollah, both entirely different organizations. The story is told of a senior government official in the Rabin government suggesting that some Arab workers sympathetic to Hamas be deported to Lebanon, not realizing that they were Palestinian and not Lebanese.

The crucial point is that there is a major mutual mistrust within all elements of society, government and politicians in Arabia and the West. In some measure, this emerges from the lack of knowledge and a lack of interest concerning the region. In addition, given the schisms that have become more apparent within

Arab and Muslim societies, there is a growing mistrust of the leadership within these countries.

While acquiescence to the rule of dictatorial governments is often mistaken as a support to governmental policy, a number of leaders in the Arab world assume their own popularity to be real and well founded with the people. This is all the more true for the authoritarian regimes of the Arab world as can be seen in the case of Syria under the late Hafez Al Assad, and Iraq under Saddam and a number of other countries. Even as Saddam's last days loomed on the horizon, he believed that he was a truly popular leader amongst his people and any change of order within Iraq that deposed him would not be welcome.

The reality remains that in a sea of corruption and repression such perceived popular adulation is scarcely sincere -- and certainly not sustainable as indeed Saddam was to find out. People applaud their leaders in public because they are scared – and because they know that their every movement is being monitored by the state. Part of the problem remains that there is no social contract of governance between the people and their rulers that can be put to test.

There are exceptions, of course. In some of the monarchies where the system seems to have worked -- and trust for the ruling elite has been sustained -- have been the smaller sheikhdoms of the Gulf States, such as the Unitd Arab Emirates. Even though there has not been a formal social contract of governance between the people and the hereditary rulers, the fact that by and large the ruling families of these states have embraced their own form of social welfare and created a benevolent system of sharing the wealth from oil trust in government has been understandably well received.

It is here that the transition from tribal society to modern state has been achieved with less pain and social dislocation. Mohammed Abdulla Al Gergawi, Dubai's minister for cabinet affairs, told me recently that the emphasis of Sheikh Mohammad bin Rashid Al Maktoum – Dubai's ruler – has consistently been on enlarging the capacity of his people to absorb change and to prosper by it. Sheikh Mohammad has created an enabling environment in his emirate, one of seven that constitute the federation of the United Arab Emirates.

"We embrace change and modernity, but not at the expense of our traditional values," Gergawi said. "You could call that the 'Dubai Model.'"

Whatever one calls it, that approach works. The smaller population of such countries has presented fewer problems in terms of cohesiveness and administration, to be sure, but nevertheless the challenge of creating modern states has been well managed by these states. In comparison, the larger body of Arab society has grappled with the issues of trusting their leadership and at the same time trusting the world around them.

It would seem that the Arab and Muslim worlds have major trust issues at different levels -- and this is more the norm; only in some societies and states the social contract for governance and trust has worked well. In general, the centralization of government without accountability in some cases has meant that a broad based consensus is absent on the form and substance of governance.

From a Western perspective, the notion that a Western style democracy will resolve these issues is very naïve as it fails to accept that the fact that underlying conditions for nurturing democratic traditions just do not exist. The failure of the "democracy" process in Iraq highlights the limitations of the process as people not educated in democratic values cannot suddenly embrace them and discard their tribal and religious loyalties.

Wherever the push toward democracy is imposed through force, the result will be a greater resistance and, indeed, more mistrust for the intentions of the major powers. Eventually it would seem that the element of trust between the rulers and the subjects in the Middle East will be generated by a gradual process through which experiments in limited democracy are tried out.

Countries like Bahrain, United Arab Emirates, Kuwait, Jordan and others have tried to introduce local elections at the grass root level, and in some cases a proportion of the legislative councils have been open to elections. While these may not be perfect democratic practices as judged by the Western standards, there is no denying that these are very vital initial steps in introducing democracy to the people.

Introducing full-fledged democracy to the Arab and Muslim worlds is not going to be an easy process; it may even turn out to be an impossible mission. Still, the global behavior of the United States concerning the pursuit of democracy in lands unaccustomed to it has been less than laudable. While the advent of social media and open platforms of communication, like the internet, the youth of Arabia have instigated massive and far reaching change, in Egypt and Tunisia, and on going attempts in Bahrain (more an religious-ethnic divide) and Syria, these are technically at best movements of change and not backed with cohesive policies and plans for managing a democratic process. This is not to suggest that the Arab world cannot manage a democratic process but merely to show that such democratic change will be slow, painful and will meet resistance from the old order, even when its figureheads have been removed.

The United States has pursued the war on terror with little or scant regard for the very principles of democracy and justice that they want to see around the Middle East. Most leaders in private wonder how the US could tolerate and even encourage "extraordinary rendition" -- a policy of sending high-level terror suspects to countries like Egypt for harsh interrogation prior to being handed over to the United States. American insistence of moving more power into the executive branch of their government in the pursuit of terrorists has meant that from an Arab perspective "democracy" is pliable to the extent that it can, under some conditions, represent a dictatorship.

In this sense it is not surprising that some of the leadership in the Arab world does not see any sincerity in the call from Washington for democracy and reform in the Arab world. In addition, in the current environment there is a clear-cut mistrust for the very reforms that the US wish to impose, partly because of the perceived lack of sincerity and more so because there is a belief within the Arab leadership that the current set of players in the US and some other Western countries do not fully comprehend the nature of Arab society. On the one hand in some countries like Yemen, Egypt (only recently), Syria and Libya the US call for democractic practices is clear and crisp. However, when it comes to allies of the US where demoractic practices are far from present the tone and tenor of the US message is down played.

An influential player within the region once told me that in the political and emotional psyche of the Arab leadership there is a long history of US denial and side stepping of their own promises on crucial aspects for the region.

Back in 1973, at the height of the OPEC embargo on oil shipments to the West, Secretary of State Henry Kissinger approached the Saudi royal family through Prince Saud bin Faisal bin Abdul Aziz Al Saud (then, as now, the foreign minister) and Prince Turki bin Faisal Al Saud – then the head of the national security service -- to speak to King Faisal about lifting the embargo and that then President Nixon wanted to announce this at the State of the Union address.

The Saudis insisted that the lifting of the embargo could only be linked to a fresh and open acknowledgement by the US government of United Nations Resolution 242, which called for an Israeli withdrawal from captured lands. Nixon wrote a letter professing neutrality on the subject and in the letter even suggested a quid pro quo on the subject of embargo for support for Resolution 242, and the letter was handed over to the two princes to be delivered to King Faisal. The Saudis agreed to support a lifting of the embargo "subject to President Nixon using the same words as in his letter to the King supporting Resolution 242."

Dr Kissinger was conveyed the message and it was assured that President Nixon would do as agreed. Imagine how stunned the Saudis were when President Nixon announced the understanding with Saudi Arabia for the lifting of the embargo and said that he was "hoping there would be peace within the Middle East" -- and nothing more. In fact, the president went on to actually say that the US would do what was in its best interests and would not be dictated to by anyone. This was almost like a rebuff to the Saudis, and was contrary to the understanding they had brokered with Henry Kissinger.

Episodes like this -- and many more -- have brought about mistrust for the US leadership from an Arab perspective. The fact that various assurances are given to the Arabs by leading US politicians and then these are rescinded points to the fact that even though there are pressures on the US leadership they create an air of mistrust between the two sides.

While there is a "special" relationship between some elements of the Saudi leadership and the US leadership -- especially the Republicans, as is evidenced by the close relationship that Prince Bandar, the former Saudi Ambassador to the US had with the Bush family and other presidents -- it would seem that the benefit of this relationship is not fully felt by both sides.

As US forces poured into Iraq in 2003 and it was becoming evident that the Iraqi armed forces and the regime of Saddam Hussein was crumbling, Prince Bandar met with President Bush and other US officials, giving them advice on the transition process in Iraq. The Saudi suggestion was that only the senior Baath Party members in the government and the Iraqi armed forces be replaced, but that the middle tier should be retained and paid for maintaining law and order and the continuation of the government.

Prince Bandar suggested that the existing apparatus be kept in place for another six months and the bad guys be used to get the bigger bad guys who would try and elude justice. In a surprising move after the fall of Baghdad, one of the first decisions made was to disband the Iraqi armed forces, sending home a large number of young Iraqis who were trained in the use of weapons and were now jobless.

Putting 500,000 soldiers out of a job and into a system where their loyalty could be bought by groups and political parties who would employ them for subversive activities was not a smart move on the part of the American viceroys. Equally importantly, it would seem from a Saudi perspective that their advice was not being taken on a matter of Arab affairs. As one high-level diplomat told me, "US officials would accept the advice of Spain on Arab affairs rather than listening to Arab friends tell them what to do in the Arab world."

It is important that confidence has to be built around those aspects of interaction between the Arab and the West where there is a consensus of approach. For trust to be built there has to be a major mind shift in all aspects and on both sides of the fence. There has to be a realization that the Middle East has become a very dangerous and fragile place, and that the geopolitical pressures on the countries of the region will be very different than what they have been used to.

While there is a risk that the US may in time become more disengaged with the region, it will not be some new-found isolationism that will prompt it. What is more likely is that as home-grown solutions for stability and peace in the region emerge, the US and its partners will be more inclined to step back from the high level of intrusive presence they have at the moment. This will mean that Washington will have to trust the process that the Arab's choose from them even though the texture of the political message from these changes may not be to the liking of the US and the West. This will allow, in the long run, a paradigm shift to occur in Western thinking resulting in a more equal dialogue between the Arabs and Muslims on the one hand and the Western governments on the other.

However, there are some keys aspects of policy and practice that the US will have to revisit in the coming years, and these may be radical changes from the way that the US has seen the Middle East for the last four or five decades. Crucial to this process will be major policy rethinking about the region and defining the goals of political change. It will mean a shift away from state-centric changes Washington seeks to more of a customized, culturally sensitive blueprint for the region as a whole.

For the Arab mind, the important change will have to be in a perception that the US is willing to play an honest broker in the region; this will imply a toning down the "war on terror" rhetoric, and seeking a more viable change-for-peace type of approach.

Central to this policy shift will be the way the US has approached the issue of Palestine and Israel. While it might be a little too late in some respects, it would be important for the US to sound out a revival of the King Abdullah proposal on the issue of peace with Israel.

In essence, what the Saudis were proposing was really for all sides to recognize that while Israel is in the midst of the Arabs it needs to be recognized -- and in return Israel has to recognize that a Palestinian state is also a reality in fact, if not yet on paper. There are a number of elements of the Saudi initiative that can be hammered out but none of them are frankly show-stopper; the US must exert pressure on the Israelis to embrace the peace initiative that has been offered from the conservative elements of Arab politics.

While we may argue that Saudi enthusiasm may not be the same as in 2002 when the proposal was first made, there has to be a show of trust by the Americans and the Israelis for the Saudi intent. In addition, there has to be a clear toning down of the noise created by the West about reforms and democracy in the Arab world.

It is not that these goals should not be pursued but at the present moment the conditions to bring about those changes just do not exist within the Arab and Muslim worlds. In time, these changes will occur; indeed, some important aspects of this change have already started within these countries. Bahrain, Kuwait and the UAE have undertaken varying degrees of reforms where their legislative councils are getting more representative and having more say within the state machinery. However, such changes must come from within the Arab world and not seen to be imposed on them. Confidence and trust-building work also has to take place between communities and leaders of faith from all sides. We have to understand that this is no longer just a political issue but the process is complex on many counts and is all the more complicated by society, religion and decades of mistrust. The leaders of both communities have to understand that so long as there is strife within the region the conditions for their own people to prosper will simply not happen. The situation in Iraq is perhaps the best litmus test in understanding the complexities of the Arab and Muslim worlds. There is a line after which the "Arabness" of the people mixes with the ethnic and also religious compulsions creating cocktails where clichéd solutions cannot simply work. There is a point beyond which a Sunni or Shia is Iraq will have to make an emotional choice as to what is more important; his religious affiliation or his being an Iraqi or his being an Arab? These are competing sentiments that create pressures and choices on the psyche of the Arab mind that cannot be easily resolved. An Iraqi national from the north will be a Kurd, a Sunni and an Kurdish nationalist all in the same breath, being no different than an Iraqi from Basra who will be Shia, an Iraqi and also be against the Americans and the Sunni leadership from Central Iraq. The trouble is all these sentiments come out at the same time and in often-contradictory ways. When we widen this thinking across the Middle East, the complexity of dealing with the region is magnified a great deal, to the point where some it doesn't make sense.

It is important for the US and its partners to understand that getting into this quagmire of contradictions will erode their credibility because without taking sides some of their actions will be perceived as that. It is more conducive for American policy to take a higher moral ground in the region and bring about an element of fair play into the equation and stress that it will broker peace rather than try and be the architect of peace itself.

This would require US policy to be not so hands-on. It would require the reduction of American military presence in the region. It would require generating mutually trusting arrangements with the governments of the region and, perhaps more importantly, with the people of the region through civil and nongovernmental organizations. President Obama's call for a pull out of Iraq is ofcourse welcomed, but in equal measure, his intention to increase troops in Afghanistan creates a fundamental policy contradiction.

The question remains whether a new approach can be created by the current US administration, especially given the impact of previous neoconservative policies on issues of global politics and terrorism having left a sea of suspicion that exists between different segments on the international political scene. There was too much inflexibility within the past policy makers in Washington to make any serious modifications – let alone turnarounds -- on Middle East policy, and one may doubt if the new fresh approach of President Obama will be enough to bring trust back to the equation of peace. In other words can the Obama administration change eight years of policy when the rank and file in the administration may be the very people who inherently have bought into the neoconservative philosophy?

However, should there be a change in sentiment and intent on policy, if policy were to become more balanced, transparent and fair, it might well create a major step forward toward bringing a situation of mutual trust with the Arab and Muslim worlds. If peace is to be injected in the Middle East, it must start with a major effort toward bringing confidence back to the negotiating table. A resolution of the Palestinian statehood situation and the recognition of Israel by the Arab states would be a huge coup for peace, and most importantly, it would take out the sting from the radical Islamists and deprive them of the one issue that they frequently exploit with the masses. It would perhaps be the foundation for resolving a number of other social and governance issues within the Middle East, and without a doubt it would set the pace for peace and progress.

The crucial question is whether all sides -- the Arabs, Israelis and the Americans -- have the political and emotional will to build the bridge of trust that is so vital to make this happen?

3

FRACTURED HISTORY.

I was vacationing with my family in Langkawi, an island resort off Malaysia in August 1990, when a friend called me from Abu Dhabi. He asked if I was near a television set and, if so, that I should switch it on.

CNN was showing extraordinary pictures of Iraqi tanks on the streets of Kuwait City. My first impression was that this was some sort of a bad movie, but I had turned on an international news channel so there could be no doubt that these were live images being beamed from the heart of the Middle East. Within an hour, my bank – where I was to later serve as the chief executive officer – called to say that the chairman wanted me back at the institution's headquarters in Abu Dhabi at once. That was the end of my much-needed vacation, and my wife and two sons were understandably upset that we would leave a luxury resort in Southeast Asia and fly for several hours back to the blazing heat of the Middle East.

By the time we landed at Abu Dhabi's airport, there was already an exodus out of the emirate, one of the world's wealthiest countries on account of its reserves of oil and natural gas. Many of my European friends were outbound, some citing Saddam Hussein's threat to continue the advance of his tanks beyond Kuwait to Saudi Arabia and Abu Dhabi. Irrespective of the fact that my British friends thought I was mad coming back from Malaysia -- and more so bringing my family in tow -- I had a sense that something vital within the heart of the Middle East was being altered in a way that was to have a profound effect on Arabs and the region forever.

As it happened, Saddam's invasion of Kuwait in August 1990 was more than a milestone in the region's history; it marked a permanent turning point for Arabs, and for the West. It changed the political landscape of the region, especially after President George H. W. Bush put together an Allied force to liberate Kuwait in January 1991. For some four decades, the Palestinian issue had been the centerpiece of the Middle East political agenda in the eyes of the world. The invasion of Kuwait in 1990 brought to the forefront a new dimension, a new crisis that has indeed changed the way the world is. Earlier – in the decade starting 1980 -- Iran and Iraq had fought a senseless and bitter war in which millions perished on both sides. But the direct impact of that war was largely local, and neighbors such as the Gulf Arabs watched those two big countries slug it out over a petty issue, control of the Shatt Al Arab waterway. Saddam's Iraq had tried to settle an old border score with Iran and initiated an invasion in September 1980. Much of the West, and even Arab countries, privately rejoiced as Iran -- ruled by the ayatollahs, against the backdrop of the Shah of Iran's ouster in 1979 -- was seemingly being humbled.

With moral and financial support for Iraq coming from countries like Kuwait and Saudi Arabia, Saddam Hussein was suitably equipped with an assortment of Russians tanks, American helicopter gun ships, French fighter aircraft and an assortment of weapons that he chose to gather from all possible sources. My friend Pranay Gupte, then a foreign correspondent for the New

York Times, recalls being at a rare news conference given in Baghdad by Saddam at which the Iraqi dictator openly boasted that the destruction of Iran was inevitable, a matter of days. Heralded as the modern day Saladin fighting not a crusade against Christianity but a war against the radical Shia rulers of Iran, Saddam Hussein felt he held a messianic appeal to Muslim world. No sooner had the guns gone silent on Iraq's eastern front, the issue of money owed to Kuwait and the delicate issue of the use of Bubiyan island, owned by Kuwait but leased to Iraq for building a naval base to fight the "tanker war" with Iran, cropped up between the allies.

Whether Saddam was misled by the then US ambassador to Baghdad – a hapless career diplomat named April Gillespie -- into believing that "any dispute between Iraq and Kuwait was a matter that did not concern Washington" was true or not, the invasion of Kuwait could be attributed to the intransigence of the Kuwaitis to negotiate with the Iraqis, and to Saddam's belief that he was master of the region. Moreover, Saddam had internal pressures within his army after the ceasefire in August 1988 with Iran, leaving him vulnerable to discontent within the ranks. The invasion could well have been a much-needed distraction for a large but tired army.

Whether the invasion of Kuwait was a premeditated act or merely one of Saddam's many strategic follies in which he allowed emotion to dictate his decisions, will never be entirely clear; yet in effect those sizzling days of August changed the regional and international topography in a profound manner. Saddam after all, was tacitly regarded by the Gulf Arabs as their guardian, and he was the man with the most powerful military in the region, and the protector of mostly Sunni Arabs against the Shia Persians. Now here he was invading his very ward, Kuwait, and threatening to continue marching toward the oil fields of Saudi Arabia and the United Arab Emirates on the pretext that they had taken advantage of the Iran-Iraq war to over-produce oil under the OPEC regime.

What exactly Saddam hoped to achieve with such a reckless act of invasion will never be clear because he never directly addressed the issue during his lifetime, let alone writing his memoirs before being hanged on December 30, 2006 in an Iraqi prison after a trial during which he showed no remorse for ordering the murder of hundreds of political opponents.

At best the threat of the Kuwaiti invasion was a more powerful political statement then the act itself, and it would seem that Saddam was not, after all, the strategic thinker he had been credited with during the war with Iran. If Saddam hoped he could negotiate a withdrawal in exchange for the write-off of debts and settlement of the border dispute with Kuwait, he was sorely mistaken. That's because the United States suddenly realized that it was losing a valuable source of oil supply.

Looking back from the perspective of nearly two decades later, there is no doubt that one of the most unresolved aspects of that period of Middle East history will always be the motives that pushed Saddam into his military adventure. Some insiders of the Iraqi regime of that time have suggested that dissent within his ruling cliché was on the rise; disbanding a large army after the ceasefire with Iran was weighing heavily on the strategic imperatives that faced the military dictator. Once negotiations were stalled with the Kuwaitis and the possibility of a financial "reward" for the war with Iran coming through dissolved, the politics of brinkmanship were set in motion. As the Kuwaitis stalled in the search for a solution, Saddam upped the ante by bringing out Iraq's historical claim on Kuwaiti soil, previously asserted by Baghdad under different regimes. It was clear that Saddam had left himself few face-saving routes to backtrack once he had made the claim on Kuwait as being Iraqi territory.

Fractured History

When American policy makers in Washington belatedly woke up to the dramatically changing situation in the Middle East, they discovered how little they truly knew about the region and its leaders; they seemed puzzled that the motives of such rash actions as those of Iraq were equally matched by the muted reactions that came from Arab leaders within the region. This was no more a region where peace would prevail in some strange quagmire of a regional balance of power. Over the recent past, Arab nations had resolved their disputes without necessarily resorting to force.

While Syria and Jordan and Iraq and Syria have had bitter territorial and/or political differences, these disputes have never really erupted in hostilities. The Libya-Egypt border dispute as indeed Sudan's border issues with its neighbors, while carrying the potential of a full blown military confrontation, each has kept force and saber rattling at a minimum. I do believe that a large measure of this restraint is embedded in the Arab nature and its tribal history. By and large state to state disputes have been handled within the context of a give and take or in some cases even a pretense of the issue not being important. The exception has been Lebanon where a fifteen year civil war was an excuse for all parties to exert their influence and test their resolve and influence in the region.

Saddam's move into Iraq was so atypical to what we had experienced in terms of inter-Arab relations that it did throw one off completely. What was perhaps more surprising to everyone was that since the Iranian revolution of 1979, which ousted the pro-West Mohammed Reza Pahlevi, the Shah of Iran, there was a widely held view that regional threats came from Tehran -- and that Baghdad was actually the bulwark against Iranian export of Islamic revolution and any attempts of military adventures by Iran. That notion sadly crumbled in the early days of August 1990 as Russian and US-made tanks supplied to Iraq by Kuwait itself were rolling into Kuwait City.

Saddam calculated that his stand-off with Iran had at least earned him respect amongst other Arab nations -- and especially the West. He thought that presenting them with the fait accompli of an Iraqi-held Kuwait would perhaps be considered a reward for the hundreds of Iraqi soldiers who died during the eight-year Iraq-Iran war, ostensibly "protecting" the region. This was an astonishingly naïve view; it is more likely that after the policy of brinkmanship having failed in talks with Kuwait, for Saddam any backing off on the threats he made to Kuwait would have meant political suicide for him.

As Washington started to recognize the possibility of its economic and oil interests being threatened in the region, President Bush – egged on by Britain's Margaret Thatcher – saw no other way but to organize the coalition that eventually liberated Kuwait through a war that began on January 16, 1991, and ended on February 28. Some 30 nations joined the UN-led coalition; perhaps for the first time since World War Two and the Korean War, the media started using the term "Allied coalition" in characterizing the 883,863-person force that forced Saddam's military of 360,000 poorly equipped soldiers out of Kuwait. The Allies lost 378 men and women, and another 1,000 were wounded. When asked about Iraqi casualties and fatalities, General Colin Powell, then the chairman of the U.S. Joint Chiefs of Staff, told reporters, "That isn't my problem." It may not have been, but a conservative estimate of Iraqi casualties suggests millions of civilians and soldiers were wounded or killed.

The Gulf war, termed Operation Desert Storm, could have been avoided. James A. Baker III, President Bush's Secretary of State, even held face-to-face discussions in Geneva with Saddam's envoy, Deputy Prime Minister Tariq Aziz, in Geneva. But Saddam was unwilling to abandon Kuwait, perhaps believing that the Americans simply wouldn't dare to take him on militarily in a region where the US had few historical ties.

The Kuwait war resulted in a degrading and humiliating loss for the Iraqi war machine. In the wreckage of tanks and strewn Iraqi bodies on the battlefield, a lot more of Iraqi pride and resolve was lost than most would have imagined only a few years earlier. An enduring image from that war was one of a kneeling Iraqi soldier touching the boots of an American soldier in obeisance – a photograph that seemed to many Arabs a symbol of American neocolonialism and of the projected superiority of the white man over a brown one.

It was obvious, too, that in the wake of Operation Desert Storm many Arab leaders questioned military preparedness in their own backyard. They had always thought that their armies and security forces were more than adequate for domestic surveillance and for keeping a tight lid on domestic dissent. But taking on the world's only remaining superpower, the United States, was something else. Of course, defeat on the battle field was scarcely a new experience for Arab forces: they had lost successive wars with the Israelis since the Jewish State was established on May 14, 1948.

The Gulf war of 1991 created an opening for a continuous American military presence in the Middle East. It was a precursor of the Second Gulf War, which began on March 20, 2003, when more than 300,000 soldiers of the "Allied" forces – again led by the US, backed by Britain – toppled Saddam Hussein and "liberated" Iraq. That "war" has yet to end, and American deaths are now approaching 5,000 with close to 32,000 wounded. Iraqi casualties? No one really knows.

The Iraq wars have meant not only an unprecedented intensification of America's direct involvement in the region. They have introduced an unexpected element in the traditional issue of the region, the Arab-Israeli conflict. Never before has the Middle East seemed so complicated: the Palestinian quest for statehood continues; Israel's conflict with Lebanon's Hezbollah continues; Hamas's frictions with Israel continue; and America's contretemps with Iran continues.

The issue of Iran is particularly thorny. Prior to 1990, the widespread assumption among Arab leaders was that between Saddam's military might on the one hand, and Saudi Arabia's oil resources on the other, the assured containment of Iran was in place. The assumption also was that Saudi Arabia – under the aegis of the Vienna-based 12-member Organization of Petroleum Exporting Countries – would continue to be the main oil trading partner for the West (OPEC members account for 41 percent of the world's daily supply of crude oil). The assumption among many Arabs also was that the gradual but halting peace process between Israel and Palestine, while a thorny issue, could, in American eyes, be eventually worked out under the Oslo Peace Accord framework.iv

Saddam's recklessness with respect to Kuwait altered this set of assumptions dramatically. In effect, Saddam inverted the security logic upon which the region was supposed to run. Suddenly, the Palestinian issue with Israel took a back seat and the peace process was derailed with the focus shifting to Baghdad and the emerging rouge elephant that Saddam was becoming. Israel realized that technology and air power would play an increasingly decisive role in maintaining military dominance in the region, and that conventional land warfare would be increasingly subject to the calibrations of high-tech strategies.

Ironically, it had been the Palestinians who rejoiced most at Saddam's seemingly short-term victory of taking over Kuwait. They did not realize in the least bit that he had stolen the limelight of the world political stage from the peace process in Palestine. Any thought that Saddam could broker a strategic withdrawal in exchange for an Israeli pullback from Palestinian territories was more public-relations wishful thinking, especially as America would not allow that linkage to emerge, given Saddam's aggressive posturing toward other Arab states in the Gulf.

However, understanding Saddam's posturing and motives had always been a problem for many Arabs – and Muslims across the world – and it is more likely his perceived role of a champion for the Arab cause was simply wishful thinking on the part of a constituency yearning for strong leadership in the face of American domination of the world stage after the collapse of the erstwhile Soviet Union in 1989-1991. The sad part for the Palestinians, of course, has been that their cause of statehood has been used for political gain by many of Arab leaders without sustained contribution for the cause or political nurturing of it. From the ayatollahs in Iran, to Saddam and all the way to Muammar Gaddafi in Libya and the late King Hassan II of Morocco, the cause of the Palestinians has figured in political rhetoric. Measured against actual tangent support for the Palestinians, such rhetorical endorsement has largely been little else but an assortment of continuing platitudes.

Like many like-minded Muslims, I have long been troubled by the fact that while Arab-Israeli conflict had occupied over half a century of world attention, it never really created any urgency regarding its solution, at least in Arabia. It was almost as though Arabs – and Muslims in particular – had reconciled themselves to a measure of timlessness about the issue. Until Saddam's invasion of Kuwait in August 1990, however, the Arab-Israeli issue was perhaps the only major foreign policy issue for the Americans to really deal with in the Middle East. After all, it was directly connected with the question of supply of crude oil from the region. While Arafat perhaps opposed the war against Iraq to liberate Kuwait on grounds that it should be the last resort, it did seem to him, too, that Saddam was not going to back down through negotiations. For Arafat, the promise of stalemate between the Allies led by the United States and Saudi Arabia on the one hand and the Iraqis on the other hand, would have been the best outcome. It might well have offered the possibility of Arafat being propelled to be the peacemaker between Saddam and the others. It was, however, not to be so as Arafat by choosing to support Saddam, was immediately marginalized and even ostracized by most of the Arab leadership. The late King Hussein of Jordan suffered similarly. His support of Saddam resulted in an immediate suspension of aid from neighboring Saudi Arabia; to this day, relations between the two kingdoms aren't quite what they were pre-1990. Memories are long and unforgiving in the Middle East.

From an American perspective, the objective was to defeat Saddam speedily, with a minimum of casualties. However, Saddam was to occupy the center stage of US policy priorities in the Middle East for another 15 odd years bringing about a huge reversal of US policy toward direct intervention in Arab affairs. If the feeling after the war in Vietnam – which ended in 1975 after America's humiliating departure from that Southeast Asian country -- was that US forces not be committed to protracted intervention in overseas wars, the events of 9/11 created the mood for enough fear within the minds of the average American to allow George W. Bush to pursue direct military conflict in both Afghanistan and Iraq.

The ongoing conflict in Iraq has practically assured that the peace process in Palestine is unlikely to be the number one priority for American foreign policymakers. With a large number of ground troops based in the region, the American public is obviously more concerned about their safe return than what happens in Gaza and Ramallah. But if the long-term goal of US policy is to bring stability to the region through an Arab solution to issues in Iraq, this aim also rests upon the premise of a long-term presence of American forces within the region. Surely the Americans know that the longer it takes to stabilize Iraq the higher the degree of risk not only to the US presence in Iraq but also US interests in the Middle East. To put it another way, President

Obama is not in an enviable position. At the same time the commencement of negotiations with the Taliban in Afghanistan and the commitment to a reduction in troops there all indicate that the Obama Administration has tacitly acknowledged that its policies in the region have fall short of expectations. Conversely, in the mind of the average Muslim in Afghanistan and Pakistan the move only shows that a mullah with a Kalashnikov has out witted an American with a cruise missile.

While some American policymakers have been sensitive to the shifting mood within the Arab world concerning the presence of US troops in the region, it does not mean that they might entirely understand or give proper weight to the perceptions within the Arab world. This is mainly so because American policymakers are only recently getting to have a feel of the region and how it functions and what are the compulsions of the leaders within the region. One high ranking US official who visited the region during the period after the Gulf War asked me why some Rulers within the region had very tight security around them, while others walked around alone, with one Crown Prince (now a Ruler) actually being seeing in restaurants without bodyguards or an entourage in tow? It took a while for him to understand its not about popularity or anything like that, it's the style of the person and this is how it is. Thus understanding the complexities of how the Arab leadership views the large presence of US troops in the region is not a question that can be answered with ease.

The policy priorities in the wake of the 9/11 attacks were ambiguous in the beginning and more cogent once Afghanistan had been invaded. For US policymakers – many of whom were weaned on a Cold War mentality -- the "war on terror" implied a war against a network of terrorists who had no tangible territory to defend or claim as a nation. Pentagon planners had spent decades of strategic planning for attacking and destroying and even occupying "hard assets" such as a country or a military base. In the initials days of the US assault on Afghanistan – which commenced on October 7, 2001 – the aim was to surgically attack, isolate and capture the militant leadership that was behind the 9/11 attacks.

As it became apparent that the Al Qaeda leadership was more elusive than Pentagon planners had expected, the strategic priority shifted to the elimination of the regime, the Taliban, who supported Osama bin Laden and were his long-time hosts.

Once the emphasis, from a military point of view, shifted from attacking an elusive network of militants to a country and its military infrastructure, US forces seemed to be on more familiar ground. Back in Washington, a broader model of intervention was developed based on a new philosophy that to fight the war of terror it was "important to change the regimes in the countries that support the terrorists."

The moment that linkage was established, it was easier for US policymakers to then target Iraq as not only a terrorist state but also accuse it of supporting Al Qaeda; it was an accusation that had little truth to it. However, this crucial policy shift has given the US opportunity to balance two divergent objectives in the Middle East: one, the continued stability of its oil supplies, and two -- and more importantly -- assurance for the security of Israel. Some US think-tanks have argued that with the removal of Saddam the possibility of bringing into power in Iraq a government that's willing to deal with Israel and also have a democratic form, has increased.

A broad view of the region is necessary to appreciate the quantum of the issues that have to be dealt with. The situation is all the more complicated in the post 9/11 era as the threat of terrorist attacks against the US and its allies have consumed a huge amount of attention. If Saddam's folly in Kuwait changed the way the region was to look like in the future, there is no doubt that the attack on the World Trade Center in New York and the

Pentagon on September 11, 2001, changed the way the world will be viewed from an American perspective. Suddenly, the Middle East and the Muslim worlds are no more seen as homogenous political units that the West has to deal with. The awareness that there are components within Arab and Muslim societies which seek America's destruction has changed the way foreign policy objectives are to be considered – and constructed -- in the future.

For Arabs, the fissures within their own societies have also come to the surface; divergence of political views is no more the criterion of dissent. The prospect of an emerging militant threat that could focus its attention away from attacking US and Western targets in terrorist type attacks, and instead hit out at the soft core of Arab society itself – this is terrifying for Arab leaders and public alike. The TV images of carnage in housing complexes in Saudi Arabia, and news reports of gun battles between Saudi security forces and well-armed militants showed that there is a siege within the very society from which a majority of the 9/11 hijackers came.

At the official level also, Arab governments in general, and the Saudi government in particular, have been tested regarding the substance and depth of their relationship with the United States. On the one hand, the sheer weight of US resolve to combat terrorism on Arab soil has meant that many of the Arab governments have had little choice in anything other than to support Washington's efforts.

They are clearly alarmed that the US has moved from being a passive influence through regional governing cliques to being an active participant with troops and aircraft carriers in the region. This is a major shift, one that has occurred without a single note of admission that Washington's Middle East policy has been little more than a series of failures.

My friends in various Arab governments tell me that they see a convergence with US interests in fighting terrorism as the stated aim of the militants is the overthrow of the existing regimes of the Arab world. On the other hand, many Arab governments feel a significant loss of sovereignty on their own soil -- and hence, in their thinking, they run the risk of being marginalized by the population. That this marginalization hasn't happened is mainly due to the tactics of the militants in causing carnage on Arab streets, a tactic that's unlikely to win them long-term support within the very Arab societies they seek to influence and rule.

Like many Muslims and denizens of Arab countries, I continue to be puzzled by the American tendency to preach democracy in a region where there's widespread indifference to democratic traditions. Perhaps even more tellingly, the absence of political civic education in most Arab societies creates virtually insurmountable problems for foreigners, however well meaning.

Alliances with non-democratic governments in the Middle East are at cross-purposes with the publicly stated political aims of US policy in the region. It is not strange that amongst the reasons he offered to explain his decision to "liberate" Iraq, President Bush mentioned the creation of a democratic regime as being one. Imagine how those words sounded to the ruling monarchies in Saudi Arabia, or the Gulf States or indeed within the entire Muslim world.

Of the non-secular Muslim states, where Islam is the official stated religion, only Indonesia, Pakistan and Iran have experienced democracy that bears any semblance to proper free adult franchise. Iraq has witnessed only 11 months of democracy since 1923, when it formally achieved "independence." Even in countries like Pakistan, democracy has involved human-rights abuses; elected governments have sometimes behaved worse than dictatorships, often displaying disregard to elementary accountability.

It is ironic that the one country which has held more than seven uninterrupted elections based on universal adult franchise has been Iran, a country that continues to be shunned by the US as a rogue state. I was in Tehran on a business trip the day President Bush condemned Iran in his now infamous "axis of evil" speech. I was sitting across some influential Iranian government officials, and I could see the shock on their faces as they watched Bush on television.

Rogue state? Axis of evil? It seemed that President Bush had conveniently forgotten that this very "rogue state" had provided support to American forces in their battle against the Taliban.

One official leaned over and asked me: "If America really wanted to align itself with democratic governments, then why is it hesitant to accept Iran?"

While it may be simplistic to call Iran "democratic" – especially because it's a country where the theocratic Supreme Council has more power than elected officials -- the fact remains that Iran's experiment with democracy is more progressive than the likes of Saudi Arabia and other allies of the US. At least they hold elections, and at least there are multiple candidates.

For the Iranians, there was expectation that the post 9/11 scenario would involve much work done behind the scenes by US State Department officials to ensure that an easing of the tensions would occur between Washington and Tehran. Some Iranian officials even told me that US helicopters had been given permission to use an Iranian forward airbase near the border with Afghanistan for refueling during the early days of the US attack on Afghanistan.

In addition several knowledgeable Iranians reported to me that there was heavy truck activity moving north to the Afghan border in the days before the attack on Afghanistan, some even suggesting that US forces had sought and obtained Iranian help in allowing non-lethal logistical support equipment to be shipped through Iran. Against this backdrop, I could well understand the shock that was felt in Tehran the day that President Bush inducted Iran into the "axis of evil."

Whether it is Iran one day, or Iraq on another day, Arabs feel that American foreign policy regarding the Middle East has simply been unreliable and inconsistent. On a broader platform, the issue of Palestine has been integral to Arab thinking – and the position that the US has taken on the question of peace between the Israelis and the Palestinians has, for Arabs, been a litmus test. The peace process has stalled so many times that many progressive minded Arabs wonder if in their lifetime the issue will ever be resolved. While there have been historic moments in this arduous journey toward peace -- moments like the Camp David Accord and the Oslo Peace Accord -- these have been few and, as it turned out, mostly illusory. My own view is that an enduring peace between Arabs and Jews is unlikely to be established any time soon; the historical and atavistic antagonisms are too deep to be resolved by the diplomatic tools and mechanisms currently available to all concerned parties. Worse, there are scarcely any visionary leaders capable of taking the bold and dramatic steps necessary to break the impasse.

From an Arab viewpoint, American inability to understand their position on the issue of peace with Israel no doubt frames the way they view American policy motives in the region. If eventually America can achieve a seemingly balanced outcome of its adventures in Iraq and the region, the Arabs know that Washington's decision makers will eventually have to re-visit the question of Palestine.

Arabs also understand that America alone cannot bring about a permanent peace between them and the Israelis. They know that they will need to sustain or expand on steps toward diplomatic relations with Israel. It is therefore no surprise that four Arab nations have either diplomatic relations with Israel or a commercial trade-office relationship with Israel. While for countries like Egypt and Jordan their common border with Israel and the pressures of the peace process brought about diplomatic links with Israel, Oman and Qatar adopted a more accommodating view at a time when they really believed the Oslo Accord was the defining moment for peace in the region. That's why they established trade links with the Jewish State.

While that calculation was based on the exigencies of economics, virtually all Arab states have come to accept the realities of the stop-and-start nature of the peace process between Israel and Palestine. There is no doubt that once a Palestinian state is formally established -- and the peace process between Israel and Palestine is successfully codified -- then a large majority of the Arab states will have to make their own bilateral accommodation with the Jews. From the Israeli perspective this might be welcome as oil-rich states pouring in petro-dollars into Palestine will ensure economic progress, more jobs for Palestinians and, in the long term, hopefully the reduction of unrest among the Palestinians. A legitimate Palestinian state is also likely to be the beneficiary of largess from wealthy industrialized states of the West, plus Japan, one of Arabia's biggest customers of crude oil and natural gas.

But Arabs continue to be perplexed about just how Washington approaches the issue of peace in the Middle East. Take, for example, the issue of nuclear weapons. Barring Pakistan, each Muslim state that has sought to develop nuclear weapons has been reigned in through either active negotiations (Egypt and Libya, and to some extent Iran) or through aggressive means (Iraq). On the other hand, Israel is known to possess more than 35 nuclear warheads and has a very advanced high-tech weapons program -- which in some aspects even rivals that of the United

States -- and yet not once has the US even indicated it is willing to admonish the Israelis. Of course, Israel has never formally acknowledged its development of nuclear weapons, nor has it indicated willingness to join 189 other nations in signing the Nuclear Nonproliferation Treaty.v

Arabs see the American insistence that Arab nations –and Iran – not possess nuclear capability, coupled with Washington's tolerance of Israel's nuclear stockpile, as a double standard. Israel's superior military strength, nuclear capability and the political support from Washington, ensure that its sovereignty will not be compromised too easily. It is this military strength that has been an important factor in creating the deterrence it feels is necessary for its own survival. Hezbollah's military successes against Israel during the Lebanon skirmish in 2006, however, clearly alarmed both Israel and the United States. The radical group demonstrated that it knew how to target and exploit the underbelly of the heretofore mighty Israeli war machine. Surely, this leaves little doubt that Israel will step up its nuclear program; its very survival depends on its ability to ward off military attacks, and the slightest setback can seem magnified.

While some Israelis – and their rightwing supporters in the United States – continue to contend that the Arabs are determined to obliterate the Jewish State, Arabs have resigned themselves to the presence of Israel, some 60 years after its creation in their midst. Why else would at least four of their leaders sat across the table and held peace parleys? Why else would there be private peace missions, such as those initiated by the late King Hussein of Jordan? One cannot talk to someone that one does not recognize; one does not sign peace accords with a state that one does not recognize. Indeed the emotional embrace of this reality is as much a function of Israel's desire for peace as it is a question of acceptance for the Arabs. The two elements go hand in hand, and that is something progressive thinkers on each side of the debate generally concur with.

I keep returning to the role of American foreign policy in all this because of Arabs' conviction that without an intelligently sustained strategy by Washington, there's unlikely to be any permanent resolution to the Arab-Israeli problem. This problem cannot be approached fitfully. Yet, Washington policymakers have rarely articulated to domestic and global audiences a compelling vision that America has for the region, or even iterated the self interest that the US needs to pursue in the region. Even though an effort by the Arab League to seek Palestinian statehood at the United Nations may well succeed at the General Assembly stage, the more curcial acceptance of this by the Security Council is a more delicate and ambitious undertaking.

Having met many soldiers who were stationed in the region during the Gulf War in 1991, I could not help notice the utter confusion in their minds as to the reasons for their presence in the region. This is borne out of the fact that a large number of Americans have never viewed foreign policy as a major priority in their personal political universe. America, after all, is a self contained land of plenty, bracketed by two enormous oceans, and its natural beauty and resources are bountiful. The notion of "manifest destiny" historically harbored by Americans, applied more to domestic consolidation of territory than foreign colonial adventures.vi

But since Operation Desert Storm of 1991, the continued presence of US troops in Arabia has spawned mounting uncertainty about American intentions. Did Washington only wish to rid the region of weapons of mass destruction? Well, none were found in Iraq, despite earlier assertions by the Bush Administration that it had incontrovertible proof of their existence in Saddam's land. Was the American intention to eliminate Al Qaeda? Well, so far there's been precious little by way of a linkage between Saddam's Iraq and Osama bin Laden. Was the goal to rid the world of a dictator like Saddam? But how about other authoritarian leaders in the region – like Muammar Gaddafi, whose human-rights records is scarcely salutary? Since the United States is the world's sole military superpower after the collapse of the erstwhile Soviet Union, it can conceivably choose to pursue any military campign it wishes, however unilaterally. But short-term campaigns – such as those that toppled Panamian dictator Manuel Noriega – are one thing; sustained presence in a geographically and politically fraught region like the Middle East is something entirely different. The Vietnam War showed that the price America paid – 56,000 soldiers dead, thousands more wounded, many grievously maimed – was so heavy that no administration could sustain a permanent foreign presence militarily. Such a point is rapidly approaching in Iraq.

Moreover, many Arabs ask why, if America's stated ambition is to export and institute democracy worldwide, Washington continues tolerating brutal regimes such as the one in Myanmar, which has imprisoned or put under house arrest Nobel peace Prize laureate Aung San Suu Kyi for the last 17 years. What about the colonization of Tibet by China, which has systematically sought to wipe out that region's local ethnic culture? What about Zimbabwe, where President Robert Mugabe has governed with a ferocity and disregard for human rights and civil liberties not seen since the days of Idi Amin Dada of Uganda and Haile Mariam Mengistu of Ethiopia?

Of course, no modern nation, however powerful militarily, could embark on so many campaigns at the same time. If one were to tally up the list of brutal regimes, then the list would include nations in Asia, Africa and South America, not to mention some of the "republics" of the former Soviet Union. The purists of internationalism would always argue that once a moral thread of logic, or the absence of it, is applied to a situation then the length of that thread cannot morally be restricted. It is not any more a question of being selective, and in their eyes being selective about nuclear non-proliferation and human rights by the very nature of its selective process suggests hypocrisy. The end of the Cold War initially brought to the forefront the moral imperatives of how America conducts its relations with other countries. Indeed, the scorecard might not be balanced in this respect; but support for the end of apartheid in South Africa, the involvement in ending the war in the Balkans, and coming to the aid of and leading the liberation of Kuwait, were highlights of the very moral imperative that most world watchers would have liked to see. It seems that in the post Cold War era these episodes were the high points of a moral imperative that frankly deserves due respect. Although skeptics might attach an ulterior motive to any of these basically good acts of leadership, the fact remains they were done for a good cause. But it's hard not to factor in some of downsides of American policy making – most significantly, its lackadaisal role in pushing for a permanent peace between Arabs and Jews. What is difficult to comprehend is how these differing high moral actions and political indifference can coexist in such a contemporary mix of policy actions?

The simplistic answer might be the competing demands of domestic politics that effect foreign policy, and while this may be true on a number of critical issues, like the Kyoto Protocol (the clean environment pact which America did not ratify), and the silence over China's human-rights abuses given corporate America's stake in the Chinese consumer, a more baffling picture emerges concerning global "political" issues, particularly those relating to Arabia. I have been around long enough to understand that nations primarily apply self interest and realpolitik when it comes to issues such as foreign-policy and trade – and that often the decisions they take need to vary substantially from historical patterns of leadership. But I also know that the world expects a certain bold consistency on the part of the United States.

That consistency has certainly been there regarding Washington's support of Israel. Perhaps that's understandable in view of the fact that more than 9 million of the world's 13 million Jews live in the United States; and indeed have been a powerful lobby in their own right. They have a strong lobby, and Jews make heavy contributions to domestic political campaigns.

But although here are an estimated 8 million Muslims and Arabs in the United States, America has sent confusing signals when it comes to Arabia. This could be on account of the fact that the interaction at the social and political levels between Arabs and Americans has been relatively new and not deeply interconnected. The understanding of the Arab perspective has been lacking within the American political mind; poor media coverage of domestic issues relating to Arab-Americans certainly doesn't enhance popular appreciation of Arab culture.

I, for one, don't think that such appreciation is likely to expand any time soon. "Arab" mostly translates into "oil." American policy interests with regards to Arab states have generally been concerned protecting Washington's oil interests, and usually have relied on friendly proxy states for protecting those interests. Only when the balance of that equation – one that protects US economic interests or political interests -- has been disturbed that direct US intervention becomes an option. It could also be argued that sometimes American military intervention has occurred on humanitarian grounds, such in Somalia in 1993.vii

The events of 9/11 forced Americans to consider some interaction with the Arab and Muslim worlds, even if the Americans have based the initial phase of that interaction upon an aggressive intervention into those seemingly alien worlds. I would even argue that eventually Americans will understand the need for a deeper understanding of the Arab and Muslim mentality and they will be forced to see beyond the barrel of their guns to deal with these worlds in a more deeper and meaningful way. There are 1.2 billion Muslims in a world of 6.6 billion people, and just about 301 million Americans – you do the political and cultural calculus.

The manner in which the war in Iraq has panned out it has shown that eventually the US needs to avoid the image of being an army of occupation – even though it is -- and gradually hand over power and administration totally to the indigenous population. To achieve this, a modicum of understanding of Iraqi society has to happen. However, American policy objectives have been in a state of flux; and while reactive to the 9/11 on the one hand, these policies need to be proactive in terms of finding long lasting solutions for countries like Iraq and Afghanistan. The way forward has been more precarious in many respects as both societies have a huge burden of their historical past to deal with; and as much as Afghanistan is an orthodox feudal society resisting change, Iraq is a country rich in culture but left deeply divided by the vacuum of power at its center.

In the post World War II era, the US was content with developing strategy toward the Middle East that concentrated on relations with the key states in the region. Afghanistan and Iraq weren't among them.

While containment of Soviet influence in the region was a priority, the continued economic links to key oil-producing countries was equally important. Policy toward Egypt (which isn't an oil producer of any consequence) and Libya was dictated in terms of the delicacy of the Cold War, while countries like Saudi Arabia were considered the more vital economic partners, especially for a future in which American policymakers assumed that the domestic thirst for oil would increase.

Given the Islamic faith it was assumed, and quite rightly so, that countries like Saudi Arabia would not endorse communist thinking, nor would they be especially supportive of the Soviet Union in the conduct of foreign relations. While the Soviet Union had a growing presence in the more "liberal" Muslim countries like

Egypt, Syria, and Libya, their diplomatic presence in the Gulf States (barring Kuwait) was simply not there. Chinese influence in the region only picked up pace in the 1980's, and that too has been focused on commercial links rather than a political agenda. However, this does not suggest that US policy interests within the Middle East have been met with unadulterated enthusiasm.

Washington's ability to persuade Arab states to deal with Israel and assure the Jewish State of its security, was a function of how the Palestinian and Israeli negotiations progressed over the years – and, of course, they didn't progress much. Israel's political leadership has held the key to the level of acceptance that Arab capitals will enjoy in Washington; no matter what the Arab's pricey P.R. advisers and lobbyists tell them. Other than this long-standing contentious issue, the US has been able to contain Soviet influence within the Arab world through a policy of bilateralism that was successful in a number of instances. The most important of these reversals was the extraction of Egypt from Soviet influences into the American area of influence and eventually bring them to be first Arab nation to make peace with Israel. The relative indifference to inter-Arab relations has meant that Americans have not been much concerned with how Arab nationalism has developed, or Arab monarchies have conducted relations with one another; the dictum has been that so long as US interests were not directly threatened there was no need to intervene.

Iraq, on the other hand -- especially after the 1963 Baathist revolution that toppled the monarchy in Iraq and paved the way for Saddam Hussein to eventually come to power -- dictated a foreign policy based on need. While the Soviet Union, and later Russia, remained the key ally and weapons supplier to Iraq, this did not prevent Saddam from doing business with anyone he wished, including the US and the West.

America on the other hand could not define its policy objectives as clearly as it could do in Southeast Asia, (especially after the defeat in Vietnam) or in Europe. In the Middle East, the reactive mode that dictated policy with respect to, say, Egypt on the one hand, was quite different from the steadfast support for the Shah of Iran on the other hand. While the Shah was not seemingly playing the Soviets off against the Americans, his domestic track record in human rights remained appalling. His dreaded secret police force, Savak, murdered or incarcerated tens of thousands of political opponents of the monarchy.

For the most part, America's choice of allies during the Cold War had nothing to do with "good" governments; the criterion was simple: the regime had to be anti-Soviet Union in order to qualify to be an ally.

During the Cold War era, the priority for Washington was simple: containment of Soviet influence in the Middle East region. Everything else that fell outside the matrix of that central thesis didn't warrant much attention. So much so that when the Suez Canal Crisis erupted in the 1950's, the United States was more on the sidelines. And while it did support Britain's position it did in equal measure call for a peaceful solution to the crisis. Four decades later, the US was no more an omniscient observer to the events in the region; it was becoming a direct participant to the matters. What brought about this huge shift?

While the reasons could be many, some of them can be summed up below.

The gradual diminishing of British influence in its former colonies, and the emergence of strong nationalist feelings in the new emergent nations of the Middle East prompted them to be ripe for Soviet influence. America acted through most of the Cold War period as a counter balance to fill the vacuum being left by the British, and at the same time work for the containment of

Soviet influence in world politics. However, unlike the British involvement in the past, America sought a sphere of influence in terms of the conduct of foreign relations of the newly independent countries of the Third World, and not only Arabia.

Countries like Iran, Turkey and Pakistan were considered important to America's containment policy. Thus when Iran seemed to move out of the US orbit of influence under Prime Minister Mohammad Mossadegh in 1953, he was dismissed by the Shah of Iran with American compliance, (Mossadegh was later tried and found guilty of treason; he was spared execution, but kept under house arrest near Tehran until 1967, when he died.)

British influence in the region, meanwhile, severely shrunk with the Suez Canal crisis and its earlier handling of the creation of Israel. Nevertheless, British historical knowledge of the region was paramount in maintaining a presence and influence in countries like Oman, Saudi Arabia, UAE, Bahrain, Qatar, Iran and Jordan. As Britain moved away from being an imperial power, and former colonies attained independence, the British influence was more through its past than the promise of a future. Unburdened by the weight of its colonial policy, Britain realized it had no need to play an imperial role but seek a better working relationship with its former colonies. More specifically, Britain realized that it could conduct healthy commerce with the developing economies of its former territories.

Even though independence for most Arab countries came at the height of the Cold War, there were few concerns that the newly independent nations would have fallen into the Soviet sphere of influence. Given the social and religious characteristics of these new states, it was highly unlikely that they would follow the Soviet Union. However, some of the more republic minded states like Syria, Libya and Egypt did steer a course of their own. But none of these states looked to the Soviet bloc for a political philosophy that they would adapt for their own societies, but more as a tool for leverage in their foreign policy toward the United States.

For most Muslim countries, and especially Arab ones, the character of their society, and the role of the religion within society, made it impossible to even consider an alliance with a country like the Soviet Union where religion had no role in society. Thus the United States always did seem to have an advantage knowing that Soviet doctrines would not really penetrate the social fabric of these societies.

For America, Israel assumed significant importance to its foreign policy and public opinion; its political contacts within the region had been mediocre and yet seen through the prism of its Cold War policy. The exception remained Iran and Saudi Arabia, upon whom the dependence for oil was long established; American and Western commercial oil interests were well entrenched in both countries. As Egypt's call for the Nonaligned Movement (NAM) in concert with India, Indonesia and Yugoslavia gathered pace, it was still seen as a marginal political positioning on the world stage; it did not seem in any way to pose a challenge to the American policy of Soviet containment.

American contacts with the region remained rather broad-based, and both defense supplies and commerce remained the cornerstone of US policy up until the period between 1967-1973. The two quick wars between Israel and the Arabs in 1967 and then 1973 suddenly changed American political thinking about the region. While the 1967 war was a swift victory for Israel, the humiliated Arab populations were quick to see their loss as an outgrowth of US policy rather than success of Israeli weapons on the battlefield. For the first time America realized that the prospects of a peaceful Middle East were illusionary; even though the Arabs were defeated in the war with the small Jewish state, its presence in the midst of the Arab world would refuel Egyptian President Gamal Abdul Nasser's call for Pan Arabism.

Suddenly, Arab states were divided into frontline states like Libya, Egypt, and Syria – who were relentless in wanting to confront the Israelis -- and the others who morally, if not financially, were willing to support them, such as the Gulf Arabs who had seemingly endless oil revenues.

More importantly for the long term political map of the region, the 1967 war created a large number of Palestinian refugees, who spread out into countries like Jordan and Lebanon. They joined the tens of thousands of Palestinians who'd been displaced from their homes when Israel was created in 1948. And since 1967, these refugees have become an integral part of the political history for not only the region but also for the countries that have accommodated them.

The emergence of a Palestinian resistance characterized by various shades of militancy was perhaps the most significant development of the political process for the Middle East after the 1967 Arab-Israeli war. One might argue that in those early days when Palestinian commandos hijacked planes, the complexion of future political behavior was being shaped. Ironically, four decades later those acts -- which many Arabs deemed at the time as patriotic acts of freedom fighters -- would be portrayed in broader terms as the precursor of contemporary terrorism.

The nature of this militancy and its far reaching effects on Arab and Muslim societies was also perhaps the singular reason that established Western political processes could not identify with what they saw as brazen – and unforgivable -- acts of violence.

For the Arab mind-set, the lack of Western and American support for their acts of "patriotism" were in sharp contrast to the way the violent actions of the Jewish Brigades formed in 1944 and led by Ezer Weizmann, and others during Israel's struggle for statehood, was seen in Western eyes. Arabs to this day argue that while Weizmann and others were branded terrorists by British courts, they were still welcomed into the political process. Such arguments also ignore the manner in which Yasser Arafat was also subsequently welcomed into the political process, but yet such feelings highlight the huge political and emotional divide between the West and the Arabs.

The displacement of Palestinian refugees also created politically militant populations in countries like Jordan (which in 1970 had to crack down on the Palestinians) and Lebanon, where the Palestinians were an integral part of the 15-year civil war that ravaged the country from 1975 through 1990. The domestic political mileage that the Palestinians accumulated in countries like these also led in part to the impetus for these countries to support a separate homeland for them carved from the Israeli occupied countries. To put it another way, Lebanon, Jordan and other Arab countries where Palestinian refugees had camped would be only too glad to get rid of their involuntary "guests."

American political linkage with the Palestinians or the Palestinian leadership never ever emerged till 1978, when Jimmy Carter was president of the United States. There was now recognition that American policy was not encompassing the whole range of the political process needed for achieving peace between Arabs and Jews. The emergence of the Palestinian leadership as a party to the political peace process was a painful one both for the Palestinians themselves and for the West. Part of the reason for this was that the Palestinian leadership was very "Arafat centric" and other political figures within the Palestinian leadership were never really exposed to the US political leadership till another decade. The evolution of the Palestinian Liberation Organization (PLO) into a political machine rather than one geared for armed resistance also meant that it had to seek deep within its ranks to find the leadership more suitable not only to negotiate the peace process but also to represent a more broader political view point of the Palestinian people. The maximalist approach of leaders like Arafat – the "all or nothing" approach – was hardly proving productive; the Jews were not about to vacate the land they'd been given in 1948, nor much of the territory they'd seized during the conflicts of 1967 and 1973.

The 1973 war with Israel in some measure restored Arab pride as the Israelis this time suffered setbacks on the battle front, and for the first time saw Arab armies effectively using Soviet weapons against Israeli weapons supplied by America. One has to wonder if this was an incentive for Soviet presence and influence in the region. Suddenly, Russian embassies sprung up everywhere in the Middle East, and even the Chinese established a token presence in Cairo and Damascus.

America under President Carter realized for the first time that its involvement in the Middle East could no longer be one of a distant party. The stakes went well beyond the simple commercial interests of oil; the West suffered a massive shock when the Arab oil producers imposed an oil embargo on exports in 1973, disrupting Western economies. Suddenly, the convergence of oil as a weapon for political ends was a reality and perhaps a vital element in making the American political leadership understand that a simplistic view of the Middle East and the Arab mind was not going to work.

The oil embargo of 1973 was also a moment of empowerment for the Arab oil producers in particular, and the Arab population in general. The fact that it was the only way the Arab nations could reinforce the message from the battlefield, where for once Arab armies had a modicum of success. The embargo also broke the pricing cartel of the major oil companies, who in some cases welcomed this free movement of oil prices given their huge concessionary interests in oilfields.

It eventually gave a strong and enduring political voice to the Organization of Petroleum Exporting Countries (OPEC), and within it the Arab voice now carried weight. The resulting economic wealth that came to the Arabs also meant that a huge development and spending spree by these newly empowered nations would accrue to Western suppliers of goods and services. In this emerging scenario, the United States had to accept that its role in the region and its role of managing Cold War politics was rapidly changing.

The resulting economic boom from the 1973 oil crisis created amongst the Arab nations a sharper difference between the haves and the have-nots, as small but increasingly rich Arab nations – particularly in the Gulf -- emerged. On the other hand, countries like Jordan, Syria, Egypt, Lebanon, and a few others not having the oil resources that Arab OPEC members possessed, continued to grapple with the economic ill-effects of war and poverty. Countries like Saudi Arabia, UAE, Qatar, and Kuwait – which had relatively small native populations -- suddenly emerged with huge financial surpluses; their ability to provide financial aid to the poorer Arab countries increased dramatically. For the poorer Arab countries, the promise of US aid or World Bank assistance was now substantially complemented by the prospect of their rich cousins not only providing developmental aid, but also direct investments in their economies. In addition, all the newly rich Arab countries required both skilled and unskilled labor -- the demand for which was enormous in creating a huge float of petro-dollars coming back to the poorer nations through worker remittances. Egyptians, Moroccans, Tunisians, Jordanians, not to mention Palestinians, started pouring into the oil-rich countries, often to accept menial jobs, but also to take up lucrative managerial positions.

While the assistance to the poorer Arab countries was in more in the form of financial aid, it did reduce the US leverage into the poorer countries, especially those bordering Israel. For America future dealings with these countries would have to rely more on political savvy than merely economic aid. However, the decline of US aid as a means of influence on political outcomes did not mean their influence was eliminated.

In some cases the money given to them by the rich Arab cousins was spent on US technology and, in some cases, on US-made weapons. The political tack that US policy had to take was more centered on the issues that concerned Israel and its neighbors. American interests in the region were actually helped in the long term with the emergence of rich Arab nations as they remained in the mainstream; they were the non-radical states and also physically distant from Israel.

These Arab countries often provided a voice of moderation and brought about a greater degree of balance within the Arab League, while certainly calling for Israeli withdrawal from Palestinian areas captured in 1967, but falling short of calling for another all-out war.

America's commitment to preserve the State of Israel has been the uncompromising cornerstone of its policy within the Middle East since 1948. The 1978 Egyptian-Israeli pact – brokered by President Jimmy Carter, and which he should have received the Nobel Peace Prize along with the eventual recipients, Egypt's Anwar El-Sadat and Israel's Menachem Begin -- was designed to achieve a status where both sides of the dispute could respect the policy imperatives of the US and provide recognition of Israel by Arab nations.

Though only two Arab countries -- Egypt and Jordan -- have established formal diplomatic relations with Israel, the eventual inclusion of the PLO in the peace negotiations, and certainly the accelerated determination to create a Palestinian homeland, have been significant achievements in the path toward to peace in the last few years. While the seemingly difficult part of the journey toward peace was to get the Palestinian leadership to the same table as the Israeli leaders, the more difficult task has been to put the frontier posts toward Palestinian statehood into place. Thus the creation of a Palestinian state, and independent in the true sense from Israel has simply not happened. The long-drawn process of bringing about peace through negotiations has spanned long decades, resulting in a ticket of political pressures that might well be responsible for tangible results being slow in coming.

While one may argue that peace between Israel and the Palestinians has no direct bearing on the Arab countries of the Gulf, or indeed other than the states adjoining Israel, it does have enormous psychological importance. On the one hand, it shows a concrete move towards creating peace, but on the other hand it serves as a barometer for judging the fairness of American policy in the Middle East and acts as a gauge for Washington's sincerity and evenhandedness. The fact that Israel is heavily armed and possesses nuclear capabilities is something not ignored by the Arab leadership; and as much as it serves as a deterrent for rash moves against Israel, there is a quiet acknowledgement that it also has the potential to be a flash point in the Middle East.

The presence of nuclear weapons in Israel acts as a clarion call for the nuclear ambitions of Muslim and Arab countries. Prior to American intervention in Iraq, the question of peace in Palestine was the only issue of serious importance for the Arab world to consider on the world stage. Resolving the Palestinian issue would surely create for the United States a huge degree of acceptance within the hearts of the Arabs.

The developing world is often amazed at the manner in which Iraq, Iran and Libya are being targeted by US policy makers to come clean on their nuclear-weapons policies, while Israel which is a non-signatory to the Nuclear Non Proliferation Treaty continues to develop and hold nuclear weapons. Even when revelations came up that Israeli agents had been stealing defense secrets from the United States, the ensuing uproar was short lived and muted. As one Arab diplomat told me, "Imagine the trouble if an Arab secret agent had been caught stealing that kind of information?" It is this feeling that is at the heart of how Arabs in general, and their leadership in particular, feel about the unfairness of their treatment on the world stage.

A major problem exists among Arabs in understanding the policy bias that the US has toward Israel. A largely uneducated Arab population subscribes to the conspiracy theory of an American-Israeli axis determined to destroy the Arab world. The educated middle class and the politically astute in the Middle East acknowledge that ignoring the presence of Israel and not seeking a workable peace with Jews is a folly; but few would, in the face of public opinion, openly advocate their views. In so far as selling any peace accord to the public is concerned, the view remains that once such a peace is achieved it would fall upon the Arab leadership to sell that peace. After all, in Egypt where the population was resolutely against peace with Israel, the eventual outcome was a quiet acceptance of the realities of the region.

There is a quiet acceptance within the Arab mind that reforms are needed within their system. The debate that ensues is more over the direction and content of these reforms. The Western view remains that political reforms will usher in democracy that in turn would lead Arab societies to a more participative and responsible role in regional and world affairs. This view is radically different from what Arabs within their own society see as the crux of the issues. The search for a democratic system within the Arab world lends itself to essentially a more secular definition of the society; Arabs see virtually no room for a secular state order where the role of Islam is absent from the main fabric of social, and where possible, political life. Liberal Arabs would gladly embrace a democratic system within the realm of a more liberal interpretation of Islam; however, this is subject to pressures from within Arab societies for which the solutions do not necessarily exist in think-tanks in the United States.

In fairness to Washington, American involvement in the region post 9/11 and the actions it has taken with respect to Iraq, suggest that its choices of not being involved have diminished. It would seem therefore that there are two currents affecting US policy from Washington's own perspective. On the one hand is the traditional and historical relationship with Israel and the need to find solutions within a Middle East perspective for peace within the region. On the other hand, America has to deal with the larger Arab world and pursue a policy which is bilateral in emphasis as it would wish to be aligned with the overall goal of instituting stability within the Arab world. It is finding a balance between these two competing dictums where the problems for US policy makers have been the most difficult to handle. While in extreme situations of conflict, like the 1991 Gulf War, an element of restraint was easily applied on Israel not to react to the Scud missile attacks from Iraq. But it is in relative periods of "peace" that the task of marshalling the different pressures on US policy seem to be stretched to the limit.

The regional issues that concern the countries have taken a back seat to the way the US perceives the region. The concept of "allies" that was seen in 1990-1991 has not perceptibly changed in the way America deals with countries like Kuwait and Qatar in particular. The fact that both countries have very small populations, large financial resources and inherent security concerns of their own, means that both countries have been more agreeable to the mutual containment of the "rogue" nations in the region.

While the rich Arab nations have always welcomed American presence in the region on a political level, some of them have been uneasy about the presence of military forces on their soil. This concern has come more from domestic pressures than from other countries. Hence, countries like Saudi Arabia have had to rethink some of the aspects of their relationship with America, particularly when it has concerned the stationing of US troops on Saudi soil.

Within Arab societies there is a perceptible change, as countries like Saudi Arabia cannot be sure of a monolithic social acceptance of the current order. American reactions to developments within Saudi society are not unfortunately seen from a Saudi perspective but from an American perspective, and while this is normal and expected in the light of the events of 9/11, American policymakers must understand that their tackling of the "terrorist" threat has to be a function of understanding the way Saudi, and other Arab and Muslim societies are undergoing changes.

It is the failure of modern societies in the Arab world to deal with the reasons for underlying anger against the regimes and in large measure also an American failure to understand the region that explains why a great deal of that anger is projected toward the US. The fact remains that most of the regimes in the Middle East are walking a tightrope in their support for the US and UK coalition against "terrorism."

The rank and file in the Arab world certainly deplores the attacks on the US, but in equal measure they either feel that the reaction and incrimination of Muslim militants was too swift, or at best they equate the US reaction to the events with their lack of action against Israeli actions against defenseless Palestinian refugees.

On both fronts the US and its allies in the region lose the crucial battle for the hearts and minds of the Arab in the street. It is here that the future of the Arab world will be framed, whether it is through the imposition of democratic traditions or through the voice of the unheard.

American policymakers seem to have initially imbibed the views of Samuel Huntington's concept of a "Clash of Civilizations" and saw the need for a crusade against the "evil of Islam."

It was only after stumbling on the part of President Bush by his equating the attacks on the US as the "evil of Islam" was seen as nothing more than stupidity that a more marginal view developed of dividing the Arab and Muslim world into "good" and "bad" Muslims. Muslims were to prove they are "good" (i.e. by the rigorous standards of the Patriot Act), and on the international scene the "bad" Muslims like the Taliban and Saddam Hussein were singled out in a strategy that clearly suggested that the US was going to rid those countries of the "bad" Muslims so as to allow democracy and freedom to flourish.

In any case, that at least seemed to be the core of the philosophical message that shaped American policy in the aftermath of the events of 9/11. The whole premise of this line of thought ignores that the battle that will ensue in the coming decades will not be between Western Civilization and Islam, (hence most Arab states), but within Arab and Muslim societies themselves. That is where the battle lines will be drawn and the solutions for this have to be found within the Arab mindset and not necessarily the political will of the West.

While America's stated aim seems to be to install democratic regimes in countries like Iraq and Afghanistan, there is scant understanding in Washington that a democratic process in both countries will either bring Islamic oriented leaderships (the sympathy vote) or certainly nationalist (and eventually anti-American in sentiment) governments into power.

Since 9/11 Pakistan, Turkey, Morocco, Kuwait and Bahrain have had varying levels of elections where the results have clearly yielded pro-Islamic gains; even though the platform may not have been openly anti-American, the interpretation of the results are unmistakably different then what was expected.

Admittedly these were knee-jerk reactions in these countries to the events unfolding on the world scene. But those reactions highlight the huge effect that religion can have on these societies. Indeed, most Arab and Muslims societies, contrary to popular Western belief, are very welcoming of foreigners and indeed very hospitable. By the same measure, when Arab and Muslim societies have been faced with dangers and external threats they have almost always reacted by having a more fundamentalist approach which by their nature has been less tolerant.

The inclusion of a democratic emphasis as one of the US foreign policy objectives for the Middle East may well be a naïve approach to the region. Given the lack of education, and the absence of reliable institutions of good governance, which would support a democratic representation in these countries, the adult vote would clearly be a vote of illiteracy and emotionalism. The democratic experiment in the Arab and Muslim world has been fraught with obstacles and false starts that begs the question whether these countries would ever have a represented democracy?

Some have drawn the parallel that Islamic societies are not fundamentally suited to democratic ideals and if they are to incorporate them then, like Turkey, they need to develop secular complexions. The issue of religion and state are indeed complex within societies where Islam is the official religion of the country, and simultaneously where the Muslim clergy has entrenched itself in the social fabric of the country.

America's relationship with the underlying narrative of society has been difficult to maintain. Unlike the British, who had a battery of Orientalists who spoke Arabic and had established themselves as authorities in Arabic and even Islamic studies, America has lacked a deep tradition of contact with the Muslim and the Arab world. Only in the past two decades have American intelligentsia realized that if the Middle East and the Arabs have to be contended with in the landscape of American foreign policy, then an understanding of them beyond the cursory stereotype has to be developed.

Arabs believe that it is this lack of placing the Arab and his culture in a historical context that causes a major part of the perceptional problems towards Arab nations. This also lends itself to considerable confusion between the reference to Islamic societies and to Arab societies, and quite often the terms are used to mean the same, when that may not, and usually is not, the case.

For the Arab mind, too, there is considerable confusion over the use of the word "Arab," and more often the reference to Islamic societies.

Within the Arab world, the mind-set of the Arabs is radically different region to region, as can be seen from the Lebanese Arab's distinctly Westernized or rather modernized outlook, in contrast to the Yemeni tribal outlook.

Interestingly, the 22-member Arab League – founded in 1945 -- is best representative of this wide contrast within the Arab world, as African "Arab" nations like Mauritania and Ethiopia claim membership to the League with the same gusto as Saudi Arabia and Iraq. The slogan for Arab unity therefore has been as confusing to the Arabs as it has been to the outside world. At various times it has served as a moral meeting place for opinions that concern the "Arab" world, and yet it has never really displayed any degree of serious unity on issues within the Arab world.

While Islam as a religion has been most prevalent in the "Arab" world, its binding influence has been at the social and emotional plane; in times of crisis a "political" Islam has found favor amongst the people. Yet Islam in most Arab societies has not had to compete for space with any strong secularist creed; this has been one of the more obvious features of Islamic societies.

However, to claim at the nation-state level that emergence of an Islamic political philosophy as being the main guiding principle of inter-state relations would be quite off the mark.

America's dealings with the Arab world have been restricted to the core of what one would consider the Arab world, namely, Saudi Arabia and the Middle East in general. In so far as the perception of a pan-Arab nationalism is concerned, there is scant regard for a political pan-Arab sentiment. In sharp contrast, amongst the Arab masses, especially the "voice" of the street, there is more rejoicing at American failures in the region than there is applause for Arab success.

It is precisely this sentiment that has been sympathetically garnered for causes like those of Osama bin Laden and his followers. To them an Islamic revivalist movement is based more on a hatred for the West than actually on the essence of the movement itself.

Osama bin Laden had managed to create amongst some of his followers a distinction between what the people of the region want as opposed to what the governments and rulers of the region are doing. Even radical Islamist thinking since the times of Syed Qutb, the Egyptian fundamentalist thinker of the 1950's, has created concepts that make the distinction between "pure" Islamic societies and "impure" Islamic societies. This form of thinking has been the basis of the radical Islamists' battle with the established regimes of the Arab world where the concept of

"Jahilyyah" (ignorance) -- where Syed Qutb argued that non-theocratic Islamic states were perennially in a state of ignorance -- was placed as the foundation for a Islamic revival.

The view of Syed Qutb and his followers differed radically from the more political stance of Pan-Arabists. This constituted the foundations of what were later to be a replacement of the Pan-Arab ideal of 1950's with the 2000 ideal of Islamic revivalism through the guise of fundamentalist movements. It is dealing with this phenomenon that America and its allies have the toughest task ahead as winning the minds and hearts of people will always require a deeper and more patient understanding of the region.

It would be wrong to argue that thinkers like Syed Qutb saw their own views as radically fundamentalist, when in reality through his writings such as "Maalim-fi-l-Tariq," he tried to explain the condition of Islamic societies and asserted the concept of legitimacy of regimes as measured against the yardstick of a theocratic, and therefore Islamist, outlook.

The fact that the Muslim Brotherhood and later Osama bin Laden followed the percept of their philosophical outlook from Syed Qutb's views, while not a coincidence, is nevertheless as clear cut as it sounded.

Indeed, the connection was rooted more through Syed Qutb's brother, Mohammed Qutb, (author of the book "The Muslim Path") who, while preaching in Saudi Arabia, was the teacher to Ayman Al-Zawahiri, the second in command to Osama bin Laden and now its new leader after death of Osama bin Laden in a US Navy Seals attack in Pakistan. Islamic scholars, nevertheless, provided the emotional net for the movements that were born to follow them; it was not as if the scholars themselves formed the movements, and therefore it is not clear if the radicalism came from the philosophy or from the interpretation of the thought.

Needless to say that while in the 1950's through the 1980's the Islamic revivalist movement was turning to scholars for inspiration; it was also being nurtured to replace the failed zeal of Pan-Arabism of people like Nasser of Egypt.

In a sense President Nasser's flirtation with Pan-Arabism and the Soviet Union, at times under the suggested guise of a broad socialist platform, caused enormous distress in the minds of the fundamentalist clergy and scholars who had positioned the Muslim Brotherhood more on a social rather than a political platform. It would seem the clergy itself was split on how to react to Nasser's professed nationalism and encouragement of ties with the Soviet Union, some arguing that the politicization of the Brotherhood was inevitable, while others wished to stay in the agenda of "Tabliqh" (preaching) and reinforce the social agenda with the people.

Nasser's witch-hunt of the Islamic clergy and imprisonment of scholars and Brotherhood activists accelerated in October 1954 when he used the pretext of a failed assassination attempt on himself to purge not only the Brotherhood but also remove his mentor, President Mohammed Naguib; that way, Nasser effectively became Egypt's leader till his death of a heart attack in 1970.

While a number of pro-Brotherhood scholars went abroad after their release from jail, mostly to Saudi Arabia, those who didn't believe in the politicization of the Islamic movement stayed on in Egypt to form the core of what remains till today a scholarly community with good standing in circles of Islamic theology and jurisprudence.

The likes of Osama bin Laden never did receive support from this elitist clergy who continue to believe that Ayman Al-Zawahiri's influence on Osama and the radical youth was actually counter-productive to the agenda for social and Islamic revival within Muslim communities.

The radicalism that confronts the world today and is perceived in the West as a broad-brushed result of Islamic fundamentalism is actually only a threat from political Islam that has used the appeal of Islam to garner support from the Muslim youth.

This entire process was going on at a time when the Big Powers were embroiled in their control of influence over regimes of the Arab world. The Cold War and the lack of knowledge of the underlying social dynamics within Arab society resulted in a general perception of things being fine within the Arab world. In a sense, one can argue that the revivalist Islamic movement, which soon became more radical and fundamentalist, emerged from belly of Arabia with no birth pains and generally unnoticed.

Even regimes that could have been threatened by this radical Islamist thought did not notice the long-term implications of what seemed like scholarly diversions toward Islamic philosophy. In the West, the people most familiar with the Arab world and Islam had been sidelined and the new emerging powers of the New World, like the United States, had little interest in a deeper understanding of Islam; what mattered to them was the geopolitical picture, and not the tone and texture of how it was composed.

The model for dealing with the Arab world during the 1960-1980 period was based either on government to government interaction – where social problems of poverty and neglect existed, and the sanctioning of new aid packages were considered adequate to win the hearts and minds of the people.

In so far as dealing with rogue governments was concerned, the US policy in the region was pretty straightforward and in large measure was dictated by the needs of foreign policy objectives. The allies of the Cold War became the rogue states of the post Cold War era, and containment of Iran was more vital than the issue of democracy in Iraq or elsewhere. However, the emergence of a fundamentalist Islamic anti-American sentiment has changed the nature and substance of the reaction that is expected of American foreign policy in the region.

It is arguable whether America's engagement with such forces within the Middle East, and the Islamic world would have happened were it not for the events of 9/11. Given that the main thrust of the ideology of people like Osama Bin Laden and his followers was the removal of "corrupt" regimes from the Middle East, while their focus has remained on a change within Saudi Arabia, it was only a matter of time when US policy would have had to take cognizance of the growing instability within certain key Middle Eastern countries.

For Osama bin Laden particularly, the aim of his activity has principally been a messianic mission to replace the House of Saud in Saudi Arabia, while at times he has seen himself also as a leader for the Muslim Ummah. Eventually Osama bin Laden and his followers would hope that as the threat to Arab regimes from within emerges, America will work harder and closer with those regimes to protect its economic interests in the region, giving a widespread legitimacy amongst the masses to the movement against the existing Arab regimes.

The fact is that this has not happened and while the battle for the hearts of the masses may not be over, regimes have embarked upon limited reform programs of their own to satisfy the pent-up demands within their own societies.

The problem for some countries has been that the Islamists from within have attacked them as vehemently – just as they have been by the US for not undertaking radical reforms. The problem of pressure from Washington became so acute that at one point Saudi Arabian insiders had to ask the US to downplay the "reform" slogan as it was making the task of reforms all the more harder.

American policy planners have been bothered by their inability to understand the domestic forces what work within the Middle East that might destabilize what seem to be robust and stable governments. The suddenness with which the Shah of Iran was toppled in what was initially a populist uprising funded by tehran's bazaaris – one that later got hijacked by the clerics -- astonished most within the State Department. After all, the Shah of Iran had invested huge sums of money not only to build a military force to play a role within the region but had also spent a huge amount on domestic security forces and the police to ensure precisely that a street uprising against him would not succeed.

Were it not for the fact that the Shah's policies had no domestic following, and were it not for he fact that the ruthlessness with which opposition to him was crushed, perhaps the face of the region might have been different.

In contrast, in Egypt the emergence of an intolerant regime of President Nasser also created the breeding grounds for an opposition that used religion as a means of protest and more importantly as a rally call for the people. Unlike Iran, the Egyptian movement never had the chance nor the in-depth public sympathy to turn to a street led uprising; yet movements like the Muslim Brotherhood were extremely well organized and exported a large part of their thinking and philosophy into the region.

It would not be wrong to suggest that a large measure of the philosophy and passion in fundamentalist movements within the Islamic world come from an Egyptian component, which can be traced to the early years of opposition to both President Nasser and later President Sadat. Even when in August 1966 Syed Qutb, the scholarly mentor of the Muslim Brotherhood, was executed, there was no uprising on the streets of Cairo.

I would argue that if Saddam's 1990 invasion of Kuwait had not happened and the subsequent direct involvement of the US in the region would not have been so pronounced, the eventual conflict between fundamentalist militant organizations and Middle Eastern regimes would have occurred in any case. All that the American presence has done has given such movements an impetus and a rallying call that was previously solely directed at Israel.

It is however unlikely that the broad-based sympathy of the youth that exists for such movements would have been so obvious; indeed one can also see that such youth have two driving thoughts -- a hatred for the likes of Saddam Hussein and other dictatorial rulers in the region, and a hatred for the American presence.

It is this difficult combination to deal with that makes them a potent threat to American policy in the region. Recent detailed accounts of the US administration set up in Iraq highlights the inadequacy of understanding of the way in which Arab societies and their political systems work. Prior to handing over power in Iraq, at least nominally, to the provisional Iraqi government, the Coalition Provisional Authority headed by L. Paul Bremer controlled Iraq soon after its invasion in 2003, but such control was exercised from a heavily protected – and therefore severely insulated -- Green Zone in Baghdad; it was common that CPA officials had never been outside Baghdad for months. It was no surprise that their decisions to fire all school teachers because they were Baath party members ignored the fact that during Saddam's rule you could not be a teacher unless you were a Baath party member.

American policymakers perhaps smile at the irony that on the one hand these movements are the ally of the US in wanting to get rid of the corrupt and dictatorial regimes in the region; yet the State Department would list only a handful of the countries in that strain.

To the fundamentalists it would imply a widespread change in the region whereby from their perspective every government within the Middle East would need to be replaced with an Islamic government. The fundamentalists know that as things stand within Arab societies today, any move toward elections based on total adult franchise would result in perhaps a sweeping electoral victory for pro-Islamist candidates. To that extent the fight for the future of the region cannot be conceived as a military battle but one that is dependent on many factors -- from economic well being, to education and, most of all, long-term confidence building. Islamists shun the modern notion of reforms as this would imply secular education, preferring instead a wider notion of an Islamic welfare state where the notion of education would be non-secular.

In a reformed Arab world under an Islamist notion, the concept of electoral reforms would only mean a victory by the ballot for the fundamentalists who, after achieving power, would commence on a social exclusion of any secular thought, particularly if it came from liberal minded Muslims. It is here that the battle for ideological dominance will be fought over the next several decades.

4

UNDERSTANDING THE DIVISIONS.

There are Muslims, and then there are Muslims. A question I have been asked persistently during my years in Arabia has been to explain the difference between the different sects of Islam and, perhaps more importantly, to try and fathom the differences that go beyond theology to the ethnic and cultural distinctions. One would think that such a query would come mostly from non-Arabs. But I remain surprised how many Arabs themselves turn to me – a Muslim-born non-Arab – for insights into their society and history.

Perhaps I shouldn't be surprised. Arabs are bewildered on account of the upheavals that have upended their longstanding assumptions about themselves, especially in the wake of the American forays into the Middle East in recent years. Those forays have done more than just rend the physical fabric of places such as Iraq; they have created – and perhaps even sustained – myths about Arabs and Islam that are turning into dogma. It is thus commonplace that a large segment of Western society has a rather clichéd view of Muslims, some of it fed by the superficial casting by the media of Muslims and Arabs into stereotyped roles.

Understanding the Divisions

For example, would it be wrong to assume that the Shia of Iraq will embrace the Shia of Iran, as some in the Bush Administration had suggested? Somewhere along the way, the fine line of religion and an ethnic sense of belonging becomes blurred and we have a totally different perspective on the people and the region. While in some ethnically diverse countries like Iraq, only the removal of a central authority has brought out the schisms within society, in other countries harsh divisions have been created from absolutely nothing. As one prominent Iraqi physician told me recently, "I am Shia, I am married to a Sunni, and it never really mattered to me other than the fact I am an Iraqi first and last. But today, who knows?"

Arguably today Islamist political parties are as prone to exploit these ethnic and sectarian differences as indeed the West is naïve about the over simplification of the religious divisions within the Muslim world. While on a macro view most Muslims will be highly emotional and united about what they perceive as attacks on their religion, and yet at a micro level the deep suspicions of sects within Islam become very obvious, as highlighted by the Shia and Taliban (who belong to a Deobandi school of thought) hatred for each other.

Against the backdrop of a changing Arab and Muslim world there has been the undercurrent of a movement born out of an Islamic zeal mixed with the anger of the "unheard" that for close to five decades that had been simmering below the surface. The emergence of a militant Islam within these societies has caused distress as much on the inside as it has on the international scene. The presence of the Muslim Brotherhood in Egypt, for instance, is not something that cropped up in the last decade, but its effect, while persistent for some years in Egypt, now has come to the forefront under a radically different set of circumstances born out of the 9/11 events.

When in 1998 members of the Brotherhood attacked tourists in Luxor killing 68 and wounding scores more, the potency of their message was highlighted, more so as the attack was perhaps the largest single attack at that point in time targeted against foreigners. And strangely enough it was the broadening of what they called their Jihad that actually triggered revulsion within the masses. The very masses from where they drew, at least notionally, sympathetic support, suddenly felt that the message of the Brotherhood movement was not supposed to involve attacks on tourists.

Yet movements like the Brotherhood in Egypt were localized, at least initially, and their export of ideology was limited. They took their ideology to some Gulf States through the Egyptian-born teachers that were recruited in to the school system there. In time this "export" of ideology was either purged in the Gulf States or could not be nurtured in societies where the presence of a deprived class was not as strident or apparent as in the slums of Cairo.

The exception to this, of course, was Saudi Arabia where the blend of anti-Nasserite sentiment within the Al Saud ruling family and fear of his pro-Soviet and secular thinking, created an atmosphere that proved hospitable for radical thinkers and leaders of Egyptian fundamentalist movements. It was the Saudi government who were the first to welcome the expelled scholars and rank and file of the Muslim Brotherhood of Egypt into their society as it served the twin purpose of getting back at Nasser of Egypt for his support of the Soviet Union, and also allowed the Saudi's to find a resource of teachers and scholars for their emerging educational system.

However, the growth of militancy -- much credited by Western scholars and commentators to the likes of Osama bin Laden -- could be actually attributed to three key political developments in the Muslim world.

One was the changing nature of the Palestinian and Israeli conflict; another was the civil war in Lebanon; and the there was Russian invasion of Afghanistan.

All these spawned conditions from which emerged irregular militias most of whom professed as being Islamic. While in Lebanon the 15-year civil war was fought across religious and ethnic lines – between Muslims and Christians, for the most part -- it also helped shape Shia and Sunni Muslim militias that in time were to serve perhaps as the most fertile source for the emergence of an armed militancy within the Arab world. Yet the Lebanese civil war had dimensions of conflict that never really nurtured fundamentalist trends other than the emergence of the Hezbollah, whose appeal was localized in the south of the country. In contrast, the Israeli-Palestinian conflict and the Afghanistan war presented less of a dichotomy for the Muslim militias as they were organized against a common foe. In both cases, the zeal of these armed struggles was against non-Muslim states and hence not internal to the Muslims.

The Civil War in Lebanon also demonstrated for the first time the use of proxy power in the context of the parties involved. Both Syria and Iran became strong players in the context of the Lebanese civil war and each exerts to this day an element of control which is obvious to the political system within Lebanon. Syria's role in ending the civil war, albeit it at its own terms, and Iran's influence on the Hizbollah show that where social and political cohesiveness has been absent the use of proxy roles has been not only easier but highly effective. Interestingly Iran has not managed to have such an influence on the Shia in Iraq even in post 2003 perhaps indicating where nationalism was strong, as in Iraq, the influence from external powers on domestic politics has been either absent or marginal.

In the case of the conflict with Israel, the leadership of the radical Islamic organizations that emerged was drawn originally from the Muslim Brotherhood. Leaders like Ahmed Yasin, the eventual leader of Hamas, were originally active members of the Muslim Brotherhood, and even for a time were permitted by the Israelis to be politically active in the occupied territories. These was in contrast to the armed movements of the 1960's and 1970's, and were led by Yasser Arafat's Al Fatah wing of the Palestine Liberation Organization, and by George Habbash, who headed the Popular Front for the Liberation of Palestine. There were several splinter groups within the Palestinian movement, of course, and even more factions in those groupings. Outsiders to the Middle East – and especially many policymakers in Washington – had a tendency to assume that the Palestinian movement was monolithic, and a behemoth, to boot.

Radical Islamic parties have followed very different paths with regards to the Palestinian movement (which has a number of non-Muslim adherents as well), and while in the case of Afghanistan a semblance of unity was simpler given the enemy was Soviet Union. Nevertheless, for Palestinians the dichotomy has been more difficult to manage – you need look no further than the disputatious, even violent, manner in which Arafat's Fatah and Hamas typically dealt with each other.

While Hamas has been singularly targeting the Israelis and building its own political appeal with the Palestinians, other radical Palestinian groups like Islamic Jihad (not to be confused with many similar sounding organizations around the world) have acted pretty much on their own. The Palestinian Islamic Jihad, as it is commonly known, is fiercely committed to the destruction of Israel; not surprisingly, it is also against the modernist and moderate Arab governments, who, the Jihad believes, have sold out to Western secularism. The dogma of these radical parties sounds very similar but their tactics are different; the notion that a central chain of command governs the activities of all of them is not true. At times the political face of these organizations and movements are different from religious leadership, from which the inspiration is derived -- as can been seen in the case of Hamas. However, the more radical and professedly militant organizations have kept the political and religious leadership unified. As the events following 9/11 have shown, this seemingly unified approach in these organizations has become more pronounced.

The main difference has been that the Afghan war brought about the theological emphasis of the war by portraying the struggle against the Russians as a Jihad. It also set the ideological basis of testing, and more importantly, justifying the struggle for these militant parties. The fact that the Russian ally in Afghanistan was an Afghan government -- and at times the Afghan fighters were killing Afghan government troops -- needed a justification. The Jihadists needed to justify the killing of Afghan government soldiers; who like the Jihadists, were Muslims too.

This is where the concept of a "just" Muslim government was developed. Under such a concept, it was perfectly permissible to kill fellow Muslims if they worked for an unjust Muslim government or aided an infidel regime. This concept was to have a major impact on the thinking of the young Muslim fighters who flocked to Afghanistan, especially those from the Arab world, and it honed them in not only the skills of warfare but also set the ideological and philosophical foundations which were instrumental in their thinking in the years ahead.

The application of this concept within the context of the Arab world itself, would have serious implications on the Muslim and Arab world more than a decade later, well after the Soviets had fled Afghanistan. The dictum that was developed to distinguish "them" from "us" was based on the political affiliation of the particular Muslim; thus if he donned a uniform and supported the Afghan government, he was considered a legitimate target by the radicals. It is interesting that today the Pakistan Taliban fighting the Pakistan Army in the Swat Valley use precisely this argument when they justify the kidnapping and killing of Pakistani soldiers.

Indeed the Soviet invasion of Afghanistan was largely responsible for a catalyst for unity between many of the Islamic political forces within Afghanistan, but it also served as the rallying call for many of the radical Islamists within the Arab world. Suddenly Afghan fighters found their ranks swelling with more than 4,000 Arab fighters from Egypt, Algeria, Kuwait, Saudi Arabia, and Yemen, among many other countries. These fighters had no particular political bias or orientation; they were mostly young men determined to join the Jihad against the Soviet troops. In many cases, these fighting groups had no central leadership even though with the emergence of a young Saudi millionaire in their midst the fulcrum for a search for an Arab radical leader was shifting toward this man, one cannot say they were politically organized to the extent that Osama bin Laden would later claim.

While Osama bin Laden was in later years able to cater to the young militants' need for a leader and also serve as an important conduit in the Americans finding a toehold in their proxy war against the Soviet Union in Afghanistan, he did not brandish a political ethos other than the need for expelling the Soviets from what was considered a Muslim land.

Indeed, Osama was content on playing the role of the Mujahid who shunned the riches of his family to liberate a Muslim land from the infidels. While his religious zeal was strong, there was no indication that a political doctrine would be born that would so dramatically affect the Muslim world and its interaction with the Western world.

Osama bin Laden's political doctrine was to be developed in the years after the First Gulf War; it was shaped by the development of his own radicalism; and was also reactive to the various forces that were affecting the Arab world. His political philosophy has been born out of the guidance that both Dr Ayman Al-Zawahiri and Abdullah Azzam, both of whom, in turn were inspired by the thinking of Syed Qutb. (In fact, a large number of militant Muslim organizations from the Middle East are inspired by Syed Qutb's thinking, and if anything, this is the one common denominator between them.) Both Al-Zawahiri and Abdullah Yusuf Azzam remained the closet confidants of Osama bin Laden, and it was only after Azzam's death in 1989 that Al-Zawahiri was able to infuse Osama with the political doctrine that has marked the man's thinking.

The Islamic ideological journey from a nationalist religious movement to a regional movement with the aim of driving the Russians out of Afghanistan and finally to being the vehicle of Osama's internationalist aspirations of Osama has been complex and convoluted. For Osama and Dr Al-Zawahiri themselves, this has not been an easy path either. A large majority of the Islamic clergy has not agreed with the radicalism that called for an all-out war, both within the Muslim world and also with the Western countries.

I would argue that Osama and Islam's radical wing have had to fight an internal battle for control. Some of the answers to understanding 9/11 and other events lie in understanding this internal conflict with the realm of fundamentalist Islam. It is highly conceivable that the 9/11 attacks were planned with the precise aim to wrest the radical Islamist movement away from the doves and give control to the hawks, knowing full well that a US reaction, as it has happened, would create the ground for the likes of Osama to have more following within the disgruntled youth of Islam.

My argument, therefore is that the battle for control of the radical movement within Islam was fought over the spoils of the 9/11 attacks and -- irrespective of who ordered the attacks -- it clearly set the pace for a non-reconcilable situation between the Western governments and the radical movements of Islam. The war between the US and Osama bin Ladin has in effect created, in the minds of the Muslim youth, a stature for Osama akin to that of a modern day Saladdin leading the Muslims into a battle against what they see as infidels. This overwhelming importance that media has placed on the persona of Osama bin Ladin has ineffect drowned the voices of other Islamist leaders and even those who are moderate and shun violence. While towards the latter period before his death Osama bin Laden's silence from the eye of the public media indicated a fading of his perceived image, there is in his death a cultish reverence that may well emerge in the rank and file of his followers.

Until the inception of the ideological struggle for control of Islam's ethos by radical Muslims, the emphasis was always on changing the Arab society from within. A major thrust of the focus was that change from within would allow the societies to reform into an Islamic mould and hence bring about Islamic governments based on Shariah law.

The emergence of the Muslim Brotherhood in Egypt and the subsequent execution of Syed Qutb brought about a major change in the thinking of the religious clergy who provided emotional support to these movements. On the one hand they realized that the Egyptian establishment was very nervous about their own vulnerability to fundamentalist Islamic movements; on the other hand through that vulnerability clergy established the possibility that more radical means could bring down these governments and create a new order based upon traditional – that is, conservative -- Islamic values.

If the ideologues of groups like the Muslim Brotherhood might have been initially concerned at losing their young firebrands to a distant non-Arab land in a war, they later were to realize the enormous value of their battlefield experience. Hence the ideological support from Cairo and other centers of radical Islamic parties continued for the cause in Afghanistan. The path that radical Islamist parties took as a result of the Afghan war was determined by the fact that, in certain circumstances, they could conceivably cooperate with one another; irrespective of the differences they may have felt at the heart of their ideological beliefs.

With the exception of the Muslim Brotherhood, which tried to project an appeal on a broader front in Arabia until the 9/11 crisis changed everything, most of the radical Islamist parties have been concerned with change within their own societies. The lines of division have been as much a function of Shia and Sunni political differences and, more importantly, religious differences, as much as the peculiarities of their domestic circumstances. Rarely have the militant organizations been able to cross the bridge of the Shia-Sunni divide and appeal to both sects -- mainly because part of the struggle of these organizations is designed to contain each other.

Hence one notices that when major regional or even international situations develop that constitute threats from non-Muslim entities or states, there is easier cooperation and rallying of these radical forces. Afghanistan and Chechnya were relatively easy rallying calls for Arab fighters to collaborate, irrespective of their political or religious affiliation. The differences become more profound when they concern mainly Arab situations. This can be very confusing to outsiders.

For example, what to make of the fact that the Shia-based Hezbollah in Lebanon is mainly anti-Christian and fiercely anti-Jewish, but receives support from Syria, where Christians and

Jews have lived in relative harmony. In Syria, the radical movements over the past many decades have been Sunni in composition fighting the minority Alawite governing class, and yet the Syrian government has supported the Palestinian Islamic Jihad, a predominately Sunni Palestinian group which seeks a forced expulsion of Israel from the Occupied Territories of Palestine. Within Iraq during Saddam's regime, members of the Shia opposition -- both reformist and Islamist -- were brutally crushed, and yet the strongman had been supporting a smattering of radical groups in Palestine and Lebanon, irrespective of their religious leaning.

The fact that Islam is knitted into the social fabric of the Muslim world cannot be overlooked when analyzing the complex politics of Arabia; no wonder that even the most reform minded political leaders need to possess a repertoire of Islamic slogans. Yet it would be a fallacy to believe that all Arab and Muslim countries are besieged by radicalism, when in fact the emotional appeal of the Islamic parties has been more a reaction to events in the minds of people. Back in 1979, for instance, a disgruntled element of the Saudi hierarchy attempted to engineer a coup. It resulted in the coup leaders taking shelter in the Holy Mosque in Mecca. The Saudi regime immediately branded them as heretics. There were massive street protests around the Muslim world against the takeover of the Holy Mosque. Scant attention was paid to the manner in which the dissidents were decimated. (Muslim traditionalists would have spun into catatonic shock had they known at the time that the Saudis called in non-Muslim French paratroopers to eliminate the rebels in Islam's holiest shrine.)

Now, 25 years later, with repeated militant attacks and gunfire on the streets of Riyadh, the recognition has dawned on many Muslims that there is a problem within Saudi society. Today there are no protests on the streets in Karachi or Jakarta in support of the Saudi regime. So what has changed?

Understanding the Divisions

It might well be that the general awareness amongst the Muslim populace around the world has increased as to the unique political pressures within Saudi society itself. Thus the Saudi ruling elite is not as seen as synonymous with the presevation of Islam as it used to under King Faisal. The emergence if a Saudi dissident segment, who are not only highly educated but also reform minded might have also been responsible for the change in perception that has taken place. This dissident element wants political reform within Saudi society and equally finds the militant platform of Osama bin Ladin to be a grave threat to Saudi society.

Much of the attention since 9/11 has been focused on Osama bin Laden and the silent turmoil within Saudi society. The Al Saud family has been shown to be profligate, with some members even living in debauchery. This hasn't exactly been received well in Muslim communities around the world, let alone in Arabia itself. Saudi society has had an ongoing influence of not only the Wahhabi sect of Islam through the alliance between the clergy and the monarchy. Over the past five decades, through Egyptian teachers – many of who have been followers of either the Muslim Brotherhood or the Jihad Organization of Al- Zawahiri -- a strict doctrinal education has seeped into the very fabric of the educational system in Saudi Arabia. Yet it would have to be said that in the past decade the Saudi Royal family has shown a remarkably more open minded approach to reforms and attention to social change within the over percepts of acceptance.

While Wahhabism and its clerics have shied away from political interference within Saudi society, the "imported" doctrine, namely the conservative theological view that Egyptian scholars, mostly Muslim Brotherhood supporters, brought into Saudi Arabia, have a clear political agenda within Saudi society. Even when Al-Zawahiri moved to Saudi Arabia after being exiled from Egypt, he continued to emphasize political change in Egypt; he was careful not to abuse the hospitality of his host country but protesting against the domstic political and social situation. Some have argued that when measured against more accomplished Muslim thinkers and educators Al- Zawahiri was basically a lightweight intellectually. He acquired heavyweight status only much later – and that, too, after the events of 9/11.

The essential element of Saudi society has been the pervasive presence of Wahhabism and its all-encompassing approach to every aspect of Saudi life.viii Given the alliance between the Saudi royal family and the Wahhabi clerics, the fabric of Saudi society for the better part of a century was well knitted into both elements maintaining the status quo.

For a rigidly orthodox society, challenges from liberalism and perhaps socialist thinking were very easy to combat. In truth, there never have been such challenges to the Saudi regime or Saudi society. While the rich and the emerging upper middle classes may have wanted some decorum of social liberalism they never did consider it a political issue, or indeed enough of an issue to be vocal about.

It would be naïve to believe that current dissent in Saudi society is merely related to the events arising from the 1991 Gulf War or indeed the 9/11 episode. Saudi society has had two mainstreams of dissent from within, namely the Reformists who through petitions to the royal family has sought change from above, and the Radical Islamists who have, since 1991, adopted violent means to bring about the change.

The presence of Egyptian religious scholars like Mohammed Qutb, who were part of the Muslim Brotherhood in Egypt, brought to the Saudi radical right a different dimension that the Wahhabi movement was ill prepared for. These new scholars were more "purist" than the Wahhabi school of thought and while their philosophy would eventually put them on a collision course with the Saudi rulers, they served the purpose of balancing the growing influence of the Wahhabis. For the Saudi ruling family the motives for bringing in the "Sawha" were mainly to counteract Egypt's growing flirtation with the Soviet Union and secular thinking.ix The side benefit to them was that it created a counter balance to the Wahhabi movement. The clash of philosophies was not all that apparent at that time. Yet it seemed appropriate that the largely uneducated Wahhabi rank and file had to face the more educated and articulate "scholars" who came over from Egypt and later from other Arab countries.

On the other side of the spectrum, the Reformists mostly belonged to the trading families of Jeddah. These families historically have not had any affinity to Wahhabi doctrines and essentially are the more liberal elements of Saudi society. Most of these families sent their children to the US and Europe for education, and by and large have emancipated views of society. The large number of other professionals also educated in the West has added to the cadre of these Reformists, and there has been a shared feeling for reform amongst them.

However, to believe that the reformists are organized as a political force would be a mistake as the only semblance of organization is from the outside in the shape of those Reformists who live in exile in London. By and large the reformists have always used the modus operandi of discussion with the monarchy for giving advice; this was tantamount to cajoling royalty toward reforms. The emphasis of the trading families remains to keep economic and social liberalization on track for Saudi society, and they have never questioned the political legitimacy of the monarchy. In contrast, the radical Islamists, who till 1991 were urging change within Saudi society, never targeted the ruling family; only after the first Gulf War was there a clearer political motive to the Islamist reformers.

While the reformist movement is based more in Jeddah and carries the tradition of openness and acceptance that traditionally was associated with the trading merchant families of Jeddah, their liberal thought has always clashed with both the Wahhabi school and the conservatism of the Saudi royal family. Yet in the pre-oil boom days, the merchant families of Jeddah were strong allies and financial supporters of the Saudi royal family, a connection that was particularly strong during the days of the late King Faisal. As other families, some of Yemeni descent like the Bin Ladens moved into the Jeddah area, commercial and business links between the region and the royal family were expanded. The result was that loyalty to the Al Saud blended well with the growth of business and a number of families; the Bin Ladens were the beneficiaries of the post-1973 oil boom.

One may argue that the decision to allow US troops onto Saudi soil to fight Iraq and expel Iraqi troops from Kuwait, was perhaps the moment that the Saudi royal family was irreparably weakened. However, it also signaled the beginning of a process of increased criticism of the way things were administered in Saudi Arabia. On the one hand, the vulnerability of the Saudi regime was exhibited during the early days of Iraq's invasion of Kuwait; but it also underscored the deeply religious divisions within Saudi society that have since plagued Saudi society. In the eyes of many Arabs, allowing non-Muslim soldiers into the Holy Land was seen as an act of apostasy; this was one of the central complaints of Osama bin Laden against the royal family. For the Wahabi clergy the presence of US troops, including women driving on Saudi streets, something Saudi women are not permitted, was bitter pill to swallow.

For many Muslims, the invasion of Kuwait by Iraq served as a watershed of indecision. It was a crisis that they were not entirely sure their own societies and governments were entirely equipped to deal with. Their defense spending on modern weaponry and sophisticated training all came to nought in the face of

Understanding the Divisions

a threat that came from a former ally. The inability to deal with the crisis within an Arab context suggested weakness on the part of the Saudi and other Arab governments; such perceived weakness has since been capitalized on by the radical Islamist elements within their own society, even though these Islamists did not have a credible solution of their own. The fact that the US took over the leadership of the global response to the invasion of Kuwait – albeit at the invitation of the Kuwaiti regime in exile -- softened some of the political responsibility of the Saudi monarchy.

In the absence of viable Pan-Arab leadership, it seemed that the exiled Kuwaiti leadership and the Saudi royal family were left to lead the initiative for an Arab response to the events unfolding in the Gulf. It seemed unlikely that the Saudis or Kuwaitis could effectively sing the right tune to lead the coalition against Saddam's Iraq. This was in effect one of the very weaknesses that were exploited by Osama bin Laden and his followers in the years following the Gulf War. In the face of objections from Egypt, Syria and Pakistan, it was agreed that a complicated chain of command be created whereby the Arab and Muslim contingents who joined the 34-nation Allied coalition against Iraq would report to a Saudi general rather than to the American and British chain of command. These were the first demonstrations of the complex nature of dealing with the realities and sensitive nature of the region, and it would seem that 12 years later the American military was still learning those sensitivities on the battleground of Iraq itself.

For many Saudi citizens, the added problems that emerged after the Gulf War of 1991 included the steady deterioration of their living standard as more money was channeled into defense spending. The burden of paying for the Gulf War sharply reduced living standards and increased unemployment.x The transition from a state of prosperity to one of austerity has not been easy on the average Saudi, especially considering the royal family and the rich have showed belt-tightening of their wasteful lifestyles . As the gap between the rich and poor has widened, so too have the accusations of massive corruption within the royal family become more vocal. In two decades, Saudi per capita GDP had fallen from $19,000 to less than $8,000. It has been reliably reported that Saudi natives have been peddling potable water in the streets of Riyadh, a situation totally inconceivable prior to 1991; such menial tasks were always done by imported cheap labor from South Asia or from poorer Arab countries in the region. The change in economic circumstances – notwithstanding the recent high revenues from surging oil prices – has resulted in disgruntled Saudi youth becoming easy prey for indoctrination by the radical Islamists. These Islamists, of course, find it easier to trace every ill in Saudi society back to the presence of US troops on Saudi soil beginning in 1991. On the public relations side, the presence of US troops was indeed a disaster for the Saudi regime as at times it put it at loggerheads with the religious clerics of Wahhabism and also brought the wrath of the more ultra-conservative followers of splinter groups like the Jihad Organization and of Osama bin Laden and his followers.

Yet the placement of foreign troops on Saudi soil was supported by some Wahhabi clerics like Sheikh Abd al-Aziz ibn Abd Allah bin Baz, who was the highest religious authority in Saudi Arabia. While this may well have put him at discord with the larger following of Wahhabi thinking, he wielded enough religious authority and respect – not the least because from 1993 until his death in 1999 bin Baz served as Saudi Arabia's Grand Mufti – that it was not openly disputed from within the Wahhabi rank and file.

In contrast, the Sawha strongly condemned the move to lodge foreign "infidel" troops on Saudi soil. The Saudi royal family edged closer to the Wahhabi clerics after decades of having encouraged the Sawha to be a religious counterweight to the

Wahhabi establishment. While religious authorities like Sheikh bin Baz could rise above the differences and commanded the authority to speak on a wider platform, most of the other clerics had, in time, to make choices. As the Sawha movement further acquired a Jihadist identity, and its preachers became more radical, the call for a general Jihad highlighted a "fight on all fronts." The distinctions between the "near enemy" and the "far enemy" began to dissolve, and it was seen more as a larger struggle to rid Arabia of the "impure Muslims regimes" (the near enemy) and also fight the "far enemy" -- the governments of Western countries, principally the United States, who had "invaded" the Muslim homelands. It was Dr Ayman Al Zawahiri who was the foremost proponent of the concept of the 'near enemy' and the 'far enemy' and has been the hallmark of the Al Qadea's indoctrination of the Muslim youth against the current order within the Arab and Muslim world.

In addition, the falling standard of living has been a catalyst for the radical Islamists to gather momentum on their promise of an Islamic revivalist movement. In the same breath that they scream for a change of regime, they also promise the youth a different Saudi Arabia. The threat of Islamic radicalism is something even the Wahhabi clerics cannot really combat on the philosophical side. These clerics feel obligated to the Saudi monarchy with whom they are publicly aligned; they need to defend the very political order that the likes of Osama bin Laden wished to demolish. The rank and file of Wahhabi clerics have been careful not to involve themselves any more than necessary in the tussle between the radicals and the monarchy, however, and it is a position that is politically most convenient for them under the circumstances. The clergy within Saudi society know that their political fortunes are tied to the monarchy; and yet they are conscious that should a political upheaval take place within Saudi society, they must have a role to play in any "new" Saudi Arabia that might emerge. The Wahhabi clergy understands history --

that the iron fist of the monarchy has managed to keep the 13 provinces of the Saudi kingdom together, given that prior to the 1930's their history as one political entity never existed.xi An understanding of this history surely leads them to the conclusion that the tribal – and feudal – society would, under any conceivable form of governance, require a strong central authority. Whether that authority continue to be the monarchy, or a caudillo of assorted radicals and reformists, the clergy's role would be vital in preserving the moral underpinning of a state whose Islamic ethos is unlikely to change with any change in regime.

Yet the Saudi Wahabi's know that should the likes of Osama bin Ladin succeed in changing the political order in Saudi Arabia they will be at theocractic loggerheads with the thinking of Osama bin Ladin's followers not because of a major schism but more because the Wahabi clergy would have to submit to the political will of Osama bin Ladin's successors. This would inevitably mean a loss of political power for the Saudi Wahabi's; a prospect that is not in the least bit comfortable for them to ponder. Interestingly, with the death of Osama Bin Laden one can argue that the political clout that the name carried cannot be inherited by someone like Ayman al Zawahiri, who is an Egyptian and cannot command latitude within Saudi society.

The rapid population growth in Saudi Arabia – 2.07% annually -- coupled with lower per capita income (currently around $13,500), has resulted in discontent through various layers of Saudi society, a factor that has been played upon by the extremist elements within Saudi society. For an economy overwhelmingly dependent on oil revenues (75% of the country's annual revenues of $190 billion comes from the sale of crude oil and natural gas), the fluctuations in oil prices have been difficult to plan around, and any diversification plan has not really been sustainable. xii

Population growth remains a problem as given a fundamentalist version of Islam any form of formal policy of family planning is prohibited. This has resulted in more than 50 percent of the population being below the age of 30, and seeking jobs in an increasingly competitive environment. In the past few years, of course, oil revenues have soared on the back of extremely robust prices and this has meant more ability for the Saudi government to tackle the issues of growing unemployment (currently 13%, but most outside scholars contend that it's more like 25%), and unbalanced resource allocation. The economic planning and the implementation of sustainable economic-growth plans will also play a crucial role within not only Saudi but all Arab societies in the next few decades.

The impact of the Afghan war against the Soviet Union and the participation of Arab youth in that war changed, in a radical way, the expectations of many of youth in the Arab world. They saw the humbling of a superpower. Its eventual collapse was inextricably linked to the Soviet failures in Afghanistan and hence seen by these youth a direct result of the victory of "Islamic" forces against one of the world's two superpowers. The empowerment that these youth felt was not universal in appeal to many of the other Muslim societies, who, while rejoicing the Soviet defeat, didn't see it as having deep implications within their own societies.

The civil war in Afghanistan after the Soviet defeat confused the radical elements within Islamic movements even more. Suddenly, the seven groups of Afghan militias who fought to oust the Soviet Union were destroying Kabul and the country in a mad thirst for power. It perhaps was a period of disillusionment for people like Osama bin Laden and other "Afghan Arabs" who had gone back home elated but couldn't see the results of the victory fully come through in the form of acclaim in their home countries. Surely, the ensuing civil war in Afghanistan wasn't what Osama and other "freedom fighters" had in mind when they'd embarked on the campaign against the Soviet Union. The emergence of the Taliban changed the domestic situation in Afghanistan fundamentally and perhaps decisively for these radical elements, even within Saudi Arabia. Wedded to an extremely orthodox style of Islam, the Taliban were in some ways even stricter in their interpretations of the Islamic laws than any of the radicals or the Wahhabis. The Taliban occupied a power vacuum that had been created by the United States, Saudi Arabia and Pakistan. In fact, the conduit of cooperating with the Taliban was mainly through Pakistan. General Zia ul Haq, the then military dictator, saw himself and his country as needing to be fundamentalist in creed. The general viewed his own role as one of an Islamic revivalist who envisioned both Afghanistan and Pakistan as the bulwark of Islamic virtue and polity. The Pakistan military intelligence agencies, funded by Saudi money and directed by United States interests (although not entirely) supported the Taliban as a means to end the civil war and introduce a unifying force within war torn Afghanistan.

The strategy worked for everyone, particularly since the United States was uncomfortable with an unstable civil war-ridden Afghanistan. Saudi Arabia found itself as becoming the harbinger of support for Islamic regimes – and, after all, who else but the Taliban would be better as an indigenous faith-based movement, a Taliban that was theologically even more to the right than themselves? For Pakistan, the reasons for supporting the Taliban were obvious, given its long held desire to influence the outcome of events in Afghanistan. It was sheltering some 3.3 million Afghan refugees who come across during the 1979-1988 period of the Afghan war. (Pakistan has a 1,615-mile border with Afghanistan, one that's mountainous, largely porous, and with much of the territory occupied by feudal tribes whose loyalty is local, not necessarily to any central authority.)
The Afghan war seemed to empower Muslim youths in two important ways. It taught them that regime change could be

brought through extreme means such as warfare. It also taught them that it was possible for a diverse group of young Muslim men to come together for a common cause under the banner of Islam.

There was a third lesson that these youths learned. It was that poor but proud Afghans could attain parity with rich and proud supporters of the conflict such as the Saudis, through their battlefield glories. While the Arab-Afghans – including Osama bin Laden – may not have had any extended agenda at the time beyond the "liberation" of Afghanistan from the Soviet Union, the Saudi intelligence apparatus was viewing them with increasing concern. Surely, some of these officials thought, young Arabs armed with both sophisticated weaponry and religious fervor could take on a state such as Saudi Arabia that had a conspicuously vulnerable underbelly?

While such concerns were undoubtedly articulated within the precincts of the Saudi – and perhaps other Gulf – intelligence agencies, the officials need not have feared the Afghan-Arabs too much – at least not at the time. They were exhausted from a long and brutal war that began when the Soviets invaded Afghanistan on Christmas Day 1979 (and quit only in 1988).xiii It's doubtful that the ragtag band that defeated the mighty Soviet Union (which suffered fatalities and casualties of more than 30,000 men) entertained any expansion of their military efforts to the region.xiv Moreover, the Afghan-Arabs were by no means a united, unified group with regard to their geopolitical aspirations. The Saudi intelligence authorities need not have feared that the House of Al Saud would be toppled any time soon. Indeed, opposition to the Al Saud family even today is fragmented and divided. While it would be an exaggeration to assert that the Saudi leadership is widely admired, it would also be erroneous to conclude that it is widely hated. While today's leaders – including King Abdallah – may lack the charisma of King Faisal and certainly don't invite popular devotion, there is acknowledgement that Saudi Arabia is cemented together in its tribal diversity by the House of Al Saud. The likes of Osama bin Laden have articulated the concerns of the radical religious element of the opposition, whose agenda for change is merely one of replacing the Al Saud with a system based presumably on Islamic law. Even though King Abdullah has seen the need for not only rapid reform of Saudi society he has also seen the push towards economic prosperity and job creation as the best means to combat the influence of Osama bin Ladin upon the youth of the country.

In contrast, the more established opposition to the Saudi regime has come from the reformists who represent a section of the intelligentsia, people who are mostly well traveled and in many cases foreign educated. Interestingly this reformist group draws its inspirations from models of democratic traditions based on human rights, representation and liberty. Yet, curiously enough, these reformists do not call for an outright change of the Saudi ruling structure – yet. They are a mix of urban and affluent people from the newly emerging middle class and from the wealthy trading families. It's clearly not in their self-interest to upset the camel cart, so to speak, just yet. And even if they wanted to trigger a revolution, how would they do it, and with what means? The House of Al Saud isn't going to be brought down by a guerrilla war featuring words and ideas alone. One should also remember that amongst the tribal elements of Saudi society the House of Saud has been more popular and this is where decisive power of the Saud family comes from.

Much of this reform movement has remained outside Saudi Arabia, nested comfortably in Western cities such as London. Beyond a broad reformist call their political message is not revolutionary and, indeed, it accepts the realities that a change of regime may not necessarily mean a more stable environment. The reformists want the system to be changed in emphasis rather than in structure. In contrast, the Islamist opposition is composed of two widely contrasting views: those who, while fundamentalist in approach, object to the Saudi regime on a broad front of issues and yet in essence want a stricter regime embracing something akin to a broad-based Islamic democracy; and those, like Osama bin Laden, who clearly see a radical change of the political order through even violent means as the only solution for Saudi Arabia. It would seem the fundamentalist reformist can see a Saudi Arabia where the monarchy has a continued role to play side by side with a reformed political system. In contrast the likes of Osama bin Ladin's militant Islamists saw no compromise on the elimination of the monarchy, even though by implication they desired that Osama himself be installed as the 'Caliph' of the Muslim Ummah.

The radical fundamentalists clearly have evolved an agenda that goes beyond simply Saudi Arabia. It is Pan-Arab in nature. It calls for a change within the Muslim Ummah where embracing the notions of a vast Islamic Caliphate is considered to be the only political solution on the table. Beyond this general call for political change, there is little thought given as to how the leadership of this Ummah would be selected. Such ambiguity over key issues such as leadership and governance is what undermines the credibility of Islamist revivalists with the burgeoning middle class in the Arab and Muslim worlds.

Nevertheless, this radical movement of Islamists shouldn't be underestimated. It draws support from the growing numbers of the poor and dispossessed in Arabia, people who view Islamic radicalism as the means for societal and economic change. In a classic sense, the appeal of Islamist radicals can be seen as being at a grassroots levels. The affluent Saudis who profess varying degrees of radicalism often give the impression of having picked up their creed – and rhetoric – from other Saudis whose were exiled to the United States and Europe, and who used local mosques to influence the affluent who studied there.
A Saudi from an affluent family recently told me about the time when he was visiting Oregon in the United States. He said he

was surprised to find the local mosque prayer leader exhorting the youth to join an Islamic revival movement and to bring about a change in the Saudi regime. When I think about such situations, it doesn't surprise me in the least that various US surveillance agencies and law-enforcement organizations keep very close tabs on mosques around America.

These mosques may or may not provide the next generation of leaders for Saudi Arabia. In any discussion of who might lead an organized opposition to the Saudi regime, only two names crop up. One, of course, is Osama bin Laden, whose whereabouts – as of this writing – are unknown. The other figure who also calls for a radical change within Saudi Arabia is Saad al Faqih, currently exiled in London. Other opposition figures are more of a reformist leaning who call for an adjustment to the system whereby there is a modernization of the Islamic system to accommodate Western political practices – such as local elections -- and the introduction of accountability into the system. Most reformist movements accept the Saudi royal family as a political entity integral to the process of national governance, and do not seek any change at the very top of the pyramid. They are mindful of Arabia's history. The reality of the lack of unity among Arab tribes prior to the House of Al Saud seizing power is a fundamental fact that does not drop off of their radar.
Radicals such as Osama bin Laden rarely display this understanding of Arabia's history. His central contention had long been that by allowing non-Muslim troops on Saudi soil in the wake of Saddam's invasion of Kuwait, the Al Sauds became apostates. Hence, in Osama's view, they lost their right to rule the Holy Land. It's doubtful, in my view at least, that everyday Saudis would like to see the institution of a Taliban-like system in their country. Globalization has made everybody more aspirational in a world where modernism, not recidivism, is the goal. Moreover, my view is that the call for modernism within the Islamic society of Saudi Arabia, while muted, is not to be construed as a call for Westernism, including Western-style de-

Understanding the Divisions

mocracy. People do want more financial security, if not prosperity, in their own lifetime, and not just for their children. Osama and his ilk don't seem to offer anything other than a socially harsher system than currently in place in Arabia.

For the Saudi government, the issue of social governance has been an important one; its record has shown a consistency in maintaining the puritanical creed of its social and political administration. Threats to the system were in the past reformist in nature, while the clerical call for an even more puritanical idiom was met easily by shifting the axis of social administration even further in to the conservative bandwitdh.

Saudi Arabia's realization of its strategic vulnerability in the wake of Iraq's invasion of Kuwait caused new pressures within Saudi and Arab societies. It was never really conceivable that an Arab Muslim country, in this case Iraq, would attack another Arab country even though it had been the reciepient of massive financial aid in its war with Shia Iran from Kuwait. The mass stationing of foreign, and essentially non-Muslim, troops on its soil brought about a mix of challenges to the government. The reformists welcomed the social implications of seeing women members of the US armed forces driving military vehicles on Saudi roads as a sign that eventual liberalization of the puritanical code – in which Saudi women are not permitted to operate cars on the road -- will happen. On the other hand, the radicals for once felt the Al Saud could not maneuver further to the right and their call, largely echoed by Osama bin Laden, seemed more rigid and critical of the regime. Yet the Wahabi clerics were not overtly demonstrative of their objections other than in sermons and direct appeals to the Saudi ruling family. Indeed, when Saddam's invasion of Kuwait took place, Osama bin Laden was already in Saudi Arabia and his call to the Al Saud not to invite foreign troops but allow him to arrange a similar army as that which defeated the Russians in Afghanistan was largely ignored. Osama's eventual exile from Saudi Arabia to Sudan was a direct result of his criticism of the way the Saudi government handled the whole Kuwait issue. Yet it remains debatable if a Muslim militia backed by the armies of the Gulf countries, and of Egypt and Syria, could have expelled the Iraqis without extensive damage to the region's infrastructure, including oil wells in the six member-states of the Gulf Cooperation Council.

The message that Osama bin Laden and Saad al Faqih broadcast for the establishment of a theocratic state as an alternate to the Saudi monarchy is muddled, at best. Both men lack the political and indeed even religious credibility to persuade Arabia's general populace. Osama came from a Yemeni background, while Saad al Faqih is of Iraqi origin; neither enjoys allegiance from the strong tribes of Saudi Arabia. It is there that the future system will be decided, irrespective of the denomination of the political message that either man may have. Even though both may have banked on the urban youth of Arabia as their constituency to whom their appeal has largely been directed, it is the tribal allegiances, which for the moment, provide the color and complexion to any possible change in most of the Arab world.

The events of 9/11 may have made Osama into a larger than life political figure. But, in my view, his public persona is more the creation of the Western press; the political realities of Saudi Arabia suggest a far more limited appeal for Osama's brand of nihilist radicalism. From an emotional viewpoint, Osama was more of a hero to radical Islamic youth in Pakistan, Afghanistan and Indonesia rather than in his home country. His political message remains fragmented and disjointed. There's only so much that can be done with the singular call for a Jihad against the "far enemy." Besides, even those radicalized youth love Madonna, and want to wear Benetton T-shirts.

One could argue, of course, that just because Osama didn't enjoy mass appeal in Saudi Arabia it doesn't mean some conditions for revolution don't exist in the kingdom. The Saudi situation may be analogous to that in Iran, where the Shah was deposed in 1979 and where the ayatollahs subsequently established an Islamic theocracy that flourishes to this day. As in Iran, there's an authoritarian government in Saudi Arabia; there's an economy that is not only unbalanced by rising unemployment and poverty, but also by rampant population growth, and by stark disparities in income levels; there's political myopia; there's the strong structural and diplomatic relationship with the United States. But it's difficult to conclude from these similarities that Saudi Arabia may be vulnerable to the onset of an Islamic revolution. The revolution in Iran was actually a broad-based nationalist movement, funded by the merchants of Tehran and even supported by the middle classes. It was hijacked by the clergy when the revolutionaries realized that a national icon was needed to symbolize the struggle -- and hence the selection of Ayatollah Ruhollah Khomeini as the "Supreme Leader." Within a predominantly Shia Iran – where the Shah of Iran was head of state but not head of church – it was possible to institute parallel hierarchies of religious and bureaucratic leadership. But the Al Sauds, who are Sunni, are both temporal leaders and "Custodians of the Holy Shrines" of Mecca and Medina. In that sense the Al Saud claim a unity of political and religious sanction in their role within Saudi Arabia. While they do not, importantly, assume the role of a religious clergy, by being the 'custodians' of the Holy Shrine's they ensure that challenge from a religious orthodoxy will be seen also as a challenge to their religious role. This is a role that is reinforced through tribal allegiances and alliances that run deep into the social and emotional fabric of Saudi Arabia.

In contrast, the Shah's regime had no tribal or social links with the Persian society. This alienated the monarchy with the people it governed. In contrast -- and with credit to the Arab social polity -- the Saudi and other ruling families of the Gulf are drawn from within the fabric of the tribal social structure. This structure is cemented through complicated alliances, marriages and appointments, which, when all put together, create a massive social stake in the system that the radical Islamists – who are proletarians in the classic sense -- seek to challenge but will be hard pressed to replace.

It will be interesting to see how the battle between social allegiance and Islamic fervor unfolds within these societies in ensuing years. In the case of smaller oil-rich Arab states, the problems have been handled with greater ease as the economic benefits of oil have largely been passed to the population through jobs, medical care and significantly better living conditions. In Saudi Arabia, only in the past five-odd years has the need for social and economic reforms been felt more strongly, resulting in a longer-term strategy for social reform. This is not to suggest that the problems of economic disparity in Saudi Arabia, for example, have been solved, but significant steps are being taken in this regard. In a broader sense socio-economic welfare has been finally been seen as a main ingredient for social and even political reform across the Arab world. However, the capability and resources of each nation vary vastly in being able to deliver a model of a social welfare state.

The impact of these social and economic dislocations within some of the Arab countries has provided the nesting ground for the militant Islamic organizations to set their roots. In some cases, as in Egypt, Palestine and Lebanon, these organizations have even managed to set up parallel administrations to the state apparatus posing a unique challenge to the established order of the State. Nevertheless, militant Islamic organizations have been gaining influence in a number of regions of Arabia. In most cases, the militancy of such organizations has been associated with freedom struggles in Palestine and Lebanon. In some cases, the experience of traditional liberation movements – such as those in Palestine -- has spawned a religious dimension to these struggles.

Three cases in point are certainly those of Afghanistan; the Himalayan territory of Kashmir, which is claimed by both India and Pakistan; and Chechnya. In the case of Indian-held Kashmir (roughly another third is held by Pakistan, and China has occupied part of the Siachen Glacier area) and Chechnya the inspiration that came from the successful defeat of the Soviet Union in Afghanistan by militant Islamic Mujahideen cannot be underestimated. The local appeal of these movements was tremendous and remains perhaps the central feature of these struggles. The Afghan war highlighted role of the Muslim fighter who fought for Islam rather than a country. Why did Muslim fighters succeed in Afghanistan, while they failed in the case of both Indian-held Kashmir and Chechnya? The conventional political view would have us believe that the support of the US in the case of Afghanistan made all the difference. While partially true, this explanation couldn't possibly tell the full story. In the case of Afghanistan there was a clear cut invasion by the Soviet forces whereas in the case of both Kashmir and Chechnya one notices that the historical context of the 'freedom' war is blurred.

It was not unusual to see Egyptian Muslim fighters in Chechnya who believed that with a victory for Islam there would be one more Islamic country. The post 9/11 defeat of the Taliban in Afghanistan may well have dented the ambition of these young radicals to dot the world with puritanical Islamic states, but emotionally it certainly is a cause they consider dear to their heart. They also believe the defeats against the United States in military battles does not mean that the war has been lost, and given their ability to blend back into society they feel its patience that is needed for the tide to turn.

For many of these fighters the idea of being a martyr for Islam in any land is more important than merely dying for your own country. In that sense the Arab-Afghan fighters set the tempo of a zealous struggle that continues to this day. One has to wonder if the 9/11 attacks on the United States were reflections and, in essence, extensions of the same struggle? In a sense I do feel that a great degree of the motivational elements for the hijackers who carried out 9/11 came from the concepts of martyrdom for Islam, while the frustrations that provoked the attacks are more political in nature.

Today in Pakistan there are more than two-dozen fiercely militant organizations that have aims ranging from establishing an Islamic theocratic government in Pakistan, to the liberation of Kashmir. They see themselves in a struggle-unto-death with all non-Muslim forces and complexions of faith, even with moderate Muslims. These groups have a firebrand leadership, very conservative outlook on social values and most importantly a deep contempt for any view that does not agree with their view. Even though some of these Islamic parties have used the political platform in elections based on adult franchise, their success has been very limited. Only in the elections held after 9/11 events and the US invasion of Afghanistan have we seen a sympathy vote swing in their favor, but only marginally. The recent emergence of the Pakistan Taliban, has however, irked political Islamist parties within Pakistan as the Taliban model would have no place for Islamic political parties thus seeking to have a monolithic view of Islam as the Talib see it.

Militant Islamic movements have one ingrained advantage in most Muslim societies and that is the fact that the general public cannot criticize anything in the name of religion. In most Muslim societies, religion has held a public appeal and respect that allowed the radical elements more leeway in expressing their view knowing full well that secular criticism will be limited from within the society. Very few moderate Muslims will dare to publicly question some of the precepts of these militant organizations -- and that, too, at the risk of immediately being declared an apostate.

Added to that is the tendency in such societies for people not questioning the clergy; this tacit silence is used by many militants to their advantage. Because these organizations were led by a charismatic Muslim figurehead, who also had a clerical appeal, more often than not opposition to their views at the social level, of say a village, never emerged in the sense to be a challenge. This also explains the reason why in countries like Pakistan the elected Islamic party leaders rarely speak out against militant Islamic groups. The militants take advantage of such silence to their maximum. Indeed, when the established political system does not offer solutions for disputes – such as in Indian-held Kashmir -- as well as for societal ills, militants see it as yet another raison d'etre for extending their militancy.

Miltant movements, to be sure, vary in their intensity and modus operandi. They tend to be culture specific. And sometimes their methods are virtually impossible to grasp. Take Algeria, for example. What would explain the massacre of a large number of innocent Muslim villagers by Muslim radicals? As the Algerian Islamic parties got fiercer in their retribution against basically innocent people, the Algerian government began to win the war against them. Today, radical groupings such as the Islamic Salvation Front (FIS) are largely discredited.

The Algerian situation showed that militant Islamic organizations need to be careful of their actions because, at some point, the population they profess to save through an Islamic revolution is the one that turns against them, too. Everyday Muslims, contrary to the extremist view of some right-wing commentators in America, do not condone senseless killings, whether of non-Muslims or Muslims. In fact, the beheadings that are carried out by radical Islamic groups in Iraq and elsewhere, broadcast widely on TV networks, have not won endorsement from Muslim masses. While there may be emotional justification of what is called the "Jihad," the reality is that educated Muslims and the Muslim leadership around the world finds no place in their religion for such heinous acts.

Even from the most radical interpretation of the Koran one cannot deduce that the wanton murder of bystanders or noncombatants can be considered a part of Jihad. This is the fundamental weakness of the radical militant Islamic groups; they know that other than sensationalism, the beheadings of truck drivers and civilians have no place in everyday Islam. It is for this reason that in the long run these acts will have to stop -- either because they yield no lasting results or because their own theological leadership will see the senseless of these acts. Part of the problem, at least in the context of Iraq, could well be that Saddam Hussein's feared Fedayeen militia has donned the garb of religious splinter groups who are exploiting Islam as a weapon in their attempt to destabilize Iraq.

On a broader front, the idea that the militant Islamic movements have a central leadership command is only partially true. While Osama bin Laden's call for a Jihad in 1998 against "the Jews and the Crusaders" may be seen as a symbolic message, its emotional appeal is stronger than the actual following it might conjure up. Even amongst the ranks of militant Muslims there is acknowledgement that Osama's war against the Saudis and Western interests has been the result of a personal feud between him and the royal family.

One must not forget that Osama was part of the system, which he later opposed. One of his closest friends was Prince Turki ibn Faisal al Saud, who was the head of the Saudi intelligence service until a week before the events of 9/11. During the formative years of Osama's blending into the Afghan war, it was Prince Turki who was an important conduit to both the Saudis and the Americans to get funding to Osama and his Afghan resistance camps in Peshawar and within Eastern Afghanistan. (Prince Turki is currently Saudi Arabia's ambassador to the United States.)

Osama's falling out with the Saudi Royal family was over the handling of the Iraqi invasion of Kuwait. In a crucial meeting days after Iraqi tanks had rolled into Kuwait, he met with Prince Abdullah, then the Crown Prince, and tried to persuade him not to invite American forces but to let Osama raise an Arab militia of 30,000 fighters, who, supported by Syrian and Egyptian troops, would liberate Kuwait. Osama sat quietly listening to Prince Abdullah lay out the plan for calling in the Americans. In his typical non-confrontational war, the Crown Prince was, in effect, rejecting Osama's offer. Meanwhile, Osama was fuming with anger. Days later, audio cassette tapes appeared in major Saudi cities with Osama bin Laden declaring that allowing American troops on the holy soil was an act of apostasy -- and it was to be that he never again referred to Saudi Arabia by its name but henceforth referred to it as the Land of the Holy Mosques.

It has never been clear why Osama's offer was never accepted; was it because Crown Prince Abdullah thought it would mean a long struggle to liberate Kuwait? Some may argue that a Muslim army fighting on the ground with US and British air cover was not a bad long-term solution. It might also be that allowing Osama to lead a Mujahideen army of irregulars into Kuwait city as a liberator would have made him too powerful within the domestic political scene of Saudi Arabia. In many conversations wth high Arab officials, the impression I've gotten is that the House of Al Saud did not have confidence in Osama's ability to fight a conventional protracted war in Kuwait and that, in any case, support from the Americans and British would be required.

The eventual house arrest and subsequent expulsion of Osama from Saudi Arabia, are all narrative aspects of history. It was only in 1996, when Osama returned to Afghanistan as an exile from his homeland that his contact with clerics like the Egyptians Abdullah Azzam and Ayman Al-Zwahiri was re-activated. That's when he developed a broader view of what was considered the Muslim struggle. The Egyptian radicals were instrumental in showing Osama that the issue was not only of Saudi Arabia but of fighting on all fronts against what they called the Jewish and Christian conspiracy against Islam.

Mohammed Atef, an able military commander, and also an Egyptian who had fought in the Afghan war, was to be perhaps the most crucial element of the triad that made Osama understand that the battle had to be fought in military terms. This was the turning point in the re-shaping of Osama bin Laden, as Abdullah Azzam had always been his ideological hero. What is ironical that all this transformation was taking place in Afghanistan, which was ruled by the Taliban who, while more radically fundamentalist that the Wahhabis drew their ideological roots from the Deobandi school of teaching and did not necessarily agree that Wahhabism was puritanical enough for contemporary Islamic societies.

It is still not clear how many of the terrorist attacks carried out against Western and other interests can be attributed directly to Osama bin Laden. The issue becomes all the more complicated in the manner in which Osama bin Laden praises these attacks with the constant use of the term "we." Hence when he says "We never imagined those planes would do so much damage," it leads one to believe that it is self-praise for something he may or may not have ordered. Radical Islamic organizations rarely work in terms of issuing direct orders concerning specific attacks, and it's unlikely that there will there be a direct order from the top.

What is more common is that a fatwa, or a religious commandment, is issued in the broadest of terms, like the one in 1998 when Osama called for a Jihad against Jewish interests and the Crusaders. The use of the word "Crusaders" was important because it signaled a war having started, and perhaps in it was the message to step up the attacks.

The actual tactic is left to the militants in the field, and how it is conducted is not something that is elaborated prior to the attack. It is this element that was inherited from the tactics of the Afghan fight against the Russians; the rebels' high command never specifically planned attacks, but left it to the commanders in the field to pick the targets and their timing.

This is why the weapon of terrorism is so potent in such a structure of command and control. It also leads one to believe that while the leadership of the militant organizations may lose contact with their operatives, the acts will and can continue as they follow a highly decentralized command and control structure in terms of tactics. In so far as the inspirational leadership is concerned, and the macro message in the fatwas, the adherence to a central leadership has been apparent in the ongoing Islamic militancy.

Yet, according to confessions by captured Al Qaeda members, it has emerged that within the organization's Shura council (Shura being the equivalent of an advisory council), there was intense debate about the attacks. Sheikh Mohammed Omar, the Pakistani cleric and strategist who is credited with being the mastermind behind the attacks of 9/11, was at one time instructed by Osama bin Laden to just hijack the planes and crash them "anywhere."

It has also emerged that through six years of planning the attacks, a number of would-be hijackers dropped out of the plot, and some diehard members like Mohammed Atta kept the group going. It is also now clear that as Osama bin Laden met with the Shura Council to discuss the attacks in his search to obtain a consensus between the hawks and the doves, he was criticized by both sides. Mohammed Atef also known as Abu Hafs and considered by many as the head of operations of Al Qaeda, felt that the attacks were not being carried out fast enough and too much time was going into planning, while Ayman Al-Zawahiri, who today is a militant firebrand, was advocating not attacking the US on its soil because the response from the US government would be "strong and overpowering."

At times when Osama seemed to heed the call for caution; Abu Hafs would get frustrated; and it seemed there would be fissures within the Al Qaeda ranks that would split them into distinct groups. Many would argue that, with Abu Hafs' death on November 16, 2001 from a missile strike on his home in Afghanistan, perhaps while Al Qaeda lost its operational chief, it is also possible that the movement lost Osama's designated successor.

To my mind, there's little doubt that Al Qaeda commanders and their immediate superiors would have used modern communication methods and even the Internet and couriers to get messages on the timing of certain attacks. But it would also seem that the idea of cells operating on their own is more the order of the day. The use of modern communication technology, including the internet, seems to have been embraced by this warriors of God with relative ease, at times creating very clever means to hoodwink the intelligence agencies who they knew were watching them closely.

Eliminating cells might mean that others would take their place but the process would be slowed down, as has been seen in some cases. Militant Islam's battle is no more with just the Jews and the Crusaders, so to speak, but has extended to all governments they see as allied to those two elements of world geopolitics. Hence, the regime in Pakistan is as much a target as indeed is the regime in Saudi Arabia. Yet one has to wonder if the widespread attacks against civilian targets in both these countries have not alienated the masses from the emotional appeal that might have existed of a militant Islam asserting itself in a world of rapid globalization.

It is also unlikely that the loose network of command and control within these organizations will ever allow for concrete evidence to emerge about the origins of specific orders. The United States intelligence network has been caught between a model of blaming "state sponsored" terrorism and an organized Al Qaeda network, when in reality perhaps the foundations of terrorism within the realm of Islamic organizations is more nebulous that such an assertion might sugegst.

While the initial assumption of state sponsored terrorism emerged in the aftermath of the 1979 revolution in Iran and the taking of 52 American hostages by what was essentially a state set-up group called the Pasdaran, or Revolutionary Guards, the subsequent events of bombings of US marines in Beirut in 1983 was also linked to Iranian proxies operating in Lebanon. Still, one cannot be sure to what extent the direct involvement of state-led or state- planned terrorism continued. From a political perspective, the Iranian revolution showed to the more militant Islamic thinkers that in a world dominated by the Americans and the Soviets, there was a chance that a pristine Islamic movement could find a place of its own. Within months of the regime change in Tehran, the Soviet invasion of Afghanistan in December 1979 set the stage for testing the notion of Islamic militants' assertion that they could draw a zone between the Americans and the Soviets based upon a new radicalism that was not seeking Arab nationalism but instead desirous of projecting a more powerful message of Islamic resurgence.

I believe that had it not been for the Iranian revolution, radical Muslims elsewhere would not have subsequently felt empowered. The events in Tehran in 1979 gave them a wholly new perspective on Islam, their own history, and perhaps even their sense of destiny. To put it another way, if in the 1990s the Iraqi invasion of Kuwait changed the Arab world, then the Islamic revolution of 1979 in Iran changed the Islamic world in similar measure.

I've always found it strange that on the one hand the American intelligence community was advocating a hard line against Iran, but at the same time was willingly forming plans to arm and support the Islamic groups that were assembling in Afghanistan to fight the Soviet invasion.

That, of course, is what realpolitik is all about. But realpolitik aside, the underlying dichotomy of the situation never seemed to have dawned on successive administrations. As the war in Afghanistan intensified, the funding of the freedom fighters increased and new channels of support opened up with Osama bin Laden. Even the Saudi intelligence agencies became conduits for American money and arms.

About the same time, the region was becoming intensely embroiled in conflicts that were adding to the puzzle of what was to be achieved.

Lebanon was becoming a testing ground for all sorts of militant ideologies and thinking in the wake of a senseless and mindless civil war that had lasted 15 long years (and ended, ironically enough, when the Saudis brokered the Taif Accords in October 1989. Into that mess, the United States jumped in with a presence of Marines and other armed forces, with objectives that were not even known or clear, resulting in their withdrawal in 1983 after 300 American marines were killed in a terrible suicide bombing of their headquarters.

At around the same time, Saddam Hussein decided to invade Iran, and encouraged subtly by countries like the United States felt it could not only settle old scores but also keep the Iranian revolution from spreading. With regard to Palestine, it was evident that peace was not in the offing, and while the threat of war may have abated in the wake of peace efforts of the late 1970's, there a proxy war going on between Syria and Israel in Lebanon with all the fury of an all-out conflict.

Between the events in Afghanistan and Lebanon, a radicalism that they had not been accustomed to was being acquired by the youth of the Arab and Muslim worlds. Their emotional and political rhetoric was finding a channel to express itself -- and that, too, through the barrel of the gun. It is interesting that in the 1980's the call to arms to the youth of the Islamic world was more widely welcomed than the late 1960's when Yasser Arafat's Al Fatah movement was hard pressed to find a mass radical following. Part of the reason for this could well be the particular change in the socio-economic demographics of Arab youth, who faced with bleak economic prospects and an ever encroaching political climate, found militancy for an Islamic cause as the best way to survive -- especially if it was laced with the prospects of heroism.

Perhaps the exception to this phenomenon have been the youth of Saudi Arabia who, while coming from a rich country, did not have any tradition of political and religious militancy. Even during the early years of the Soviet occupation of Afghanistan, the Saudi economy was relatively stable; joblessness was nowhere near the subsequent levels of the late 1990's. The initial attraction to an armed involvement in a cause flowed more from the Islamic romanticism of fighting a Jihad -- and nothing more than that. Eventually, of course, the deteriorating conditions within Saudi society created an environment in which a more inward looking radicalism was born. Now this appeals to a wider audience than it did perhaps 20 years back.

It is interesting to note that from the hijackers who were involved in the events of 9/11, only a small percentage came from poor backgrounds, and many of them had studied in the West -- particularly the United States -- some even being exposed to the radical teachings of leading Islamic dissident scholars who had been expelled from Saudi Arabia.

The long-term landscape for radical Islam is very difficult to predict. It is not simply a question of modeling an outcome for these militant organizations because a great deal of what will happen to them will depend on factors within the society they operate in.

In addition and more importantly, the geopolitical picture in the region and the world will determine whom the major powers, especially the United States, deal with. There is no denying that the American actions in Afghanistan and Iraq have given rise to radicalism and militant attacks against a variety of targets, and that, too, with growing impunity. That the war against terrorism has closed the ranks amongst the terrorists rather than driven them into the woodworks is not merely a liberal view but something that merits a sustained discussion. To the extent that George W Bush acted ostensibly to protect America, the actions of his administration have made American citizens and American assets more vulnerable to attacks in many countries, and yet deflected the battle against terrorism away from American shores.

One would argue that understanding the roots of this terrorist activity is as important, if not more, than fighting the terrorists in a variety of theaters of "war" around the world. An act of understanding cannot, by definition, merely be an intellectual process; such understanding would need to examine the causes of the growing resentment among the masses in the Islamic world. The current situation is not solving the issues but merely containing the world that America fears. It is more importantly a situation which needs urgent solutions within the societies from where this anger is being bred.

Understanding the Divisions

This is a task for both the regional powers and the societies within the Islamic world to resolve. It is also required of the United States to understand the "Arabia" problem better. One of the associated risks most certainly remains that if the current war on terrorism results in a stalemate, the chances of which are high, the militancy will then turn to regimes within the Islamic world and seek Islamic-style revolutions. In those countries where there is an electoral process, there will most certainly be a greater degree of political success for the radical-style Islamic parties. From the point of view of the militant organizations, the realization that they can achieve more from attacking the softer domestic targets than the more distant US holds a better prospect for success. It will happen sooner or later. It is this scenario that is most dangerous for the Islamic world.

For those who believe that the events of 9/11 and the bombings in Spain and London will not happen again, there has to be an understanding that the nature of this battle is not rigid; it is more fluid than we imagine. It would be fair to say that with the death of Osama bin Laden movement has lose an important figurehead. But given the nature of the leadership structure it is likely that other leaders will take his place and indeed Al Qaeda as we know it will perhaps also be fragmented. There are within Al Qaeda enough zealous leaders who can continue the struggle as they see it under Ayman Al Zawahiri's leadership, but without the persona of Osama bin Laden looming in a larger than life role in the minds of the youth it would seem that eventually new recruits to their cause would be harder to enroll.

A fragmented Al Qaeda whose satraps are vying internally for political leadership will doubtless conduct more external attacks on the "far enemy" (the US and its Allies) and the "near enemy" (the Arab leadership of the Middle East) in a bid to show their muscle and strength. Such attacks, in these leaders' view, will also win admiration from within the young cadres of other Islamic militant movements. In the immediate aftermath of

Osama bin Laden's killing in Pakistan the reprisal attacks were all conducted against targets within Pakistan and killing dozens of innocent people and some paramilitary troops, bringing home the ferocity of the anger.

While eventually the lack of a central leadership will affect the movement, this might be a slow process during brutal attacks are bound to take place out of sheer desperation, if not necessity. On the other hand the militant organizations do feel that the cohesiveness following the events of 9/11 has grown within Al Qaeda, and the adversity it faced from America and the West has brought them closer for "eventual victory." An eventual victory does not necessarily mean a military or political defeat of the United States but could also mean a US withdrawal from the region due to change of political realities within the US itself. The results of the 2008 US presidential election will influence American foreign policy in Arabia profoundly.

The fact remains that the divide within the world of Islam is serious. As much as there is a move toward regarding it only as a militant world, there is hopefully a realization that a more moderate face of Islam is also present and perhaps is the majority of what Muslim societies are all about. The world at large will have to invest considerable time and effort in understanding the compulsions and dynamics of this world because one way or another it will have a profound effect on society in our lifetimes – and for the next many decades.

THE ARAB NATION-STATE.

Just who is an Arab? I have been with Lebanese who have claimed to be Arab at moments and French descendants at others, or Gulf Arabs who stress they are "Khaleeji Arabs," while Iraqis who are caught in a myriad of definitions, particularly during these calamitous days, define themselves differently at different times – but almost always within their particular ethnic matrix.

I once asked a prominent North African personality, a Muslim who went on to become president of his country, about the concept of an "Arab Nation." He alluded to the common history of the Arabs, the bond of religion, and then said indeed in a number of cases the ethnic, cultural and social bond seems to be discordant but that "We Arabs realize that being anything other than an Arab nation will not work for us."

I am not sure to this day if he implied that the moment a Moroccan or a Mauritanian considers himself as not being an Arab he becomes an African. Or was he implying that having created the bond of religion and the common history of being under Arab rule, the only way forward was to embrace that history and continue -- or else the "Arabness" somehow erodes to leave nothing else there. I wonder if many Arabs realize that in truth the "Arab Nation" is a work in continuous progress, although Arab society has been around for centuries. Yet through various stages in history being an Arab was at times only a question of the commonness of language; thus the Arabs accepted Wilfred Thesiger as much as he assimilated into the Arabs as he spoke Arabic fluently. This has, in the modern day, become less of criteria and today being an Arab and belonging to an Arab Nation-State are all blurred concepts at times.

The common bond of Islam has indeed been not only the central point of gravition for the 'Arabs' because not only did Islam bring them a common unifed faith it also brought with it the Arabic language. In most cases Arabic was adopted with ease into the social and administrative fabric of these countries, like Morrocco, Tunsia, Libya and elsewhere adding to the 'Arabness' that characterized these societies which were later to be become nation states in their own right.

The creation of the concept of the modern Arab nation-state was the result of the after effects of World War One, when the Ottoman Empire collapsed, and the eventual roll back of the empires, especially the British. While the traditional Arab states were based on monarchist models that emerged from deeply tribal systems, the advent of the modern nation-state was and remains a challenge to Arab societies. A cursory look at the map of Arabia of the 1950's shows monarchies literally doting the political landscape: Saudi Arabia, Iraq, Jordan, United Arab Emirates, Oman, Bahrain, Kuwait, Qatar, Libya, Morocco and Egypt, some of whom remained British or foreign protectorates, but nevertheless were monarchies.

The Arab Nation-State

The emergence of Egypt as a republic with the removal by the military of the debauched King Farook, followed by the military coup in Iraq, began a period of state building that was not linked to monarchies or indeed a foreign imperialist rule. Yet the emergence of the non-monarchist Arab state has not been on the back of republican revolutions or philosophy but, in many cases, the result of political power struggles that needed to reinforce nationalist sentiment under the guise of an Arab nation-state.

In these independent Arab countries, both republican and monarchist, there wasn't any rollback of the legal and administrative systems that were essentially the legacy of the colonial period, indicating that the making of a modern state was very much an issue of nation building for the Arabs.

Nation building, in an Arab sense, has been as much a function of creating the state machinery and the legal and administrative systems as it has been a matter for defining a sense of Arab "belonging" among the Arab people. When the Libyan leader Muammar Gaddafi complained of the lack of an Arab unity and interchanges his identity to be African rather than Arab, the problems seem to be deeper than one can imagine. In a similar sense, the task of building Arab nationhood has been challenged by ethnic and cultural diversities that normally Arabs only talk about in a limited public platform. Is it the Islamic "values" that bind them as a nation, or is the common language of Arabic that binds the Arab nations, or is the general sense of geography that makes them feel they need to define a sense of "Arab-hood" into a nation?

The diversity that internally divides the Arab "nation" also unites it when perceived threats to the "Arab-ness" of the area emerge, and in a strange way nationalism of specific nations has been a stronger focus than Pan-Arab nationalism, which has remained an emotional plea. At times the emotional appeals of Islam have been the strongest, but more at the social level without necessarily bringing a political definition to the elements of nationhood. Nevertheless, the actions of the United States since 9/11 have been seen as much as an attack on the identity and polity of Iraq and Afghanistan as they have also been seen as an attack of Islam. Even though the US has taken pains to show that this is indeed not the case, but it would seem the treatment of prisoners from the war on terror tend to have been seen by the US interrogators more as 'Islamic jihadists' rather than combantants in the two theathers of war.

The confusion for Arab nationhood is as much a problem for Arabs with their history as "nations" as it is a testimony to the political mapping of the region. The colonial history of the Arab nations has dictated to the way modern states were born, in large measure with their former colonial masters drawing lines across maps to carve out countries. There is thus a disconnect between the history and the concept of a modern nation-state that is fundamentally contrary to the idea of history in the many centuries prior to the granting of statehood to many territories. Thus for an Arab the transition from a tribal society to suddenly a modern Nation-State is disjointed and in clearly discernible as an event that was not smoothly connected to his tribal past. Prior to the creation of modern states, local feudal lords governed most of the Arab lands or tribal leaders who then owed allegiance to the Caliphate or any other superior power that had the trappings of an Empire. In some cases, like the Turkish Caliphate, a system of governance and law was also in place for the governed territories, but the power flowed through the local social and tribal structures. The tribal structure was -- and one may argue still remains -- an integral and vital part of the tools of governance within the emerging Arab nation-states. It is as much a necessary bond for political legitimacy as it is a yardstick for loyalty in a political power structure where failure of regimes is often fraught with the danger of physical extermination.

The Arab Nation-State

There have been instances in Arab history, when nationhood was stressed through strong social links and emotional ties of Islam. A case in point is Sudan under the Mahdi; this was where a tribal structure and the emotional appeal of Islam, albeit the Dervish philosophy. While strictly speaking, a "Dervish" is an ascetic religious fraternity largely inspired by Sufi philosophy, where spirit is more important than form, in the context of the Sudan Mahdi uprising British historians tend to misuse the term "dervish" in this context and broadly described the movement meshed together against British presence. Yet to give it any Pan-Arab connotations would be wrong as the bulk of the soldiers who defeated the Mahdi army, in revenge for the ousting of the British from Khartoum in 1885, was composed of Egyptian and Sudanese forces, led by two brigades of British troops.

But instances of such uprisings, whether in Algeria against the French, or against the British in Sudan, were more assertions for power rather than assertions for Arab statehood. They might well have carried the nascent history-making epochs that bind the romance of nationalism into the next generation but there is little evidence that these uprising were motivated by a philosophy toward independent statehood in the sense we saw in the British colonies of America and India.

The defeat of the Turks in World War I by the Allied Powers, led to the British and the French directly governing a large part of the territory formerly belonging to the Ottoman Empire, and which constitute present-day Arab nations. With the exception of Saudi Arabia, most of what is modern-day Arabia was a part of the administrative set up of these victorious colonial powers; the impact on the history of these lands was shaped by the emergence of modern nation-states all over Europe. Since the defeat of the Turks in Saudi Arabia led to the emergence of a dynastic monarchy -- which the British had encouraged and supported -- its governance by a monarchy was more desirable rather than direct dependency status. xv

However it is curious that the new powers did not immediately move toward creation of modern nation-states but installed monarchies in a number of these countries, Iraq, Jordan, as an example, perhaps out of concern that the machinery for modern nation-state did not exist within these societies. It is also interesting that some of these monarchies – such as those in Iraq -- either vanished within 60 odd years or were modified to fit into modern state mechanics.

Today the issues that face the Arab "nation" have radically changed as there is a whole set of new dynamics in play. The main impact of factional and communal infighting, the religious issues and the current state of world politics are the dynamics that cannot be ignored. These bring opportunities and pressures for post-colonial Arab nations that will shape the way their societies develop. In addition, the events of 9/11 have dramatically brought into focus the societal tensions of Arab societies, both internally and externally, and also at the same time forced Arabs to ask questions that they perhaps have reluctantly put aside for decades. The central question, of course, is: Who are we?

It is remarkable that the responsibility of 9/11 has been pinned on "Islamic terrorism," when in reality each and every hijacker of the planes that carried out the 9/11 attacks was an Arab. If there had been only Taliban-inspired Afghans or indeed other non-Arab Islamists among the hijackers then the notion of a widespread Islamic conspiracy behind the events of 9/11 would carry more credence. Yet the notion of the West being under siege by an international Islamic terrorist movement -- as opposed to, say, an Arab terrorist movement -- is quite widespread, perhaps because the impression it creates is more within the vein of a Crusade-like emotion that is compelling in its own realm. However, in no sense do the Arabs see the events of 9/11 and the subsequent American actions in Afghanistan and Iraq as totally connected, and even those liberal enough to share the outrage of the attacks on the US do not see the policy extension of Washington as really a war on terror. The extended US response to 9/11 in the form of the attack on Iraq is seen as an attack on an Arab nation, yet the act against the US under the 9/11 tragedy is not seen as an act of an Arab nation against the US, but of fanatics who happened to be Arabs.

The Arab nation has itself also witnessed the calamity of the terror campaign as the focus of some of the fanatical elements have moved intermittently, from the "far enemy" (the United States) to the "near enemy," (the Arab regimes they wish to replace). The impact of the war that is being waged between these two opposing philosophies has dimensions that are difficult to comprehend for the Arab moderates. While Ayman Al-Zawahiri professed that Al Zarqawi, the most militant of the fanatics in Iraq, was the Prince of Al Qaeda in Iraq, his death brought as much relief to the Shia community as it did to a number of Iraqis who clearly cannot understand how the bombing of mosques and buses and killing everyday Iraqis will expel the "far enemy" from Iraq? The Arab nation has therefore seen the challenges from within as dichotomous in the sense that they exploit the socio-religious fissures of these societies. The problem that such strategies have is that they never unify, as was seen with the sectarian violence in Pakistan between the majority Sunni and the minority Shia radical groups. Radical elements of the Shia and Sunni communities in Pakistan fought a bitter religious war for close to a decade, bombing mosques and killing each other's leaders none of these actions creating any sense of unity within the country.

Prior to the events of 9/11 the struggles within the Arab world were multi-faceted with social and political reforms enmeshed with truncated and, in some cases, failed economic plans. In addition, the seething anger of the masses in some countries was directed at times into social change. Such change was hoped for but the leadership did not possess the vision or the means to create and engineer the change. The growing role of the orthodox clergy, with its various shades, was creating and adding dimensions to the perceived agenda for reform that complicated the place that Arab nationalists could feel was needed for this political and social view.

Within Arab societies since the time from the emergence for a call for a Pan-Arab movement by Gamal Abdel Nasser of Egypt to the modern-day search for an Arab political and social identity the struggle to understand what Arab nationhood continues. The Pan-Arabists would have us believe that the social fabric for that Pan-Arab nationhood was always there and it is only the political focus to it that has been absent. The abysmal response to the call for Pan Arab nationalism, even in its non formal social sense, has shown that as Arabs have begun to embrace the concept of nations the idea of a fluid Pan Arabism is currently alien to them in so far as unions.

This is where the divide of expectations becomes difficult to comprehend, as it is not natural for most Arabs to conceive of Pan-Arabism as anything more than an emotional plea for the moment. In fact, with the current political situation, and the fragmented notion of Arab politics and society one would imagine calls for Pan-Arabism would be heard more clearly. However, this is not the case, as perhaps people understand that the notion of Pan-Arabism during the Nasser period, such as it was, did not change life for the common man.

While Pan-Arabism sought Arab governments to give up some element of autonomy for the "common good of the Arab nation," Arab nationalism on the other hand was seeking to assert a sense of Arabness within the context of the modern state. This was easier for new, and mostly autocratic, regimes to implement through massive public-relations and near jingoistic appeal. It is not uncommon to go to a number of Arab countries and see massive larger-than-life posters and statutes of local leaders, and in almost all facets of life the intrusive presence of the leadership is obvious. In the case of countries like Syria, Iran and Iraq one notices the presence of the leadership pervading into the daily lives of the people – either through propaganda, or the secret police, or various forms of intimidation. This was particularly so in the case of Iraq under Saddam Hussein as the Baath Party was so ubiquitous that it was impossible to work to obtain any government employment without being a member of the Baath Party and swearing allegiance to Saddam Hussein.

Arab nationalism has, in this respect, grappled with the 9/11 events and the subsequent American actions with many mixed feelings. In so far as the removal of Saddam Hussein was concerned, most Arabs secretly rejoiced his downfall; his brand of Arab nationalism was at best adventurous and more anti-conservative Arab than anyone else. However, the fact that an Arab nation-state surrendered its national sovereignty in the process to an invading army is something most Arabs felt utterly helpless about.

The American right wing sees the linkage between what it calls "state terrorism" and the 9/11 events to be seamless, even though no proof was ever presented of that linkage. Arabs see the two as separate elements; indeed many Arabs would argue that the 9/11 event was an excuse to violate Arab nationalism. More perversely, now fundamentalist elements within Muslim Arab states have broadened their appeal to their audiences by pointing to the continued presence of US troops in Iraq as a reason for a Jihad to be waged against them. However, not strangely, having called upon a Jihad against the US forces and their presence in the region, the Muslim Arab radicals cannot any longer claim a façade of an Arab nationalist movement fighting for the removal of American forces. The call for an Islamic war has more appeal than a war of liberation in countries like Iraq as the people, after decades of Saddam's repression are hardly likely to consider Arab nationalism (a common slogan in Saddam's rhetoric) to be a rallying point for the people.

For Arab societies and nations the situation thus presents very interesting dynamics. The call for an Islamic Jihad for removing foreign forces from Arabia can just as easily become the rallying call for change within Arab societies -- and therein lays the current challenge for Arabs to consider. The Arab societies are literally torn between the call for modernism and reform on the one hand, and the call for a return to traditional values and Islamic fundamentalism. From the perspective of the world's only dominant military power, the United States, one of the professed goals of its foreign policy is to bring about democratic reform within the Middle East. To that extent, the Islamic fundamentalists and the US government, at least on the face of it, have the same goal of bringing about reform within the Arab world. The difference ends there, as for the US the shift of its policy objectives means that "change" in governments not aligned to its policy objectives is paramount, while "reform" applies to governments that have been its strong allies. Thus, US policy directives concerning "change" are targeted at countries like Iraq, Afghanistan and indeed Iran, while the word "reform" is more typically used for the rest of the Arab governments and Muslim countries. The dichotomy of the US policy toward the Middle East and its desire to see a New Middle East is at the very core of what the Islamic fundamentalists and radicals are experiencing, except they want it to be radical, and they seek reform under an Islamic framework.

The script for the need for a change within the Arab world is common to both the US call for change or reform, as the case may be, and for Al Qaeda's call for 'change' (removal of regimes not aligned to its thinking) and for ultimate reform into an Islamic society as defined by its philosophy.

The push and pull, however, is in opposite directions and this is where the division between these approaches is tested most.

So long as the threat of Al Qaeda-led "reform" exists for current Arab existing regimes, the chances are that the only ally through whom Washington can bring about even limited reforms are the existing regimes themselves. In a crucial sense this draws the lines of loyalty and alliances very clearly. The preservation of the geo-political status quo come from existing regimes, while the broader battle with the fundamentalists is fought with the hope that eventual economic and social reform within the Arab world will bring to the Arab societies the well-being to not be pushed into the fold of the terrorists. This brings the existing regimes to loggerheads with the likes of Al Qaeda as the latter continues to draw its battle lines across areas of confrontation with both the "far enemy" and the "near enemy" at the same time. This creates pressures within Arab societies that cannot be resolved easily; it is not as if a mutual truce can be declared between Al Qaeda and the existing regimes as the nature of their struggle is now more international then ever before.

The events in Tunisia, Egypt, Yemen, Syria, Bahrain and Libya however have brought in a new twist to the paradigm of change, where people in the street have inspired a broad based movement of change. In the case of Bahrain and Egpyt the extensive use of social media platforms and blogging has highlighted the power of social consciousness over both the power of international diplomacy and the Kalashnikov. While the street power movement may well highlight the frustrations of the growing number of educated youth of the Arab world, it faces the challenge of at best being a movement for change rather than having the political structure of reaping the benefits of the change itself.

This has been seen in the case of Egypt, where the events of Taheri Square brought down the government of Hosni Mubarak, but the dividends of this change will go, through the electoral process, to the organized political parties and may not totally reflect the wishes of those who gathered in the long vigil at Taheri Square. Yet political leaders will hear the message of the power of the youth too that if they can bring down Hosni Mubarak they could just as well effect change once again.

In a sense these change conciousness youth have shown that policies of reform or change, whether espoused by the likes of Osama bin Laden and his followers, or those propogated by Washington, were inadequate to inspire effective change. Neither the Isalmic Fundamentalists nor the US policy makers could have predicted a year back that such massive and far-reaching change could come from the power of the unheard.

Arab societies must be seen within the context of a wider boundary than the Middle East, as large Arab and Muslim populations have emerged in countries like England, Spain, France, the United States and Canada, to name only a few. The battle for the next few decades will be for the hearts of these societies too, as the call of a radical Islamist movement nowadays has transformed the battle into a broader front where the territorial boundaries are undefined.

The appeal and message of a radical Islam, whose leaders are determined to bring about the demise of its enemy, namely the United States and its allies, now has taken the fluid form of using the Internet and the media in much the same, but yet brutal, methods of media engineering for maximum impact. It is this phase of the battle between the two that divides the Arab nation politically, and at some strata of its society unifies it with an emotional appeal. It's important to understand that the shape of the Arab nation will be decided as much in the streets of Cairo and Gaza as it will be in the suburbs of Dearborn, Michigan, and Edgware Road, London. This does not mean that all of the fundamentalist Islamic segments of Muslim want to adopt radical means for change, and indeed one could argue that the manner in which the Muslim and Arab world has been managed thus far these fundamentalist believe in earnest, and perhaps quite rightly so, that they could do a better job. However, for the most part these societies have a terrible track record in terms of their present governments, with a few exceptions, to have done anything significantly better for their own people. Thus Hamas and many others can claim that it is time a different approach can indeed be tried.

The fact that Arab nations are troubled by the wave of terrorism that is ascribed as much to Islamic fundamentalism as it is to the Arabs is not entirely apparent. While the initial wave of terrorist attacks on the US on 9/11 were led and executed by Arabs, the current wave, if more widespread in its choice of perpetuators, needs careful examination then merely being lumped under the generic banner of radical Muslim inspired terrorism. The impact of the universal appeal that radical Muslim terrorist organizations have covering a number of ethnic origins and nationalities is a matter of concern within the established structures of Arab society. The attacks in Egypt, Algeria and Saudi Arabia and recently Iraq, have all shown that the suicide bomber and terrorist attacker will always have the initiative of choosing his target to suit his timing and his convenience. It is the soft underbelly of Arab societies and those of Western societies that will remain the target of this form of battle, and the antidote for it is simply not a military solution. Arab societies therefore have to contend with deeper issues within their own social structure as result of this terrorism that the world faces. One is not entirely sure that Arab societies and nations are quite equipped to handle the challenges that such an unseen enemy poses to them.

One could ask a simple question whether such tactics, as adopted by the radical militant side of Islamic movements, will actually seek anything substantial within their own societies. The emotional appeal of the religiously zealous movement will always find supporters within the poor and downtrodden within these societies. However, I am not sure their call has been strong enough to muster the support for a street led rebellion, as we saw in Iran in 1979, to bring about change. The failure of the Iranian revolution to radically change the life of the common man is something that bears testimony to the fact that an Islamist revolution might only mean for the people in the street a change of one monarchy for another form of authoritarianism, even if theocratic. On the contrary the street upheavels of 2011 were as much a surprise to the radical Islamists as it was to the governments in power.

If the aim of the change is to give the "unheard" within Arab societies a better voice, then it is highly unlikely that an Islamist reform movement led by any of the current leadership of these Islamic groups will display any tolerance to dissent. While they may champion the 'unheard' there is little chance that the 'unheard' of these societies will ever be heard if they are successful in getting power; either through the ballot box or the barrel of a gun. The manner in which the Taliban government in Afghanistan dealt with its critics within the country population might have a small minority of supporters, but most Arab-based Muslim fundamentalist thinkers agree that the Taliban regime was almost insanely inhumane in its treatment of the people. The fight in Arabia is as much for power as it is a process of determining the balance between traditional values and modernism. But in the final analysis, the next war will be waged for the hearts and minds of the Muslim youth, whether they are in Arab cities or the sons and daughters of immigrant Muslim families in Western societies.

However, Arab societies also seek security and law and order; they seek an environment in which business and society can flourish. Western commentators are amazed that dictatorial regimes are accepted even when there is a propensity for some of these regimes, like Syria, and Iraq, to trample human freedoms with ease; such acceptance also comes from the educated middle class who normally would be appalled by the mistreatment of the people. One of the biggest concerns Arab societies have is security, and if this is not present they will gladly welcome back a system that is oppressive in exchange for security.

This may explain why after the ouster of the Taliban, the radical movement is making a come back in some areas; the new order in Afghanistan has not been established and certainly the security situation has got worse. Sadly, if the common people in Iraq were asked if they wanted a return to the days of Saddam Hussein, a large percentage might agree that those days, while brutal, at least didn't witness the daily bombing and insecurity that is now seen in the streets of Baghdad. Security and law and order are a major concern to the people of these countries and at extreme moments of their recent history they would accept this coming from any quarter of society.

The concept of an Arab nation-state is fragmented and divided; it lacks a coherent political voice. But when painted in the colors of an Islamic Arab "nation," it acquires a potency that I suspect is yet to be fully captured, let alone mobilized. It is this latent unifying social power to which the militants appeal, because it's the very social fabric that is seeped in poverty and neglect. The cadres that carry out the bombings under the banner of Hamas in Occupied Palestine come from these dispossessed segments of Muslim society. A vast majority of the suicide attackers who carried out attacks against the United States, Spain and Britain came from relatively better economic social strata of Muslim society. How have the militant movements have created this appeal for both the poor and downtrodden and at the same time the relatively well do from among its ranks? I suspect we will be reflecting on this question for years to come.

My own view is that later attacks on Western targets, like the London bombings in July 2005 show that support for the militants isn't contained within a conventional framework of a stereotype of a possible suicide bomber. The overreaction of Western, and particularly US, security agencies suggests that, in the view of these organizations, any Muslim or Arab within a certain age profile – meaning young and mostly male, of course -- could be a potential suicide-bomber. This perception, while embodied in the neo-conservative thinking of the US body-politic, has caused more discontent than anything; it has triggered a sense among "good" Muslims that they need to prove over and over they are "good." Part of the problem may well be the lack of deep links of US intelligence services with the social fabric of Arab and Muslim societies. This undoubtedly leads to misinterpretation of existing data, and the formulation of policies that are, at best, dubious in their value to deal with the problem of "Arabia Besieged."

At the political level, the lack of a unifying charismatic leadership, a high degree of inherent political suspicions, and most of all, the deep distrust of the aims and motives of other Arab countries leaves the Arab nation quite aimless in the context of a modern world political strategy. While at an emotional level there is a unity concerning Palestinian rights and the posture toward Israel, in reality it is merely an emotional stand rather than a coherent strategy to influence world opinion and bring about a broader understanding of the complex issues relating to Palestine. In the wake of the 1993 Oslo Accords -- signed by then-Palestinian leader Yasser Arafat and then-Israeli Prime Minister Yitzhak Rabin, and which called for a transition toward Palestinian self-rule in the Gaza Strip and the West Bank -- the Arabs' political stance concerning Palestine, while remaining fundamentally the same in terms of supporting the cause of a fully independent state, has emphasized that it was up to the Palestinian leadership to decide, negotiate and deal with their people's political destiny. It seemed that the idea of statehood for Palestine also implied that it must steer its own course of statehood, with Egypt and Jordan playing a vital supporting role, and to some extent Syria taking a less involved role in the affairs of Palestine. The old concept of "frontline" states that are willing to go to war with Israel has changed in a unipolar world, and the reality is that an all-out war with Israel in the current geopolitical framework seems unlikely. This has meant the battle for Palestinians is now either across the negotiating table or through selective violence that some of the militant groups seek.

One cannot be sure if, in the absence of a coherent policy of aggressive military positioning versus Israel, the emotional appeal of the Palestinian cause can bring about a unity among the "frontline" states, let alone Arabia as a whole. Clearly, on account of the changing scene on the global front -- where the dividends of peace have been assumed to be more beneficial in the long run – there is a growing frustration on the part of the Arabs and their leaders. Libya's attempts to be accepted back into the community of nations by shedding its militancy have been just one barometer of the changing times and the challenges that Arab nations face. Of course, there are those within Arabia – and particularly the oil-rich states – who opine that it really doesn't matter what the world thinks of the Arabs because there's little that the US or the West, in particular, could do to alter the developmental momentum of these economies. In a recent conversation with a journalist friend, I posed the following question: "Does it really matter whether or not Americans invest in Arabia, or whether American tourists come here?"

To a degree, of course, the economic and political issues that Arabs face are no different then those faced by Russia and Europe in dealing with the United States – issues whose core consists of a central question: How does one deal with the world's only superpower? Unlike the Russians and European Union, however, Arabs lack political cohesiveness. It is almost as if the Arabs assume that once the issues of Palestine are resolved, in a manner acceptable to all parties, the search for a cohesive political position in the unipolar world will become a priority. It is here that the intellectual capital has been least employed; educated Arabs and some of their more forward-looking political leaders are aware of the challenges that this situation creates.

Within the Arab world the emergence of a bloc of oil-rich nations has, on the one hand, given Arabs the resorces to better their own lot. Yet, there's a strong sense among the poorer Arab nations of being left out. Arab leaders like Saddam Hussein tried in vain to mobilize this "downtrodden" Arab community of nations. That probably explains why countries like Yemen and Jordan, and leaders like Yasser Arafat gave Saddan moral support in the 1991 Gulf War. Others like Syria and Egypt chose the Allied side, more perhaps on the principle that Saddam had invaded an Arab country, Kuwait, violated its sovereignty, and therefore needed to be expelled. It is also true that the position taken by these governments was dictated by regional politics -- and by their critical relationship of dependency with the leading GCC states, like Saudi Arabia, who obviously opposed the occupation of Kuwait. There was always a distinction in the minds of the governments who supported the United States and its Allies, between the position they took toward Saddam and the Iraqi people at large. It was not uncommon to see an Arab country opposed to Saddam issuing a tough statement against him, and at the same time sending medical aid to the people of Iraq.

One cannot talk about the state of the Arab nation without understanding that Saddam Hussein's invasion of Kuwait created perhaps the biggest schism within the Arab world in recent history. He fostered instability within the region that, over time, has seemed to erode the strength of sovereignty in Arabia. While Saddam may well have appealed to the masses that looked for a hero to stand up to the pressures on the Arab world, sadly for them Saddam was never really that hero. His status in his homeland, too, was largely built upon terror tactics and brutal suppression of his own people. The more emotive segment of the

Arab population secretly hoped in the beginning days of the Gulf war that perhaps Saddam might have the ability to stand up to the Allies and, if not win, at least be able to engage the Americans in a protracted battle over Kuwait. This was not to be, and as Iraqi armor and dead bodies littered the Kuwaiti and Southern Iraqi deserts, more than anything else Arab pride took a serious hit. His much-vaunted army lay in disarray, with a crippled command and control structure and no ability to assert any decisiveness in the outcome of any of the battles they engaged in; yet they were left to possess enough ability to continue to surpress their own people.

What Saddam truly expected to achieve from the invasion of Kuwait will always remain unknown, but it did seem that as the events prior to the invasion indicated he relied on the age-old border disputes and his own belief that he was in the right to invade his former benefactor. Given the decision-making apparatus within his Baath Party, it is unlikely there was dissent over Saddam's plans for the invasion. This surely reinforced his belief in the righteousness of his decision.

Prior to the 1991 Gulf War there was clearly a move among different Arab states to take the mantle of Arab leadership. Saddam Hussein's claim to that leadership rested upon his "resistance" to the Iranian "menace"; Hafez Al-Assad of Syria asserted his claim on the basis of his role in bringing peace to Lebanon by stationing 30,000 troops in there and by playing a crucial role in fashioning the 1989 Taid Accords -- and by being a "frontline" state in the war against Israel. Egypt's Hosni Mubarak staked his claim to the leadership of the Arab world based on what he frequently called "a new leadership for peace and moderation." Saudi Arabia, while perhaps appealing emotionally for the role of the leadership, was never active enough within the Arab political forum to stake a claim, preferring the role of an elder statesman role that was politically less hazardous for it to navigate. The exception was during the Gulf War where Saudi input into the process was vital to forge an Arab Alliance supporting the war for the liberation of Kuwait. However, within the population at large, there never has been an acceptance toward any of the leaders as being really effective in charting a course that would make sense or provide vision for Arabia. To that extent the forum for Arab leadership has had different actors on the stage with different visions, different voices, and different agendas. This has meant that the political voice of the Arab nations, while strong on the issue of the Palestinian cause, has been divided and disjointed on other world issues; such as world trade negotiations, global warming and even the future of Iraq. In the post 1991 Gulf War scenario the voice of the Arab leadership has been even feebler on issues of regional politics and reform.

Arab efforts regarding collective leadership through the Arab League have also, largely, been a failure, much like how the United Nations' role at crucial moments in history has been more moral than politically important. As the US's current political behavior -- where the United Nations has been marginalized -- continues, so too will Arab states continue to consider their own regional organizations mostly redundant. The Arab nations have looked at their own collective summits as more regional in scope rather than formulating a common approach on international issues. There is no doubt that Arab people and Arab leadership are increasingly seeing themselves as under a political siege, all the more after the events of 9/11. The "war against terror" has turned formerly radical states into docile moderate states, and, in a larger sense, has forced the Arab leadership to look within their own societies for clues about the future. While from an Arab perspective the US call for more democratic societies within the Arab world may sound nice and politically correct, there is common – if unarticulated -- understanding within the Arab leadership and neutral Arab observers that if today the Arab world were to accept a freely democratically government in each of the 22 Arab states (home to nearly 350 million people), predominately anti-American governments would most likely be voted into power. An uneducated population will ultimately cast its votes either along tribal affiliations or along religious loyalties, ignoring the fundamental issues of nationhood – let alone sustainable economic development in an era of globalization -- that confront Arab societies, as they do societies everywhere else, too.

A movement toward a democratic process for electing governments will result in radical fundamental organizations getting a better chance to capitalize on their religious appeal with the masses. In some respects the move toward a democratic electoral process will eventually graduate from municipal elections to a broad-based electoral process being implemented in these countries. However, the process of reforms has to be seen within the context of Arab nations and their position within the geopolitical framework of the region and also internationally.

Experiments with the process in Palestine have yielded an acceptance of the ballot box as a means for bringing in political change, even though the election of Hamas indicates the very challenges of nascent democracy in a society where emotional appeal runs high – perhaps higher than the notion of melding civic responsibilities and civil rights for the common good. In countries like Bahrain, Kuwait, Algeria and Palestine, reform movements are gradually bringing in change that's likely to positively affect society far more than the externally influenced "forced" reforms toward democracy like those in Iraq and Afghanistan. While the ends may be similar, "forced" reforms will not last the distance since they need to take roots in the nation's psyche. Only through such a process will change be accepted and nurtured.

I know that some commentators point to the democracy movement in Iraq after Saddam Hussein's fall and suggest that the absence of a decisive religious vote hasn't quite emerged suggesting that anti-American feelings did not marshall the religious segment to vote a fundamentalist government into power, arguing that the religious vote is an over played card to thwart democractic reform. It is correct that the Iraqi elections, at least, showed the voice of moderation seemed to have prevailed. However, concluding that the experience of Iraq would be applicable to the whole of Arabia is a serious mistake. There has to be an appreciation that within Iraq the years of Saddam's brutal rule never allowed a religious element to hold in society, and Iraq's tribal and ethnic dynamics were such that either a strong man on the top would work or a coalition of different groups emerging after an election would hammer out a way to govern the nation. It was perhaps the long entrenched secular traditions of Saddam's rule that might still influence the people of Iraq. However, in other countries the religious elements will gain from the anti American sentiment that exists in countries like Afghanistan, and Palestine.

One may argue that the failure of the Americans and the newly elected government in Iraq to bring about an end to the insurgency is largely indicative of the tremendous problems that face Iraq as a people to govern. In the post-Gulf War scenario in 1991 one of the reasons the Allied Forces did not consider moving on to Baghdad after the liberation of Kuwait was the fear that an Iraq without a central authority would crumble into a civil war. Both President George H. W. Bush and General Colin Powell – who was chairman of the Joint Chiefs of Staff at the time – came in for considerable criticism at the time. But their judgment was borne out. It's an irony of history that the elder Bush's son, President George W. Bush took the military campaign to Baghdad, toppled Saddam, and unleashed what's turned out to be a political and strategic disaster for Arabia.

The Arab as well as the larger Muslim Ummah perceives themselves as having suffered humiliations not only within the context of Arabia but also the global political scene. While the United States and Britain – among other Western countries -- see themselves under siege by Islamist militancy, the Muslims -- and in particular the Arabs -- see themselves cornered by the policies of the United States.

This divide of perceptions is widening rather than narrowing in the post 9/11 environment. The effect of the breakdown of the Oslo Accords between the Palestinians and the Israelis contributed heavily to the loss of faith in the role that the United States could play on the outcome of events in the Middle East. In 2001, frustrated with the slow progress toward the implementation of the Oslo Peace accord, Yasser Arafat upped the stakes by allowing his student wing, Tazim, to organize the Second Infitada, while Israel's Ariel Sharon didn't help matters by walking into the Al Aqsa Mosque in Jerusalem, setting off perhaps the worst unrest that Palestine and the Occupied Territories had seen in years.

Arafat had by then already rejected a major effort by President Bill Clinton in 2000 that would have guaranteed US support for the establishment of a Palestinian state. He was always the maximalist. Arafat now laid down the conditions for returning to the peace talks, which included a demand for the recognition for the right of every Palestinian displaced from what is now Israel to return to his ancestral land. (There are an estimated 4.7 million Palestinians who are termed by the United Nations as displaced persons.)

Arafat inverted the logic of the right of each Jew to return to the Holy Land and applied it in equal measure to the issue of Palestinian refugees. This did not go across too well with the Israelis. The United States, embarrassed by Arafat's new – and unrealistic -- demands, backed off any support for a new round of peace talks and, in manner of speaking, signaled to the Israelis that they could deal with the Intifada as they thought fit. The result was a terrible crackdown by the Israeli military, at the height of which even Arafat's headquarters were rocketed, and the Palestinian leader – who was among the founders of the PLO in 1964 – was a virtual prisoner in his own compound, going for days without electricity or potable water. None of these events resulted in Washington exerting pressure on the Israelis to stop their attacks on Palestinian territories. The Palestinians and the Arabs felt alone and let down, arguing that whatever Arafat's demands, the response of the Israelis was disproportionate to the situation on the ground -- something that many US commentators privately agreed was indeed the case.

The year was 2001, George W. Bush had just become the 43rd President of the United States, and in the summer the story unfolding in the streets of Ramallah and Gaza was not in any way contributing to global peace and the promise of a US-led initiative of peace after the Oslo Accord. The Intifada represented a swelling of hatred for Israel, translating into suicide bomb attacks on "soft" civilian targets, and in time, for the United States as well.

In my view, the 9/11 attacks that year weren't a coincidence. It could well be that the genesis of the attack came from the militant Palestinian groups in Arabia, and was not based on a plan hatched in the mountains of Afghanistan. While Osama bin Laden may well have had influence in the thinking and rationale of the attacks, the seed of hatred came from the events that unfolded in Palestine in the early months of 2001. Perhaps militant Palestinian elements like the Islamic Jihad for Palestine -- one of the most radical militant groups in Arabia -- conjured up the prerogative to take the battle to the "far enemy," in this case the United States.

My view also is that Osama and his team then jumped on the idea and planned the specific attacks. Suffice to mention here that the Arab nation was angry at the way it felt abandoned in the face of Israel unleashing the most vicious response to the Intifada and eventually the suicide bombings. In that sense the

The Arab Nation-State

Arabs, especially the ones who subscribed to an ultra-militant school of thought, saw the 9/11 attack as a means to punish the United States on the one hand, and on the other hand jar it into realizing that peace in Palestine was important to prevent future attacks.

I realize that this is conjecture on my part, given that there was never a statement issued in behalf of the hijackers and attackers of 9/11 as to the goals of the attacks. Indeed many claimed -- and will continue to claim – that the attacks, and indeed the emergence of the name Al Qaeda, was essentially a reaction to the coining of the word by US spin-doctors.

Insofar as the Arab nation was concerned, the events of 9/11 were as much as shock to the educated elite as to anyone around the world. While the militants may have temporarily rejoiced, the reaction from Washington was angry and unyielding, resulting in Arab governments to feel the sense of siege turn inward, as they struggled to demonstrate their alignment with the realities of a changed world order, a world order where Washington would be setting the tone.

Even radical countries like Yemen, Libya and Sudan fell into line with the realities of the new world order. There was little that could be done to present a different viewpoint to the problem that the Arab, and indeed the entire Muslim world, faced. The picture painted successfully by Washington and its Western allies is that of a radical Muslim world that is out to destroy the West. From that perspective, the voice of a moderate Islam is lost in the hype that was created in the post 9/11 environment. It isn't entirely fanciful to speculate that had the US response to the 9/11 tragedy not been an invasion of Afghanistan and Iraq, but a more measured approach to influence Arab and Muslim governments to deal with radical Islamic militancy, then perhaps the longer term benefits of fighting radicalism would have been more sustainable.

There is little doubt that the events that unfolded in the post 9/11 global environment have created a polarization that is fundamentally difficult for the Arabs and Muslims to deal with effectively.

On the one hand, it has brought about changes in two predominantly Muslim countries, Afghanistan and Iraq; these changes were secretly welcomed by the large multitude of Arab people and governments. Yet on the other hand, the means with which the change was brought, and the subsequent unsettled nature of both countries, each hosting a large number of foreign (namely American) troops, means that the radical militants of Islam have a trump card they can always play to undermine the position of the Arab governments who tacitly or openly support the change of regimes in both countries.

President George W Bush's infamous remark of "either you are with us or with them" has forced most Arab states to polarize their position on the matter. The result has been that these countries and governments are also now threatened by the consequences of Islamic militancy within their own borders – you need look no further than Saudi Arabia and Egypt. The ability to contain the spread of militancy has acquired a military or neo-military context rather than a broader, more meaningful battle for the minds of the possible cadre of the militancy movements.

As much as the war with militancy in Arabia might be fought through the barrel of the gun, it is a much deeper issue. A war has to be fought for the Muslim mind. This has to be done in a manner that seeks to bring about the creation of effective and meaningful economic and social change within Arab and Muslim societies. The strengthening of legal systems offering equality and justice to the population and the emergence of an economic model that provides jobs, medical care and social services on a broader platform, have to be considered. In the absence of such far reaching changes, the chances are that the soft underbelly of the Arab nation will always be exposed to radical Islamists who have everything to gain by exploiting the situation. The vast multitude of Muslim and Arab populations, given a decent income, and good health care and municipal services, are less inclined to support the militants. They will likely form a bulwark against the radicalization of Islam. This is perhaps the most important battlefield that the Arab nation has to test itself in. Can the moderate voice of reason be heard within Arabia?

The disjointed state of the Arab nation is fundamentally driven toward an inward view that seeks its heroes and its causes in a maze of confused political and social messages. The situation of the civil war in Lebanon, the ongoing plight of the Palestinians, the unemployment in Saudi Arabia, and so many other issues within the Arab world cause frictions and issues that are causing rifts within the Arab ranks. While Syria may emotional and politically support the Palestinians, its position would be dramatically different if the Palestinians interfered in the way Syria wished to see the development of Lebanon. The Lebanese support the Palestinians only marginally and see them as the root cause of the 1975-1990 civil war. And yet, having steered away from Syrian control, the Lebanese would perhaps position themselves more as a liberal apolitical state within the heartland of the Arab world, a task which is fraught with difficulty by any stretch of the imagination.

The oil-rich Arab states of the Gulf have taken a moderate political course in their interaction with the world on global and regional issues. But they have also been also seen as the "near enemy" through the eyes of the militant followers of Osama bin Laden and Ayman Al-Zawahiri's followers. In a socio-political sense, these relatively liberal states have to battle the seemingly disjointed aims of modernism and social reform on the one hand, and the reigning in of militant fundamentalism on the other.

These competing political imperatives have always led to a great suspicion within Arab leadership of the motives of one another's actions and intentions. It is also one of the impediments for a unified stand on political issues, in sharp contrast to emotional issues. When it concerns the emotional impact of Israeli occupation of Jerusalem, or the question of any attack on Islam, then indeed the emotional unity comes forth with ease and a considerable amount of passion. Even though it is widely acknowledged that emotional responses to the external challenges do not force political compromises thus far, there is no saying that should the populations of these countries ride an tidal wave of religious passion mobilized toward political change – perhaps along the line of the Iranian revolution -- the current moderate leadership of these countries would be sorely tested.

While some political events, like Saddam's invasion of Kuwait in 1990, united most of Arabia with the exception of two or three countries, there has been no doubt it was the single most important unifying element of their political history. Some may argue that the Palestinian question has united the Arab nations on the political front. Indeed, this may well be the case, but it has been an emotionally led position, and is significant that political action has been more toward rhetoric. Only with the Camp David meetings in 1978 between Egypt and Israel did some measure of diplomatic effort generate a political strategy toward the issue of Palestine.

Even when it was becoming clear that the way forward for a settlement on the issue of Palestine needed to be accomplished through negotiation and diplomacy, most Arab nations shunned the initiative that Egypt had made and even ostracized it for a number of years. The recognition among Arab nations that diplomacy will be the key to peace in the Middle East has come late; the message has still not got to the streets, where the general anger triggers calls for more radical steps on the issue of Palestine.

The Arab Nation-State

Western diplomats and tacticians – going back to Lord Allenby and T. E. Lawrence in the early years of the 20th century – have often expressed frustration when dealing with the Arab leadership over the lack of political engagement in the dialogue and the lack of a cohesive policy toward regional and global issues. A great deal of this comes from a variety characteristics of the Arab political mind, cultural aspects related to negotiation and, of course, the relative youthfulness of nationhood among the Arabs.

For the Arab political mind, understanding the regional issues has been relatively simple, but dealing with the interdependence of these issues with the global political dynamics seems unwieldy. As the world has moved toward a unipolar system, Arabs have felt cramped in their ability to establish more assertive positions on global and regional issues. Their traditional ability of playing one side against the other diminished with the fall of the Soviet Union; and direct engagement with the United States on many issues has been influenced in the recent past by events that have followed from the 9/11 attacks.

From a cultural perspective, Arabs have always concerned themselves with issues immediate to them and rarely bothered about tribes that were not contiguous to them. Hence for an Arab in Saudi Arabia, the issues of a tribe in, say, Oman, hardly mattered. This tendency has always manifested itself in how inter-Arab relations have been conducted. The record of Arab intervention for peaceful resolution of conflicts among Arab nations and Arab populations is actually appalling, whether it was the civil strife in Sudan, the Libya-Egypt strain in relations or indeed the long-standing ideological rift between Syria and Iraq. All these situations indicate a weakness in developing a peace-resolution policy within their body-politic. The Gulf Cooperation Council has shown a much better record of resolving issues such as border disputes among each other, and have managed to cooperate civilly on issues of common security and other issues.

It is clear that in the years ahead the Arab nation will have to dig deeper to answer some fundamental questions about the sort of society they will create. They will also have to deal with more delicate issues of their social fabric that they have been not addressing in the past few decades. Arab societies are being challenged from within by a brand of fundamentalism that contrasts with their desire to modernize, rather than Westernize. This is where the battle for the Arab mind will be fought hard.

The battle will be fought on a platform that is largely emotional, and yet the socio-economic conditions of Arab society will determine the outcome of that battle. It is not going to be an easy battle as the need for reform, in a Western sense, will compete with the fundamentalist call for a reform toward the values of what the fundamentalists call their interpretation of Islamic values. Indeed, as Western countries -- and principally the United States -- call for more democratic traditions to develop in the Arab world, it does imply that should the fundamentalists use the electoral role to seek power they stand a better chance than any other political creed based on their emotional appeal and better organization than the nascent political parties in these societies.

However, it is unlikely that the fundamentalist see the electoral route as the means to power. And the election process does not assure them of outright victory. Even in countries where they won electoral victories, like Algeria, they were ultimately denied power, and in others where they surprisingly gained power, Turkey, they had to blend into a more established form of modernism.

The battle for the Arab mind will be fought hardest where social development is least. The exception, of course, is Saudi Arabia, where the resources are large but the distribution of social welfare has been uneven, leaving a high unemployment rate among the youth. In the smaller, more affluent Arab states, all of which are principally oil-rich principalities, the battle between fundamentalism and modernism will not be so pronounced. Countries like the UAE, and Qatar have managed to balance modernism with widespread economic benefits for their own populations. The exception will remain Kuwait, where Islamists have held onto a parliamentary system that they have dominated since its inception after the liberation of Kuwait. However, it is unlikely that the Islamists will manage to hold power in the long run, given the pace of modernism within the younger generations of Kuwaitis. In Bahrain, the problems do not relate to fundamentalism but more between the Shia, the have-nots, and the Sunnis, who are more affluent and established. Yet these problems are being solved, and it is more likely that in the medium term there will be a resolution to these issues, more so because the broader base of economic welfare has implied an underlying theme of moderation in dealing with such issues. Clearly, if these countries did not possess the wealth to distribute, then one could argue that the challenges would be even more severe.

For Bahrain, the failure to be proactive to the issues that concern the Shia majority of the country have led to the demonstrations and confrontations the like of which have not been seen before. Though strong-arm tactics by the government, helped by Saudi troops, may have brought the seriousness of the violence under control, it does not solve the political issues that are beneath the surface. Eventually there will be a dialogue, even if the process is painful for the country and this is a realization that has to be embraced sooner than later. This will have to happen with the spirit that the Shia majority also wish what is best for Bahrain and the increasing sense of alienation has to be reversed with a sincere reappraochment that is meaningful and effective.

The larger Arab world is where the battle will be fought especially hard – the world from Egypt to Yemen, from Iraq to

Morocco -- and it is there that the voice of the unheard will seek platforms of expression. As the West pushes these countries to liberalize, they will also realize that democracy in some societies will merely mean a change of the battlefield to the ballot box from the streets. Emotional agendas will become more powerful political weapons, and this is where the Islamists should have an edge. Yet it is highly unlikely that they will see that shunning the radical path is going to be the way forward, leaving a moderate conservative movement to be the only possible bridge between the two divides that sit within these Arab societies. However, for a moderate movement to emerge more conspicuously, there has to be lesser polarization within Arab societies. This implies that perhaps a broader base of education will bring about a moderate voice of Islam that can then embrace the common passion and blend it with the voice of tolerance and development.

Looking at Arab societies from the outside, one is always prone to generalizations and one has to be aware that for the Arabs the winds of change have been relatively new. They have to embrace many concepts of administration and governance that while not alien to their societies in the past, now need to be blended into the modern nation-state.

It is fair to say that public accountability and transparency has increased in many of these countries, and the role of non-partisan journalism has been particularly important. There may not be a totally free press in some of the Arab countries, but there is little denying that the appalling curbs on press freedom and human rights of two decades ago have changed for the better. While in some countries the change has been dramatically healthy, in others reform has been slow in coming. While television stations like the Qatar-based Al Jazeera have been the bane for the United States in terms of its content and positioning within the Muslim world, there is no denying that such networks have also questioned deeply the state of affairs within the Arab world itself.

The fact that the staff of many of these "new" Arab media came from the Western press perhaps explains the practice of investigative reports on Arab countries. On a broader platform, there is no denying that the shrinking of the communications world has meant that censorship is not that easy as it used to be before the advent of the Internet. These are small parts of a larger picture that seems to be falling into place. It is clear that the more dictatorial regimes and the fundamentalists both share a common hate for the free-press movement, and perhaps this is why the press in the Arab world, while very anti-American on regional issues, still remains quite liberal on the domestic front.

Arab societies have a difficult task ahead of them as the call for reform, whether from the outside or inside, as this intensifies the rising expectations of the populations. These expectations will have to be met. There is a constant debate at some levels on how these winds of change are to be absorbed and dealt with. In some cases, existing regimes and potential successors of existing regimes, have embraced the need for change -- but within their own framework and rationale of liberalism and reform. Thus, in Bahrain the previous order was changed to reflect a monarchy under which then provisions for change within the government were considered, allowing some flexibility of elected governments to emerge. In Syria, with the death of Hafez al-Assad, his son, Bashar, took over government with a more relaxed grip on the country. A former ophthalmologist who was trained in Britain, he brought in more openness and reform to the system; even though the task is far from achieved, it would suggest a mind shift is underway. Nothing in this suggests that all is well in terms of reform but merely that the leaders realize the paradigm shift that is underway in their societies.

It is impossible to accurately predict the course of Arab societies in the next few decades. However, there are a number of scenarios that could unfold, all of which are interdependent. As a underlying hypothesis we have to conclude that the Arab world will not be the same in 30 to 50 years from now, and further, the competing elements of different societal, cultural, religious and political elements will create push-and-pull dynamics which will further complicate the face of the changing Arab world.

In an ideal scenario one would presume that Arab nations will, collectively or in smaller focus groups, learn to find a better way to deal with the international political situation, which is increasingly predicated on globalization – the freer flow of ideas, capital, goods, services and people across porous borders. Whether this "better way" will be the result of an empowerment through a political process of unity or the consolidation of a cartel of common interests, perhaps around Arab oil producers, is open to question. No matter. It will be a fascinating drama to watch.

ARAB SOCIETAL RELATIONS WITH THE WEST.

With a Muslim father and a Hindu-born mother, and having lived and dealt with people of all cultures and faiths throughout my professional life, I have found dealing with the secular West to be an engaging and enriching experience for me. The tensions that characterize relations between Westerners and Muslims have rarely, if ever, come into play in my life.

However, my own "clash" with my own culture has been more pronounced, often bringing home the differences more poignantly than ever. I recall in 1999 I had an chance encounter with a sympathizer of a Lasher-e -Jhangvi (a militant anti-Shia organization that had carried out many attacks against the Shia community), and when I pointed out that it was not his place to "cleanse Pakistan of the Shia," he told me boldly that their leader Haq Nawaz Jhangvi had got "orders from Allah to get rid of the vermin Shia." In jest I asked if the orders came in an email or a fax. The man turned verbally violent, forgetting that I'd tried to introduce some humor into the situation. I do not know what subsequently happened to the man, who on hearing me speaking Arabic at Karachi Airport, had approached me, no doubt to proselytize. But that incident showed me that understanding the divide between tolerance and intolerance was -- and is -- difficult for me; I wonder how the West copes with it.

There is a common perception among many that relations between Arab states and the Western countries actually follow a two-tier approach: governments conduct a political dialogue, while Arab society has its own perception of how the West is seen in their eyes. Western societies, which have their own perceptions of the Arab and Muslim world, might well hold views that are clichéd and stunted, and which accordingly influence relations between the two societies. In some cases in the Arab world, there's a deep disconnect with the relationship, where the government might be pro-Western in its political stance but the common people do not necessarily support that view or share any pro-West sentiment. In the absence of democracy and opinion of the masses framing government policy, the disconnection is more apparent. The view from Arab society of the West is more an emotional one rather than a cogent position. In addition, the passionate anti-American feelings, in, say, a Palestinian refugee camp, cannot be compared with the instantaneous anti-American protests on the streets of an Arab city in response to something like the invasion of Iraq.

Yet for a large majority of middle-class Arabs, America in particular and the West in general are also lands of opportunity and promise. The increase in Arab immigrants in the United States has resulted in an important Arab American political caucus in a number of states like Michigan and others. On the more street level of emotion in most Arab cities, it is strange to find an Arab youth espouse anti-American feelings while wearing an American branded T-shirt, jeans, and a baseball cap. This dichotomy stares one in the face all the time. At times when one speaks to an Arab-American from Dearborn, Michigan, who may disagree with American politics in the Middle East, somehow the voices of dissent sound the same as those from the streets of Beirut or Baghdad. The Arab-American expresses his democratic right to disagree with his government, while the youth in Gaza expresses his voice, which is that of the unheard.

The transition of Arab and Muslim societies from the postcolonial docile acceptance to a more proactive view of the West has been influenced and shaped by a number of factors. In today's context, the gradual organization of the religious clergy in most Arab and Muslim societies into a potent force for social change has had the most far reaching impact on relations between Arab societies and the West. At the same time, the growth of the state administration has been gigantic as a result of two factors -- namely, the need for creating employment, and the greater need to administer a larger population with soaring birth rates. This has meant the cohesiveness of the bureaucracy of the colonial period has diminished, making it more difficult for central policies to be implemented. Imagine that during the colonial rule vast provinces were controlled and administered by a handful of civil servants, while in the modern era there is literally an army of administrators in place. The British governed vast areas of the region with perhaps a few thousand civil servants backed with conscripted local militias and some British regiments; today this force has mushroomed into massive governmental machines with the ever increasing burden of social and political administration.

The shaping of the image of the West has hence been influenced by a mixture of events and factors, and in a large sense, the framing of that opinion has been largely emotional and in a great measure totally unguided in terms of any positive elements. The social image of Arab society in the West, especially the United States, is largely steeped in a stereotype that is at best cursory and partial. After the 1967 Arab-Israeli war there was a stepped up campaign of hijackings by the Palestinian Al Fatah movement, and images of planes being blown up on runways conveyed the first powerful images to Americans about Arabs.

Thus, the early images of an Arab in a checkered head scarf portray in the mind of the average Western person the sense of a "terrorist." The 1972 Munich Olympics terrorist incident – where eight Palestinian guerrillas of the Black September movement, which had ties to Yasser Arafat's Al Fatah, kidnapped and killed 11 Israeli athletes and a German police officer -- reinforced the sense among Westerners that Arabs are violent people. The essential element that none of these acts were related to how Arabs really were did not matter, especially as the terrorist incidents occurred as the age of global television helped amplify news events. In time, the images became a haunting metaphor for Arab society, "proof" of a violent mindset. It's been difficult for the Arabs to get the West to shed those notions since.

The shaping of the Arab and Muslim attitude toward the West in some degrees reflects on how they feel about themselves. The tug-of-war for the Muslim mind between liberal middle-class intellectuals wanting "freedom, liberty and justice" as the foundations of the modern Muslim state, and the religious orthodox clergy who wish to establish a rule of Islamic law, enormously affects the way the common man on the street views the West.

For the past five odd decades, monarchies and dictators have stood in the middle asserting that justice can prevail under authoritarian rule, under the concept of a just, but absolute, ruler, (the Arabic concept of al mustabid al aadil). The reality is gradually dawning on many that the concept of an absolute but just ruler is a myth in modern times. The call of liberals for a society based on accountability, justice and freedom that will ensure the rights of the common man is beginning to elicit better understanding. However, the tone and texture of the call of liberals is very similar to what Washington and its allies also call for within Arab and Muslim societies, thus allowing the orthodox clergy to tag the liberals as "enemies" of Muslims and handmaidens of the West.

While much of the West was appalled by the hijackings in the 1970's and by the attack on the Israeli athletes at the Munich Olympics, a sense of pride emerged among common Arab people – a renewed self-confidence that they could hit back at the soft underbelly of Israel. While the West called the hijackers "terrorists," the Arabs called them "freedom fighters." It is not surprising that those earlier plane hijackings – in which passengers were unharmed, for the most part – evolved over the next 40 years into wanton attacks, resulting in no appreciation for the difference between a combatant and a civilian. Thus the militants on the Muslim (and mostly Arab) side are rarely careful not to cause casualties among civilians -- much in the same way that Israel takes no precautions to avoid killing civilians in their attacks in Palestine and Lebanon. One cannot help but conclude that both these mentalities of violence are brutal and do not provide any useful or meaningful possibilities for settling disputes and disagreements.

Arab society thus sees itself under siege, and any discussion on the subject will begin with the atrocities by the Israelis and the quiet and unwavering support of Israeli policies by the United States. It is almost as if any response – however violent -- that comes from Arabs is therefore justified. It is not difficult to assume that the view from Tel Aviv is actually the opposite, suggesting that only when the Arabs stop violence will the Israelis rein in their firepower. Unfortunately, the notion of proportional response to atrocities seems to have long been discarded.

As the lines harden, it is increasingly more difficult for the two sides to reconcile their differences. This also makes it very difficult for moderation to develop within their respective societies, resulting in a ostracizing of the voice of reason. Because the West has believed in an element of freethinking, the voice of dissent is more prevalent within its societies – although by no means influential in the political arena. In contrast, due to the lack of a liberal press tradition within Arab societies the voice of dissent is less heard and definitely marginalized. To express dissent over militancy and the path of the Islamic fundamentalism is virtually impossible for most intellectuals in Arab society -- which doesn't mean it doesn't happen, only that its effect is negligible. This could well mean that the struggle of Arab societies, which was nationalist in complexion in the 1970's, has moved toward being religious in nature in the new millennium. It's hard not to conclude that a radical shift has taken place within these societies.

I followed with eagerness the 2004 conference of the Center for the Study of Islam and Democracy (CSID) in Washington where all the key speakers were prominent Muslim and Arab professors. Each one was residing in the West, and more than likely was ostracized by the religious orthodoxy within the Arab world. What was happening to those scholars reflected the growing divide between modern-thinking Muslim scholars and the more orthodox schools of Islamic theology; the schism between them has never been so wide as has happened since 9/11 and the subsequent developments such as the war in Iraq. While Muslim scholars living in the West felt sympathy for the American people in their hour of grief, they also developed a better understanding of the anger among the radical youth of Islam who felt Israel's conduct in the Occupied Territories was being ignored by the United States. However, it is unlikely that from within the Muslim scholars of a liberal bent of mind there was any rejoicing over 9/11. There was, in fact, widespread revulsion, disbelief and shock at what happened that tragic day.

This was clearly in sharp contrast to the position of the Islamic orthodox clergy who seemed pleased that America was getting a taste of its own medicine. Yet public proclamations of support for the hijackers of the planes involved in 9/11 came from the militant clergy of Islam only after the first US bombs landed on Afghan soil. It is not true that Muslim scholars did not condemn the 9/11 attacks; liberal scholars and a number of Muslim leaders felt the attacks on the United States were a folly in terms of both religion and politics. On the other hand, these attacks have also created massive fissures within the Muslim clergy and society. The intelligentsia and the middle classes within the Muslim world clearly have been revolted by the attacks on civilians in America. While they may have a critical – even condemnatory -- view about how the US reacted to these attacks, there is clear concern and sympathy for the American people among this group. There is no denying that the attacks in terms of their planning and ferocity surprised many but even more importantly showed the vulnerability to this form of violence. The attacks also highlighted the concern between both Western and Arab people at the loss of innocent civilian lives.

I believe that after the attacks in the United States there was a rare opportunity for the US leadership to change the course of history by not reacting with violence to the events but by using a political response. This would have spurred the Arab nation to curb the internal violence of its own volition. While such a strategy would clearly be yield results only over a longer period of time, it would have drawn support from Arabs in recognizing the problem of terrorism to be a threat to humanity, and not just to America or the West. But President George W. Bush instead chose the "right to defend, and the right to hit back" route, perhaps missing a unique chance to cement the cultural divide, and bringing a better, more truly global response to the threat of terrorism.

A major problem with the Bush strategy was to determine who do you hit back at? There has never been a clear admission by Osama bin Laden that he indeed ordered and carried out the attacks of 9/11. His use of the word "we" in his declarations seems to equate "we" with the Muslim Ummah. While people close to him have allegedly take some responsibility for planning and carrying out the attack, it is more likely that while he knew the plan and his close associates the actual details were left to others. Thus the response of the US has been to organize and fundamentally change the political topography of countries where such militancy can be harbored. This means that by attacking Afghanistan and removing the Taliban, the Americans weeded out the ability of Osama bin Laden and his followers to be organized in their attacks on the United States. That, at least, is the theory.

There is no denying that since the end of the Afghan war Osama bin Laden had been offering both financial and material support for a number of jihad groups across the Arab and Muslim worlds. This support has held special appeal to the youth of Algeria, Egypt, Jordan and unemployed Saudis. There is no doubt that the way the issue of Osama bin Laden was dealt with it had an impact on the youth of the Arab world. For the moment we can see the crystallizing of opinion about the West being driven by political events; seemingly little is being done to repair the damage to societal relationships. Neither Arab society nor Western society is making real effort to bridge the gap between them, allowing misconceptions and the lack of commonality on a number of issues to emerge. One of the sad aspects of the current state of affairs is the total lack of urgency about bringing an understanding between the two societies, the West believing that Arabs wish its destruction and the Arabs believing their plight is of no consequence to the West.

The views held by Western intellectuals of Islamic societies must also to be taken into consideration. They may not fully appreciate that while Muslims who want a workable relationship are in the majority, the minority militants have stolen the limelight. The call for battling the West comes from a segment of militant clergy and followers who invoke the sanctity of Islam as the centerpiece of their argument. This leaves little maneuverability for dissenting from the militant view within a society where any perceived opposition to the theological message of Islam is considered apostasy. This gives the militant clergy a natural advantage over any liberal view as the militant view sees the current state of affairs with the West as a jihad for survival and hence expects Muslim acquiescence irrespective of a liberal belief system.

It is a failure of Western intellectual thought to fully appreciate the hold that the militant can potentially have on the minds of young Arabs. Thus books that carry the overtones of a right-wing crusade against the Muslims and warn us of a clash of civilizations do not in any appreciable measure create an environment for dialogue.

Just as the Republican Party in America had used the media to manufacture consent for its own brand of global militarism, so too does the militant clergy of Islam manufacture obedience from its population based upon the demands of a moral injunction. It is clear that in some respects, when stripped of the moral arguments of the Bush agenda and the militant Islamic mission, the underlying similarities of the fervor and lack of tolerance of both make them really different sides of the same coin.

President Obama has in a sense partially narrowed the gulf between the Muslims and the West in his approach to relations between the two. His landmark address in June 2009 to Muslims in Cairo echoed more fairness to the issue of Israel and the Palestinians than any past US President has managed. While some Muslim commentators notice that he falls short in admitting that some of the pain and agony in the Muslim world, like Iraq and

Afghanistan, has been due to the actions of the US, most acknowledge that givent the constraints of US political thinking President Obama has made bold overtures for peace between the Muslims and the West. He has admonished Israel as much as he as told the Arabs they must change too and this is a breath of fresh air in the Arab and Muslim context. The crucial issue is that do the Muslims also realize that in Barrack Obama they have a unique chance to change the way they deal with the West?

Muslims and Christians perhaps are reflexively more afraid of their similarities as indeed they have been for centuries, than of their differences, and now given a global political battle between the two those similarities are subtly clear to many who wish to probe deeper. Yet today many Muslims feel that they are becoming the new "damned of the Earth" for the events of 9/11 and the many attacks since then against Western "soft" targets. It is this sense of alienation from the mainstream of a global process that has the propensity of a spiraling out of control; it carries the danger of bringing to the forefront a new wave of militancy based on global rejectionism.

The interaction that has been happening between the West and the Islamic societies has not been a deep-rooted one. While government-to-government communication and contact has been commonplace, the reaching out among the populations has not been something that has naturally fallen into place. There has been no natural bridge of understanding between Muslims and the West that would serve as a platform of understanding. Unlike the Jews who were settled in Europe for centuries, the Muslim populations of Europe and America are only at best 50 years old, with much of the Muslim growth in these societies occurring in the last 20 years. Notwithstanding vast historical encounters – starting with the Crusades – there hasn't been enough of the kind of interaction and shared experiences on the part of the West and

Muslims to understand each other's communities. The result has been a presumptuous relationship between the masses that is concentrated upon a clichéd view of each other rather than something predicated on personal and institutional knowledge. This is all the more surprising considering that Muslim influence and presence in countries like Spain has been historical, and indeed very tolerant, yet the appreciation of the cultural divide in the post-1945 era has been marginal at best.

For the most part, the Muslim mass view of Western society is that it is morally corrupt and degenerate, and has moved away from even a modicum of a Christian definition of what constitutes a society of values and morality. The Western view of Muslims societies largely is that they are backward and exploitative, and unwilling to embrace even minimal modernism. Few within the Muslim world actually acknowledge that to become a modern society does not necessarily mean that they must take on the trappings and conventions of Western society.

It is across this divide of perceptions that both societies see each other. The lack of a broad-based dialogue between them has resulted in a widening of the gap of mutual understanding. The use of compassion as a means of interacting is absent. There is also a blurring of the issues at hand, because when we talk of an Arab society we presume a predominantly Muslim society, and the Arabs perceive of the Western society to be a predominantly monolithic Christian society, each forgetting that the issue, while religious in overtone, is really one of societies in the simplest form. The political and social agendas in each of the camps have become highly complex. There can be little doubt that in order to overcome suspicions and enhance understanding, pragmatism needs to be brought into play.

As Islamic societies become more modern, the turmoil within them will become more pronounced. The militant strain of Islam sees the twin threat of Western societies and their political ethos as an enemy; It is also concerned that as more modernism comes into Islamic societies, the battle for the mind of the next generations may be lost. The orthodox Muslim clergy does not make a distinction between modernism and Westernism, and considers them as synonymous concepts. Many clergymen aver that if modernism were to happen it is natural that the next step for the Muslim societies will be to adopt a Western complexion. If one were to examine the argument for signs of a supposed "clash of civilizations," then surely the clash within each of the civilizations is equally important to understand. Seen in this social context, one can understand what the militant Islamic clergy mean when they talk about the battle with the "near enemy," which implies that modernism is also creating Muslim societies who, by their tolerance and acceptance of Westernization, have strayed from the "path" and hence are the "near enemy" – in one's own home, so to speak.

Muslims were also increasingly worried that President George W. Bush had created a political climate in Washington that is not only less tolerant of the world, especially the Muslims and the Arabs, but has also dramatically impinged on America's ability to be a fair broker for peace in the Middle East. There is little doubt in the mind of both the Western liberal and the modernist Muslim that measures like the Patriot Act and the Homeland Security measures have strong racist tendencies. Concepts such as "profiling" of certain nationalities and ethnic groups in order to monitor whether they constitute security threats, alarm Muslims. These measures have created alienation and deep revulsion among many liberal minded Muslims; their cohort, after all, is where it would seem the bulk of the support for a modern, more understanding Arab and Muslim society will come from. The issues become even more complicated and difficult to fathom when it is perceived by the leadership on both sides that there is a clash of civilizations underway.

While President Barrack Obama won the US election partially on the promise of changing the political mentality that had gripped US decision makers through the Bush era, many Muslims are skeptical of his ability to deliver simply because it takes time to reverse the effects of the decisions that have soured the atmosphere for so long. In addition, the more critical elements of Muslim society also see the contradictions in Obama's approach that he does not acknowledge the invasion of Iraq as being wrong, nor does he accept that the further militarization of Afghanistan does not create solutions but really more essentially difficult problems for the long term. While, admittedly, such critics may not fully appreciate the difficult waters of diplomacy, both within the US and internationally, that President Obama has to navigate there is still some truth that the Obama camp may have drawn a view of the world that may be too simplistic in essence, and too difficult in action to arrive at.

For most Westerners – and certainly for most Americans -- Islam, and the Arab and the Muslim worlds are really vague notions. But do Muslims recognize that in the modern context of the world they need to develop an ethical language of their own, and that, moreover, it has to be a language that can relate to the realities of modernism? Failure to do this will essentially result in a moral isolationism that most forward-thinking Muslims recognize cannot be good for the Muslim and Arab nations. The most passionate struggle that the Muslim intelligentsia have to wage is the creation of an ethical language born from their own context but adaptable to the realities of a modern world. My belief is that the rest of the world – and particularly the echelons of social and political power -- also needs tounderstand that the messages coming from deep within the Muslim and Arab psyche can involve cooperation and coexistence. Not every one of the world's billion Muslims is seeking confrontation with the West.

I also believe that Muslims have to accept that the major impact on the Muslim nation has a lot to do with the more recent "fundamentalist" movements. Viewed through a historical timeline, Osama bin Laden and even the Taliban, are relatively new phenomena but they hold appeal to disenfranchised masses. These fundamentalist movements have cut across the historical secular nature of Islam, and today as the West explores terms like "Muslim," "Arab," and "Islam," it is in the context of 9/11. It is unlikely, therefore, that a Western audience would even accept that throughout history Islam has had a long record of secular behavior than current events might suggest.

Western audiences also need to better understand that toward Jihadi concepts, while politically and militarily enacted during the Soviet occupation of Afghanistan, have ideological foundations that are essentially Egyptian and not Saudi Wahhabi in nature.

Why is the question of origin significant? Because dating back to the 1960's, the teachings of Syed Qutb established the principles of "hakimiya" (God's authority) to change society, even when such societies are Muslim, and to rid these societies of the established order if they have strayed from the path of God. What was essentially revolutionary in Syed Qutb's message was that such change could be brought about by "any means." With it came the concepts of "takfeer" the excommunication of Muslims who have abandoned God's path and to declare themselves non-Muslims. In the 1970's, Egypt's radical Islamists were overshadowed by Shukri Mustafa who founded the al-Takfeer wal Hijra group, who preached violent means to establish a change in society. The group's activities ended with the execution of Mustafa by the Egyptian government. When Al-Zawahiri, a former student of Mohammed Qutb, (who was the younger brother of Syed Qutb) emerged on the scene with his Tanzim al Jihad, the message of takfeer was so engrained into the philosophy of the time that many observers insist that Zawahiri is a Takfeeri.

People like Osama Rushdi, who was the head of media of the Egyptian al Jama'a al Islamyia – he was given political asylum in the Netherlands -- noted in 1989 that the influences on Islamist movements were essentially takfeeri in nature to the extent that a clash with established political order with the Muslim world was inevitable. When Sayyid Imam, an associate of Dr. Ayman Al-Zawahiri and a prominent member of the Tanzim, wrote his book, "The Main Issues in the Preparation for War," his message was very clear: All Muslims must join in the fight against the "apostate" rulers of the Muslim countries and replace them by whatever means possible. It was this message that the Jihadis adopted with zealous fervor. Western societies did not figure in any of these discourses and it was clear that for the Jihadis the message of the tamer, but theologically very rigid Wahhabis were irrelevant. Whenever the Egyptian-based Jihadis met with Osama bin Laden, most frequently in Afghanistan, Abdullah Azzam, who happened to also be a millionaire but who kept emphasizing the strident nature of his ideology, influenced him first and foremost.

As for everyday people in Arabia and in the Muslim world, the contradictions of their understanding and appreciation of the West are even more jumbled. The young among them adore Western forms of entertainment -- particularly movies -- and lifestyles, and yet see American policies are out of touch with the realities of Arabia. While "hating America" might well be emotionally appealing to some, most Arabs and Muslims will make a distinction between "hating America" (which means American policies) and "hating Americans."

I am convinced that the notion of hating Americans is absent among the common people of Arabia, with the exception of the fundamentalist militant groups. For the more well to do Arabs and Muslims the liberal and humanist ideals of Western society are indeed some they would like to see incorporated within their own societies. This does not mean that they want to Westernize in their mentality but certainly these well to do Arabs and Muslims see the merits in Western society and create a reference point within their own societal context. It is perhaps more the urge to modernize rather than westernize that grips the imagination of these aspiring middle classes of their society.

Why is this interaction so important to each side? Why do Muslims need to understand how to relate to the West? Indeed, why does the West need to deal with a world where the reaction toward its societies oscillates from cold to warm within seconds?

Westerners, Arabs and Muslims, all recognize that the world is shrinking, that globalization is galloping, and that few societies are able to live in economic, political and social isolation. The increasing interdependence of the world's 192 countries, the imperative of economics and commerce, and the fact that modern means of communications and transportation have created a global township out of an assortment of culturally different nations, means that everyone needs to better understand everyone else.

Beyond these factors is the deeper concern that more than 60 percent of the world's Muslim population of one billion is below the age of 25. It is these young people who will shape the interaction with the Western world and indeed also shape the complexion of their own societies. It is perhaps the most important element of the Arab and Muslim societies that needs to be understood. The fundamentalists recognize that the battle in the coming decade will be fought for the mind of these youth. That is why in Muslim society after Muslim society, they are accelerating their efforts to indoctrinate young people

There is little doubt in my mind that caring for the way these youth are shaped will determine how Arab and Muslims societies will progress. The mass of the followers of the radical and militant Muslim organizations comes from the cohort of youth that I am referring to. While at some level economic hardships and social inequalities have driven many of them into the fold of militancy and trrorism, there is also at another level a concerted effort by fundamentalist theologians to appeal to their passion and zeal and put those qualities in service of Islam. This silent war is largely unpredictable as it is being fought in unseen battlefields.

The lack of economic opportunities has also meant that Islamic youths see themselves as having a bleak future. This means that organizations like Hamas in Palestine, and, earlier, the Muslim Brotherhood in Egypt, and other militant organizations have been able to step in and win over the loyalties of youths by providing jobs, health care and some semblance of hope for a better economic future.

What those Muslim youth will feel about the West is going to be important in the shaping of relations between the two civilizations. They need to be a part of the changes that face their world; they need to be given tools with which to shape their future with economic security; they need to be infused with confidence that they have within them the ability to chart their own course in a world of sharp competition.

But I fear that there is no significant effort on the part of Western society or the more affluent Muslims to reach out to these youth and seek some modicum of dialogue and acceptance. It is this essential failing that has heightened the sense of the alienation among the very youth that the radial Islamists wish to indoctrinate with the fervor of their radicalism.

It's perhaps understandable why the West, especially in the aftermath of 9/11, views the Islamic world only through a damask of fundamentalism, thereby ignoring the many different cultural pressures, social demographics and political and economic necessities of that world. Earlier, most educated Muslims were clear that the West and the US had merely political and strategic objectives in their region, and it mostly did not matter to them how those aims were served. Hence during the Cold War the intrusive nature of political interest from both the US and its allies on the one hand, and the Soviet Union on the other, was only to ensure the government of that time in an Islamic (and Arab) country was serving their self-interest. Thus many of the regimes that were propped up in the region were dictatorial and in many cases even brutal, and in every case the support for these governments from Washington was consistent.

For educated Muslims to now believe that the US wants to have democracy in the Islamic and Arab world seems like a farfetched idea. It goes against their historical experience. Arabs saw Saddam Hussein being tried for crimes he committed in the days when he was the darling of Washington and seemed, at the time, the only weapon for the US to contain Iran's precieved regional hegemonistic ambitions. The move toward emphasizing human rights is thus seen as a fashionable trend and often set aside for political expediency. Many Muslims point out the dichotomy of this approach when China's terrible human-rights record is ignored and in the same breath Washington now signals Muslim regimes out for chastisement. Indeed, the more glaring injustice in the realm of human rights, in the Arab mind, is the total lack of US concern when Israeli forces attack Palestinian refugee camps or their rockets kill civilians and non-combatants.

If the geopolitical spin-doctors in the US would have their people believe that the actions in Iraq have won over the Arab hearts, they are totally mistaken. The fact that Saddam was forcibly removed could well have been a welcome sign to many of the educated Arabs. But the fragile nature of Iraq's polity is something that warrants close attention. It is highly likely that Iraq will eventually crumble into three or four different countries, and this is unlikely be a pleasant process. Preventing such fragmentation through a strong federal government will mean a continued US presence for propping it up.

It is thus impossible for Arabs and Muslims to divorce their view of the West from outside the box of political markers. The inability of the US and its allies to bring about a lasting and meaningful change in Iraq and Afghanistan has meant, in the minds of the average Arab, a serious failure of their means of achieving change within these communities – and perhaps of their intent as well. No doubt the Americans assumed that hatred for the previous regimes would naturally translate into support for the American political initiative in these countries. This was clearly not the case.

Yet over the past three decades, a large population of Muslims has emerged in Europe, with countries like Britain now seeing the third generation of Muslims on their social demographic map. Switzerland has a fast growing Muslim population; so does Germany, as does France. As a result, the notion of a "European Muslim" has slowly started to work its way into our vocabulary. The term itself is a metaphor for political and cultural issues that have been transplanted to a Judeo-Christian milieu from a different culture. This is an important element of the way the relationship between the Muslim world and the West will be shaped. The interaction between the people of different faiths has created possibilities of understanding that perhaps were only present for a brief moment in history when Spain and other parts of Europe were ruled by Muslims. In essence, the emergence of substantially large Muslims populations within the European social map creates a closeness of contact that is more real and essentially more compelling.

The growth of these largely Islamic populations has taken two very interesting and diverse paths, each having its own merits and pitfalls. On the one hand, Muslim populations in a number of European countries have been settled into regions of their own choosing and in a sense a Muslim "ghetto" has emerged in these places. These aren't enclaves in the political sense but more as self styled cultural boundaries that have been laid around these communities. On the other hand, there has been a greater assimilation within the societies of some segments from the Muslims settled in Europe. It for them that the question of joining the universal appeal of Islam to a European context has been the most complicated issue. For a vast majority, the fact that they can be Muslim and also accept and adopt European social ethics has been a pleasant surprise. For Muslims living in Europe, the question remains of how to be a "good Muslim" in a society such as Europe. It creates for them the need to be self-contained on the one hand out of the necessity of cultural preservation. Yet the economic necessities and the lure of economic and social progress demand a degree of integration.

The greater challenge, then, is the assimilation of the next generation of Muslims born in European countries, and the values and ethics that they imbibe. It is normal to Muslims from this generation in countries like England and France to seek European ways of working, living and achieving greater integration than their parents. Yet, it is also natural for them to be anchored in a host of cultural traditions – such as arranged marriages — that sustain the ethos their parents grew up with.

The dichotomy for these young Muslims is resolved in coexistence within themselves that is reconciliatory, and contradictory on the outside, and yet progressive and embracing of the best of both worlds. In some cases, there are conflicts and questions of identity that are not resolved. This has also meant that for those who could not assimilate, there's been a sense of wanting to "return to the roots"; these Muslims have been the prodigal sons of Islam, ones more susceptible to embracing the radical blend of Islam. Some call them the "Born Again Muslims," and they bring fervor to the ranks of the radical elements suggesting that while they have been "European Muslims" and know what is wrong with that society, there's nevertheless an imperative for them to be more militant.

Yet most Muslims fail to readily admit that it is easier to be a Muslim in European countries than is acknowledged publicly. If pressed, Shia Muslims would say it is definitely easier for them to practice their brand of Islam in London that it is in Mecca, where the Saudi Wahhabi clergy has strictly outlawed Shia practices. There is relatively a higher degree of assurance that, in general, the freedom to practice one's religion is well protected within European societies. There's relative comfort that persecution on the basis of religion will not occur. Even though the issue of the banning of headscarves in schools in France has been contentious, there is agreement that there is a political context to the issue; in a secular society, it is easy to see why the political culture would view overt displays of religiosity with concern.

For many of the European countries, the imperative of their secular nature makes them seek integration within their own community of new cultures. Having paid the price of religious intolerance through upheavals in history, to them diversity based on religion becomes a difficult thing to accept. Thus, the French reaction to the headscarf issue is more a reflection of a threat to a national concern over secularism breaking down. It is no different than Germans and Dutch complaining about Turkish immigrants who have continued to isolate themselves in communal pockets in places like Berlin. One has to wonder if Muslim Europeans at times adopt a siege mentality as much as indeed the Caucasian (and mostly Christian) Europeans also adopt a mentality of a nation being culturally and socially invaded.

European Muslims are conscious that over the next few decades the integration of future generations into European societies will not only gain pace but will also be more seamless. It is still not certain whether Muslims in Europe see the Shariah law as applicable in their personal lives becoming the focal point of their own ethical value system. It is less likely that as more integration is achieved, there will be more adaptation of existing European law to embrace the value systems of the European Muslims. Some social commentators hope that the pursuit of the notion of what's "good" for all cultures will create a social fabric that will connote a stakeholder's sense of ownership to the European Muslims.

This new society that might emerge will then be the "our society" that both Caucasian -- and essentially Christian -- Europeans, and the Muslim Europeans will feel equally proud to jointly belong. Incidents of terror such as the London bombings bring to the fore an awareness of this "oneness" for a number of Muslims in Britain as they assess the attacks carried out by Muslim Asians, who were mostly British. British Muslims see such attacks as an affront to the social fabric of the country they adopted and want to prosper in. They don't seek confrontation with the establishment because, in any case, it will be a losing battle. Even the most rabid British-Muslim couldn't possibly expect that Britain will transform itself into a Muslim state, no matter what its demographics.

Part of contemporary Europe's problems with its growing Muslim population stems from the intrinsic nature of Islam and the expectations it has of its followers. It is a demanding religion in terms of its ritual expectations. It is a religion with a public nature in which followers are expected to openly demonstrate their adherence to the faith several times a day. While Christianity can also be a demanding religion, it doesn't require its parishioners to publoicly pray five times a day, or to fast for a full month each year, as Islam does. Christianity has had its reform movements and the place of the Church is not as all-encompassing as one would see in Islam.

It is this element that anchors the devout Muslims to the concept of their religion being a "way of life." It's a way of life that you are expected to embrace and accept fully; anything less won't suffice. While liberal and modernist Muslims would argue that the being a Muslim and a European does not in anyway clash with the religious precepts of being "good Muslims," the purist and more fundamentalist thinking Muslims would argue that eventually there will be a clash between Europeanism and Islam within the personal ethos of Muslims living in Europe.

This has not happened to the extent that the fundamentalists like to point out. But there is a strong message from their pulpit to European Muslims to recognize the conflict – perhaps even contradiction -- inherent in the concept of a European Muslim.

For Islam to adjust to being in Europe, will more likely require a more liberal shape than elsewhere in the Muslim world. This will greatly help the West understand and accept the fact that coexistence between the cultures is not only possible but also healthy in the long run. Muslim and Arab societies have to also better understand the political realities in a unipolar world in which their relationship with the West needs to constructive and moderate, not confrontational. Political confrontation is not an option to be considered in the conventions and dances of diplomacy. Social interaction and a better understanding of the imperatives of interaction need to be opened up. This cannot happen if both sides have prejudices and fears. As much as the Muslim world has to shed its militancy, so too does the Western world – or at least a significant portion of it -- have to shed it right-wing militancy, which would form the basis of a better understanding into the future.

There is a growing interest in Islam among European Muslims. But there is fear that conservative clerics will influence young minds and perhaps even nudge them toward terrorism. A growing number of orthodox Muslim scholars are also emerging from the ranks of the European Muslims; they aren't necessarily militant. Yet it is not surprising that some of these scholars who have lived in Europe for long -- some were even born there -- are tormented with the dichotomies that European Muslims face.

Take the example of Tariq Ramadan, a grandson of Hassan Al Banna, (the founder of the Muslim Brotherhood in Egypt), who is a European Muslim born in Switzerland and currently teaching at St Antony's College at Oxford. He previously taught at the University of Notre Dame in the US, until the US government revoked his visa in July 2004. Professor Ramadan is perhaps the best example of someone caught in the middle of ideologies. He has been condemned by his Western detractors for "only" calling for a moratorium on laws of stoning as applicable by the Muslim Shariah. He has been rejected by radical Muslim clerics for his insistence that European Muslims should adapt to Western cultures and lessen the attachment to their "homeland." He argues that adopting Western cultures does not mean you have abdicated your faith. His book, "To Be a European Muslim," attempts to bridge the gap of being a Muslim and a European. It has generated much controversy, all the more because the book comes from the grandson of the founder of perhaps the most important movement of the Islamic world in modern times. Professor Ramadan is involved in a dispute with the US Homeland Security Department, who never gave a plausible reason for canceling his visa other than that he made a donation to a Swiss Islamic charity, which funded a Hamas social program back in the early 1990's.

One has to ask whether the emergence of a literate Muslim intellectual class from among Muslims, both in the West and in the Muslim world, is not the one thing that needs encouragement if the hard line that separates both societies is to be softened, if not eliminated.

Islamic societies everywhere face two issues that are crucial to the norms they will establish for themselves and their conduct with the world at large. They have to contend with the internal upheavals involving the internal clash of orthodoxy and the moderate face of Islam. They also have to conduct a relationship with the more militarily and economically powerful Western world where tolerance and moderation are more likely to prevail than radicalism.

The notion that was inherited from the expulsion of the Soviet Union from Afghanistan was that armed Muslim fighters equipped with enough zeal and commitment (plus US-made Stinger missiles) could defeat a superpower. The fall of the Taliban under a barrage of US cruise missiles showed the weakness of the notion that radical Islamic fighters can "always" defeat superpowers.

There is little denying that the general populations of the Muslim and Islamic world would like to see more progress, albeit economic progress, but they would also like to see more modernity coming into society. In this context we should not confuse modernity with Westernization; these are two totally different concepts. While in the upper middle class of the Arab and Muslim world the terms are interchangeable, the reality that in some sense economic progress leads to a commensurate proportion of modernity. Yet we have to accept that given many religious and emotional sensibilities, there are limits to modernity within these societies, especially in the context of human rights, women's rights and the application of a particular school of Shariah law.

It is Islam's clash with modern laws and the code of social conduct where the struggle is perhaps most intense. It does not mean the two are irreconcilable. But the reality is that the tension that accompanies issues of modernity at some stage inhibit progress in these societies.

On the other side, there has been a conspicuous lack of understanding in the Western mind-set of the compulsions that Muslim societies face. It is fair to say that Muslims have not faced a large-scale battle, as did Christianity, to divorce the political management of their societies from religious influence. Muslim societies have not experienced an Islamic Renaissance, and this is often most frequently quoted as the reason for the "clash of civilizations."

The reality is that the ingredients for such a Renaissance within Islam's context is not that simple. The fact is that a vast majority of Muslims consider their theological code as a complete way of life. The necessity to question Islamic governance within a social context does not really arise. This implies that questioning the system would imply questioning Islam -- and this is where the inability of Muslim societies to bring any questions into the process of radical Islam is troubling. Western societies must appreciate that liberalism and protecting that concept within a legal framework has just not happened in Muslim societies. Most of them transited from their colonial experience to independence and that, too, under authoritarian regimes. Such a transition left no room for a system to develop where dissent could be tolerated.

Yet the traditions of consent with, say, tribal Arab societies is very different than the strictly autocratic systems of the modern Arab state. For a tribal leader to command respect and retain leadership within his tribe, consent was necessary. His ability to listen to the opinions of key tribal figures was -- and is -- very important to "carry" the tribe on any specific issue. When a tribal leader failed to command the respect and lead his people he was usually removed or, as is more likely, the key tribal clans moved away, chose a new leader and in a sense ostracized the erring tribal chief. This was -- and is -- the way a tribal system worked and has its own merits of being democratic.

Islam's growth within this system occurred with ease, and it never imposed a clergy that threatened the tribal system. The establishment of a clergy in the sense that it exists today within Islam happened much later. For a long period of history, Islam's proliferation within the Arab societies was actually complimentary to the tribal system. Thus the battle between the clergy and indigenous political forces never occurred in a historical context. In the modern Muslim nation state this is the battle that is yet to come.

The call for social change is not an easy one, and this is where the West needs to temper its message for change and to understand that the pace of change within Islamic societies has to be less drastic. The more sudden the changes, the reforms that could benefit these societies will become divisive issues; the reform process will play into the hands of the militants. The underlying aspect of this need for change and understanding on the part of the West has to be constructive and seriously patient in terms of results. Societies do not transform themselves without paying a cost for change. More importantly, the process is often slow and gradual, one that's influenced by factors such as education and tolerance. Arabs and Muslims often feel an innate threat to their social fabric from external pressures, especially those that they perceive as a function of an unwise and impatient political policy coming from Washington.

Moderate Muslims have been concerned that in the post 9/11 climate the view from the West of their society is one of long beards, head scarves, and militant preachers urging th destruction of the West. This is not what the vast majority of Muslims societies are about. In a large number of them there is a stronger thread of tolerance than is admitted – or even recognized -- by the West. While the images of orthodox Muslims in traditional garb in European cities do stand out, people often fail to compare those scenes with the sight of Hassidic Jews in their traditional garb around the diamond market in Antwerp or even in the streets of New York and London.

Some would argue that tolerance for Jews, even in their more traditional and orthodox presentations, is a consequence of sympathy and empathy that exists for the Jews in the aftermath of the Holocaust. Also on the face of it, militant Jewish organizations have targeted their militancy toward the Arabs within the Middle East and not against the Western governments, as Arabs are perceived as doing. The militant Muslim groups have not found their voice outside the realm of violence. This is where the acts of violence against the West by such groups have actually harmed Muslims in the long term more than their targets.

Because the large body of what has been written about Arabs and Muslims in the post 9/11 event has been more focussed on the militant aspects of their society, Muslims the world over feel that Western intellectuals and the public at large are isolating them and ignoring that the issue of militancy is as much a problem for the Muslims in their own society as it is for the West.

One of the faces of this militancy is the inter-sect violence between the Shia and the Sunni within some of the Muslim countries. This has been particularly the case in Pakistan where sectarian violence has been a regular occurrence for more than 25 years, with constant bombings and killings at times at places of worship. This sectarian violence has recently spilled over into Iraq, and we are witnessing a wider Shia-Sunni militant battle emerging on Arab soil. This will have serious consequences for social harmony within the Arab world. Throughout history there has been a modicum of peace between the communities within the Arab world, while the major element of violence between the sects has been more concentrated within Pakistan. Nonetheless, it is the lack of understanding within Western circles of the complexities within the Muslim and Arab world that is a matter of concern for observers such as myself.

That isn't to say that efforts haven't been made, however intermittently, to create a platform for common understanding between Muslims and Westerners. In Britain, for example, there have been initiatives to improve dialogue between the religions; there have been symposiums and workshops at universities to enhance inter-faith relations. However, the effects of these and other efforts have not necessarily filtered down into the community. This is not to suggest that Muslim communities in Britain are at war with the population around them. But integration has been slow to come by, and this has had a major impact on the way the two cultures have dealt with each other. In the best case, there is a respectful tolerance of each other and there is a belief that subsequent generations of European Muslims will achieve a greater degree of integration, as has been seen in the last three decades since the Muslim immigrant population increased significantly. A fair measure of this will be achieved by the fact that Muslims from Europe will get progressively distanced from their former homeland. The severing of the cultural umbilical chord will be a gradual and, at times, painful process.

Yet it would seem that from a political perspective the world seems in a hurry to reconcile the dichotomies in the Arab world. The precipitous invasion of Iraq, the half-baked peace accord between the Palestinians and Israelis – these are all evidence of a political need on the part of the West to have a presence in Arabia. However, there is little doubt that from an Arab and Muslim perspective American involvement in their region seems to lack sincerity, compassion and genuine concern for the people they purport to help. At times, in places like Iraq, there has emerged an interested concern for peace and stability but it would seem the common man is not convinced of this. The credibility gap doe'n't flow from lack of trying, but it would seem the lack of a broader engagement with Arab and Muslim societies creates a disconnect with the political process being implemented as a tool of policy and the reality of gaining acceptance within a disbelieving population.

Americans and Western commentators seem bemused that Iraqis could accept decades of brutal rule from a dictator like Saddam Hussein but be totally disbelieving of American intentions to institute a democratic government in a post-Saddam Iraq. Arabs don't know enough about American society to even understand what the mentality is that they have to deal with, and this is a crucial problem that they have to tackle. It is the political side of America and the West rather than the social side that Muslims and Arabs need to engage with in a more focused fashion.

Arabs and Muslims who have gone to the West and lived or studied there are fascinated by a number of aspects of these societies. The role of a free press, the measure of public accountability of government, and indeed the respect for intellectual capital, are all elements that in most cases have been absent in their own societies. For orthodox Muslims exposed to these Western societies, the modernism and liberalism at a social level has been difficult to comprehend, but nevertheless the progress of the society has been fascinating to them. For the orthodox Muslims within Europe, the coexistence within a liberal Europe has been easier and less of an issue.

However, for some of the militant youth, the transformation of their confusion and their identity crisis into militancy is taking place. One of the most puzzling aspects of the terrorist attacks in the United States, Spain and London, indicate that they were carried out by radical Muslim youth who seemingly had integrated in the Western society and were not hirsute or traditionally dressed zealots. None of them had shown a propensity toward radical behavior prior to the attacks, from what we know at present, to suggest that they were militants in their thinking. The theory that they were from underground sleeper cells that had been placed in Western society years ago is a bit far fetched. The militant organizations may have well planned strategies within their own societies, but for them to place and operate sleeper cells within Western societies would require years of planning and organization, which I suspect is not the case.

There is little denying that within the Arab and Muslim countries there is a great deal of anger among the youth, and it this anger that is exploited repeatedly. Just as the radical Palestinian groups recruit suicide bombers from among the youth on the basis of the promise of Paradise and continued care for their families, so too, it is assumed that same tactics are employed to bring in new entrants to the cadre of the militant organizations. This new phenomenon has far reaching implications for Arab and Muslim societies – and this troubles many people who worry about the frightening consequences for Islam in the event of a wider confrontation with the superior forces of the West. The threat of terrorism is not something that affects only Western societies; the attacks within Saudi Arabia against compounds where foreigners lived highlighted this aspect. However, it would appear when in one attack a large number of Arab workers -- albeit those who worked for Western companies -- were killed, the attacks eased. It was as if the militants realized killing Muslims in this battle was going to be counterproductive to their cause of bringing in new recruits.

It is the aspect of militancy that cannot be understood easily from the Western perspective, and indeed from the perspective of liberal Muslims as well. There has to be a way forward for both societies to begin a process of wider and more tolerant understanding between them, irrespective of what the policies of their governments are likely to be.

It would be wrong for Western societies to assume that there are no elements within Muslim and Arab societies with whom this bridge of understanding can be built. In the same vein, one is not asking that there be conformity of views between the two cultures. But it is not too much to hope for a deeper appreciation of the differences and the areas of common understanding, so that a great deal of the hate and prejudice that exists between the societies can be broken down.

Just as Muslims have to move away from militancy and fundamentalism, so too do the Western societies need to move away from the fundamentalist right-wing politics that plague their society in this supposedly progressive and enlightened age. As objective as one can try to be, it would seem that the task ahead for the Muslims is a much urgent need for change as the events since 2001 have brought to the forefront the face of Islam that needed to be seen least.

Added to the situation is the fact that speaking out against terrorism immediately draws attention from the militant clergy, with predictable accusations of being a heretic and even an apostate.

In some of the Muslim societies, such as Pakistan, where the political grouping around General Pervez Musharraf had spoken out against militant terrorists, the reaction of conservative Muslims had been of declaring him not only a political puppet of the United States but in some quarters labeling him a heretic. More dismayingly, the militant clergy designated him as a major enemy of Islam and repeatedly ordered assassination attempts on him. In other Muslim countries where the terrorist attacks were condemned by the political leadership, the reaction was as harsh, but nevertheless in some cases, like Saudi Arabia, the militant movements stepped up their attacks to weaken and embarrass the Saudi monarchy. It's among the rank and file of the Muslim population that the sense of revulsion over terrorist attacks must be stepped up -- and for this to occur there has to be a widespread reform within the society and for the vast majority of Muslims, who actually don't agree with militancy, to stand up and condemn the militants.

Interestingly, the encroachement of the Pakistan Taliban into areas like Swat, a mere 100 miles from the capital Islamabad, showed the extent to which some Muslim societies are vulnerable to a movement, which clearly does not resemble the face of Islam, but hijacks the sentiments of the people. Luckily, there has been no broad based support yet for the actions of the Taliban and the ensuing war to rid the Swat Valley of the Taliban has been greeted with consensus within Pakistan. However, economic and law and order problems, if not resolved, will give the youth of the country an added impetus to see the Pakistan Taliban, atleast for the youth, as an alternate to the current order. In this sense it is important to appreciate that the war against the Taliban in Pakistan is as much a war for territory as it is a war for the hearts and mind of the youth of the country.

To assist in this process Western political behavior has to be vastly modified with respect to Muslims societies and nations. There is no denying that the 9/11 events will be a backdrop in the Western mind in dealing with Arab and Muslims for a long time to come, but by the same measure the way the US reacted to those events and the manner in which militant prisoners in their custody have been treated by the US will color the perspective of the Muslim mind. Muslim societies will have to overcome the scars and the pain of these events. It might well seem that given the current mood on both sides this is going to take a good measure of time to heal. A process of confidence building is required, and from the infant steps of more frequent debate and contact, something big and lasting can emerge.

The role of the media in both societies will be crucial to this process of understanding, and for this there will have to a major mind shift among Muslims and Westerners. Sadly, the tone and temperament of the media in both camps suggests that this is highly unlikely. But in fairness, the large part of the Arab media's gripe has to do with American and Western political policy. In contrast, the radical right-wing media of the West tends to criticize the state of Muslim societies rather than only governments.

A dialogue of understanding must commence between the Muslims and the West -- and this must happen on all fronts. The European Muslims perhaps provide the most important bridge of understanding given their longer exposure to the West and its culture. On the broader front Muslims must, within their own societies, see all the areas where they can temper their social view of the world with moderation and tolerance rather than militancy and anger. More liberal Muslims must speak out and accept that the face of militant Islamic terrorism is as much a threat to their own society as it is to others, and to honestly ask if Taliban-style governments is what they need.

The world also has to believe that the fresh approach to world politics as initiated by President Barrack Obama has to be given a fair chance if we are to give peace a chance. It is imperative that the United States shows the world that there is a newer more compassionate understanding of the issues that confront the world. Further, with the United States as will not rely on being the only major military power in the world to resolve conflicts but will engage in dialogue and partner a new world order based on an equity for peace.

MUSLIMS IN A UNIPOLAR WORLD.

Living as I do in the heart of the Middle East, it's been fascinating to observe how Arabia has changed its perceptions about the world, and its own strategic priorities after the downfall of the Soviet Union. I always say to my friends that for Arabs and Muslims, the world changed fundamentally not on 9/11 but in 1990, after the erstwhile Soviet Union disintegrated.

The strategic dimensions of the post-1990 world – where the United States became the sole superpower in terms of military, economic and political might -- has changed geopolitics for Arab countries like Egypt, Libya, Syria and Iraq, who have traditionally managed well within the context of a bipolar world by adjusting political priorities between the erstwhile Soviet Union and the United States. In the case of Egypt, for instance, the adjustment started well before the disintegration of the Soviet Union: in the post-1973 period, its warming of relations with the United States led to its recognition of Washington's pivotal role not only in terms of peace with Israel but also within the context of a new world map. This adjustment was, initially, at a high price for Egypt as it aligned itself with Washington's roadmap of peace with Israel at a time when such overtures were not even contemplated far less acted upon.

For hard-line states, such as Libya, Syria and Iraq, the acceptance of the way the strategic fulcrum of world politics shifted toward Washington has been a slow and at times a painful process. In the case of Syria, this is still an incomplete process. For the majority of other Arab and Muslim countries, however, the adjustment has been accepted but not without considerable skepticism of whether the US truly has an understanding of the responsibility of being the major power in the world. The acceptance of the "new world order" under a single power of dominant strength has also to be considered in the manner in which Washington engages and establishes its position on regional issues that challenge Arab nations.

There is little doubt that the way the United States has conducted itself on the world scene must be seen as the barometer of the international acceptability of its world leadership. While for the moment political acquiescence has been forthcoming, many would agree that this has only been possible under political and economic duress. There has been concern in many quarters that the US political leadership's weakness in "carrying" the community of nations with it without coercion will have a lasting effect on the world political scene. That's the only way that the US will be perceived as a genuinely benign power, which it historically was.

For the Muslim leadership, the task of accepting the new world order psychologically creates enormous pressures, especially in the light of rise of militancy and anti-American feelings within their populations. Even though many knowledgeable people say that while Muslims the world over do not generally agree with the US government's policies, especially with regard to Arabia, Arab and Muslim poplations generally have a positive feeling about everyday Americans. At times they are puzzled as to why the American people had voted in a leadership such as that of George W Bush that is devoid of authentic understanding of the enormity of the role of being the sole undisputed leader on the world's political stage. In the broader perspective the Muslim world does concede that with the election of President Obama the will of America to change their support of the policies of the past has been shown to be paramount. I submit, however, that most everyday Americans simply don't give much thought to such issues. The question of America's role in the world is usually superceded in their minds by issues relating to the pocketbook.

Prior to the Iraqi invasion of Kuwait in 1990, it seemed that American involvement in the Arab and the Muslim world would be steady, with economic openness and lowering of tariff barriers being the major issues, along with, of course, the perennial question of oil prices. Even the issue of human-rights violations in many of these countries was not a matter of concern for too many decision makers in Washington, and while a convenient political weapon during bilateral discussions, the human-rights record of countries like Saudi Arabia, Iraq and others was not central to US policy interests. While the issue of Palestine was paramount on the world stage it seemed by 1990 the lack of substantive progress resulted in a shift of focus away from Palestine; which was being seen more as a problem that would need a longer period of time to to be resolved.

The Kuwaiti crisis propelled America to the forefront in Middle East geopolitics, primarily to protect a vital economic interest, oil. But the change occurred in a manner that forced the Muslim and Arab worlds to interact with Americans in a way they had never previously been used to. A direct contact within a political and military context as a result of the Iraqi invasion of Kuwait created a different dimension for the Arab people to digest. Suddenly, the Americans were not only looking at political solutions but also marshalling a huge military coalition to expel the Iraqi army from Kuwait. For the Arabs and Muslims the prospect of US military forces to be stationed enmasse on their soil and to be soon engaging in military operations against another Muslim country, albeit the aggressor of Kuwait, was a prospect that could not have been contemplated before the invasion by Iraq.

There is no denying that this was what the Kuwaitis and the Saudis wanted, but they didn't imagine that in their call to Washington for help they would set into motion a series of perceptional changes in both the Western camp and within the Arab world. This change will have serious implications for decades. American leadership of the Allied effort to expel Saddam Hussein from Kuwait created, ironically enough, strategic vulnerability for the Arab nations. It was their own regional weaknesses that "forced" the United States to set the pace for the solutions that Washington thought best, and accordingly sought. The militant sections of Muslim society have always used this 'weakeness' of the Arab countries as their argument to the youth to show that there is a need for change from within.

I'm not so sure that Arabs and Muslims fully understood or appreciated the implications of their appeal to the United States for help. In the case of the Saudi monarchy, it weakened them in the eyes of the orthodox elements within their own society, and perhaps provided the likes of Osama bin Laden the biggest impetus for militancy. The problems of legitimacy of intent became a more compelling problem for the Saudi monarchy when, after the first Gulf War, US troops continued to be stationed in Saudi Arabia and indeed within the region. It pushed the US into the middle of a complex maze of Arab politics. On the one hand, that led to a cognizance of their strategic objectives in the Middle East; on the other hand, the American presence highlighted the vulnerability of the Arabs in facing challenges to the own strategic vital interests. Given the assurance that after the expulsion of Saddam from Kuwait, American forces would leave Saudi Arabia, the Saudi monarchy perhaps naively believed that it would mean American influence in the region would be more in the nature of a Good Samaritan, leaving the Arabs to deal with the internal problems of their own region. Some may argue that after the liberation of Kuwait, the Arab nations could not conjure up and impose an arrangement for security within the region – and that this failure led to the need for a longer-term presence of US forces in the region. And there are those who argue that US failure to push on after the liberation of Kuwait in 1991, to achieve the broader objective of the removal of Saddam Hussein's regime necessitated the need for US presence in Kuwait and the region to keep the wolf at bay.

America, of course, has long held the view that its strategic objectives are global whereas most other nations have regional strategic objectives. It argues that hence its Middle East perspectives must be measured against these global strategic objectives of ensuring peace, stability and economic security. The approach that Washington took toward the first Gulf War was based on protecting its own strategic interests, to be sure: it so happened that those interests involved expelling Iraqi troops from Kuwait. Perhaps the US should have exercised more patience; perhaps it should have given diplomacy more time. Be that as it may, the end results – the forcible expulsion of Saddam from Kuwait – satisfied everybody in Arabia at the time.

In contrast, the "coalition of the willing" that the United States patched together in 2002 for the invasion of Iraq could not have been less legitimate than any in history. Not even Kuwait sent forces into Iraq, even though it seemed a number of smaller Gulf States were bullied into providing the US with military bases from which the attack on Iraq was launched. The intervening ten-odd years between the creation of the coalition for the First Gulf War and the Second Gulf War highlighted the huge change in Arabian attitudes concerning Americas. While Arab nations were always going to be apprehensive of a resurgent Iraq under Saddam Hussein after his defeat in 1991, it is evident that the means adopted for bringing in change to Iraq remain highly questionable in both political and social circles not only in the Arab world but elsewhere, too. After 9/11 it was clear that Washington was not willing to consider regional or even global concerns for its actions in both Afghanistan and Iraq; it was a situation that the Arabs would simply have to accept.

By the time those first US missiles hit Baghdad, marking the start of the Second Gulf War in 2003, it was pretty much clear that any good will that America had gathered in 1991 by liberating Kuwait had evaporated. At the same time, the myth of Iraqi military power that had been demolished in the First Gulf War, also drove home the vulnerability of even the most powerful Arab nations. The war showcased America's best weaponry -- laser guided bombs, aircraft carriers, cruise missiles – and there were times when I, like many other people of a certain age, felt that we were watching high-tech video games borrowed from our children that CNN was mistakenly broadcasting. The Arabs knew that their world was changing before their very eyes. The United States assertions of its global interests were largely at the expense of the Iraqis. Arab countries had little choice but to deal with Washington's view of things.

From the US perspective, both Gulf Wars were designed to also send a message to other Arab states with any notions of regional ambitions that their political influence would need to be filtered through what Washington saw as the regional balance of power. The American moves in Iraq and Afghanistan also had the not inconsiderable benefit of encircling Iran and limiting its influence in the region. Most of Iraqi military arsenal was considered more modern than that of other Arab armies, and while largely stocked with weapons from the former Soviet Union, it clearly showed their inadequacy for modern warfare.

Smaller Gulf States eventually succumbed to the pressure of providing bases and logistical support for American troops as the invasion of Iraq began, even though virtually every single Arab leader of any consequence opposed the use of force and certainly the invasion of Iraq. The whole approach to the invasion of Iraq was taken in a way that made it clear to the world the Washington was in no mood to seek a consensus. It asserted its argument that the invasion of Iraq was in line with the UN charter, which says that a country may act to prevent an invasion of itself.

The high handedness of the way the diplomatic effort was jettisoned to adopt a more forceful regional and international policy, created for Washington the seeds of resentment which continue to color the way the Arab world views US governmental policy. This policy has played into the hands of the radical Islamists as it created and environment of distrust within Arab and even Muslim populations the world over. Thus, the radical Islamists were handed a public relations bonanza, which was more than they could have wished for or perhaps even imagined. The voice from Washington was jingoistic, uncompromising and even at times derogatory toward Arabs, making it much easier for the Islamists to simply cite American statements as proof that the "far enemy" was bent upon war.

When the former American Secretary of State Colin Powell asserted that the United States did not need a resolution from the Security Council of the United Nations to invade Iraq, the American intention to go it alone became clear. Yet, in the name of self defense, the United States was setting dangerous legal precedents that actually will have serious repercussions in the years ahead, and also undermine the ability of the UN to sanction other smaller states, who on the perception of a threat, invade their neighbors.

This seeming castration of the United Nations process has contributed to the diminishing of Washington's position in world leadership, a fact that may not have seemed to concern the US leadership of George W Bush, but surely will one day come back to haunt it. In Arab eyes, this process has resulted in a degree of helplessness toward Washington's demands for either assistance in the "war on terror." It also represents a reaction of submission to the stature of the US that is actually resented even within the leadership of the Arab countries. America's willingness and ability to impose its political will on the Arab nations should not be confused as being entirely welcome. Much like Europe's leading nations, most if not all, of the Arab nations resent the attitude and policies of the United States since 9/11. There can be little doubt that a large consensus exists in Arabia that the US has not acted with the enlightened leadership that is expected of the world's sole superpower. Arabia values consensus – it's the tribal way, and it has stood them in good stead for centuries – before there was even an America.

When in 1978 and 1982 Israel invaded Lebanon – while the Lebanese civil war was raging -- US policy was one of "understanding" that Israel was acting out of a need to ensure its own security. It was this extra-territorial approval of military action to protect one's own interests that has shaped the thinking of a lot of Pentagon and State Department strategists. Not surprisingly the argument for intervention abroad, to protect one's domestic self-interest, was used by Washington in Afghanistan and Iraq. There have even been suggestions that in 1982, then Secretary of State, Alexander M. Haig, gave the green light for the Israelis to invade Lebanon, something that Haig has denied. Israel used the same argument when it sent its forces into southern Lebanon after Hezbollah operatives captured some Israeli soldiers. In the event, the ensuing war was widely believed to result in just a stand-off between the mighty Jewish State and the Hezbollah, and there are those who argue that Israel's military setbacks actually demolished once and for all the myth of its invincibility. Israel's action against Hezbollah drew no condemnation from Washington.

Quite ironically, when Iraq invaded Iran in 1979 the logic of Saddam Hussein was partly to settle territorial claims on the Shatt al Arab waterway. His incursion was initially blessed by the US on grounds that Iraq was ensuring its security and hence was justified in its military actions. It is policy maneuvering of this sort that has always made the Arab mind suspicious of the true intentions of US policy-making in the region.

Some Arabs have even argued that if the logic of preemptive strikes is used to ensure security, then does this imply that Washington would see actions against Israel in the same light? "Probably not" is the simplest answer -- and herein lies part of the issue of fairness that the Arab world seeks in this unipolar world. From a Middle Eastern perspective the expectation of President Obama is precisely to bring about, first and foremost, a high degree of fairness to American policy in the region.

When the pendulum of America policy will shift away from a prime focus on Arab and Muslim matters to concerns and issues that are more central to US domestic policy – such as the economy -- then any perceived diminished role on the world stage by the United States will be seen as process of "isolationist" policy resulting in more assertive state policies from the Arab and Muslim nations.

This is what I would call the "Somalia effect," where any half measures on the part of international leaders or a scattered resistance to US policy suddenly manages to undermine the strategic goals of the US. The reasons for Operation Restore Hope, under which US forces joined others to bring stability to Somalia after the collapse of the Siad Barre government, were largely humanitarian, the overarching object was not very clear to the all parties involved. If an eventual waning of interest in micromanaging the

Arab world occurs in Washington, then it is still possible that US policy makers may encounter political anti-Americanism. Acquiescence to American foreign policy seems to be glued together in the region through an active US diplomatic and even military presence in the region, and once at least the military presence were to be withdrawn through a change in US priorities, the shift in public opinion would change the face of the Middle East. Even hawks in Washington -- and their military-minded think tanks – are starting to argue that having ousted the Taliban in Afghanistan and Saddam Hussein Iraq, it wouldn't necessarily be untimely for the US to pull out of the scene.

American foreign-policy makers have entered the quagmire of Arab and Middle Easy politics not completely aware of the political quicksand. The complexities of Arab politics have prevented the emergence of clear leadership from within: this has been the common denominator of Arab politics for the past 50-odd years. For the US, a graceful withdrawal from Iraq and a lessening of its broader presence in the region seems very difficult at the moment. Promises to "bring the troops home" are likely be an issue plaguing domestic US politics in the years ahead, yet the recent elections showed that support for President Obama's victory were perhaps on the back of such a promise. Arabs are certain that the issue will be prominently featured in the conduct of US foreign and military policy in the coming years and how it achieves its objectives of withdrawal from Iraq will be a litmus test of intent.

That, in turn, leads me to raise the inevitable question: How can America stabilize countries like Iraq in order to be able to explore the option of reducing direct military presence in Iraq and encouraging the emergence of Arab forces to deal with their own issues? This implies an expectation of a mature political process to develop in countries like Iraq and Afghanistan; that, in turn, would mean that the US has developed a very clear sense of its own role and responsibilities. Is this a tall order to expect from

Iraqi and Afghan societies? My own view is that it would seem unrealistic that within a year or so this might be achieved. The hopes that removing the oppressive regimes of both Saddam Hussein and the Taliban would create the conditions for responsible government within those countries have been severely damaged by the US conduct in the region.

Most sensible leaders in the region, even if opposed to the invasion of Iraq, would agree that precipitous US withdrawal from Iraq would immediately cause major chaos within the country. Who knows what the consequences of such chaos might be? Some have suggested a break-up of Iraq into two or three or four countries, partitioned along ethnic lines. Quite possible. While some ethnic groups within Iraq and their supporters outside would welcome some element of sovereignty over their claimed parcels of territory, I believe that a weakened Iraq would never be in the interests of anyone.

Saddam and his predecessors managed to rule Iraq due to a strong central government and authoritarian command; many intellectuals philosophically argue that all that has happened in Iraq is that Saddam's Republican Guard has been replaced by the US marines. The difference, of course, is the Republican Guard and Saddam's security services were far more effective in keeping law and order, even though their means were admittedly brutal at best.

The stakes in Iraq are indeed high, not only for economic reasons, but more so the political dividends that can accrue through a Baghdad that is well governed and aligns itself with American interests. However, for such dividends it is important that the new order within Iraq, even if US imposed or guided, has to be effective. This is where the problem arises. It seems to me quite unlikely that the experiments with reforms and with reform-minded governments will work. Creating a new domestic political order within Iraq after years of dictatorship involves dealing with fundamental issues that have been created within the society. Most, if not all, institutions – such as an independent judiciary, a freely elected legislature, and an effective executive branch of government -- those make democracy work in Western countries and elsewhere are totally absent.

Saudi Arabia has been working behind the scenes to bring about diplomatic pressure on the regional parties, including major political movements, to stabilize the region, especially Iraq and Lebanon. Prince Bandar bin Sultan, the former Saudi ambassador to Washington and now the National Security Advisor to the Saudi King, has visited Iran and sought pressure from Tehran to rope in the Hezbollah in Lebanon. Saudi concerns over Iraq, and indeed the fate of the Sunni minority there, drive them toward finding solutions for reigning in Shia militias in Iraq and indeed the region.

While the Shia militias may not be getting military support as much as they'd hoped from Tehran, Iran's silence over the sectarian violence in Iraq encourages Shia militias to settle old scores with the Sunni minority who were the backbone of Saddam Hussein's reign of terror. What Riyadh fears most is a collapse of authority in Iraq and an eventual withdrawal of American forces leaving the country to a chaotic civil war. In such a war the Mahdi Army of Moqtadar Sadr is far too well organized to be easily suppressed by force. One former Saudi government official told me, "It's not when the Americans leave Iraq, its more a question of what state they leave it in." The Obama doctrine of a withdrawal from Iraq brings to the forefront precisely these fears that play on the mind of Saudi Arabia.

Clearly continued tensions in the region are counter productive to both American and Saudi interests. They are also worrisome to the established governments in the region. Little wonder then that the Saudis are taking the lead now in finding a regional solution, but behind closed doors in order to persuade the radical elements to come into line. Just which radical elements should be brought behind closed doors will pose a problem. After all, not all Shia militia groups in Iraq are pro-Iranian. Consider the example of the group led by Sheikh Mahmud Hasani al Sarkhi, formerly a part of Sadr's army but vehemently opposed to Iran and largely believed to be behind the burning of the Iranian consulate in Basra and also responsible for the attacks on British forces in the South.

There are also small, but important efforts being made for contacts between Israel and its Arab counterparts to increase contacts. There have been reports of contacts between Prince Turki al Faisal, the Saudi Ambassador to the US, of having attended key events sponsored by Jewish-American organizations closely tied with to Tel Aviv. His very presence would have sent a strong signal that the Saudi government does not support anti-Semitism. In New York not long ago, Ezra Zilkha, the Baghdad-born Jewish banker and investor, hosted a small dinner at the University Club on Park Avenue, for Prince Turki. Present were some highly influential members of the Jewish community.

In addition, there have been significant contacts between other Gulf States and Israeli officials at different levels that, while not necessarily political, do indicate some advancing of efforts to thaw relations between Israel and the Arabs. After the Hamas-PLO deal brokered by Saudi Arabia in Mecca in February 2007, it seemed that both the US and Saudi Arabia would encourage a significant dialogue to be initiated over the question of Palestine in the near future. But with the seizing of Gaza by Hamas, and the seemingly irreparable breakdown in relations with Fatah, who knows what the future holds?

Washington's role in monitoring the Hamas-PLO contretemps is going to be even more important in the months ahead. Its own tensions with Iran are getting out of hand, and any action by Washington against Iran without the Palestinian question being dealt with in a manner suitable to the Arabs will mean serious alienation from the people and the moderate governments of the Arab world.

While there is a body of political thought in Arabia that believes in overriding Washington's view of how the Arabs should govern themselves through a "democratic" process, the reality is that the jury is still out on this matter. The sight of common Iraqis to be voting three years after the fall of the most tyrannical dictator of the Arab world is indeed a small sign of the possibilities to come. US policymakers believe the lure of democracy will create the emotional and political will in the people to make the new order work in Iraq, and eventually in other Arab nations as well.

But we need to acknowledge that democratic traditions have to be embedded into the psyche of the nation -- and people should want to protect such ideals of freedom. I am not convinced yet that common people within the Islamic world -- and especially the Arab world -- totally accept and understand the responsibility of what instituting and protecting democracy means. Cast your eyes through history and every Muslim nation since the beginning of the 20th century has had a long history of being ruled by authoritarian governments. It is this weight of history that the Muslim world in general, and the Arab nations in particular, must face.

It would be fair to say that the general level of understanding and appreciation of the Islamic world and the Arabs has been low within American society, which has never felt the need to "understand" the outside world. This is a major stumbling block if both sides are to achieve a modicum of understanding of the predicaments that each society – Arab and American -- faces. The threat of terrorism has been a major reason for US government policies, both internally and externally, to be more active, forceful and in Muslim eyes, targeted against them. Americans who have not witnessed such concentrated terrorist attacks argue that they are, after all. a nation that has been signaled out for such attacks for the first time in their history, and that they have to act to prevent this from happening in the future.

The other side of the coin is that within the Islamic world, and elsewhere, terrorist attacks have been common place, be they in Colombia by drug dealers targeting uncooperative judges, or Israeli missiles on refugee camps, or militant Palestinian suicide bombers. Terrorism as a phenomenon has been on the rise irrespective of the political dimension. Terrorism analysts would agree that the US response to the 9/11 attacks was far from being a proportional response. This resulted in greater resentment in Arabia against Washington. But from a security point of view, the 9/11 events have also ensured that governments of Islamic countries suddenly realized they had a problem within their own precincts. While terrorism has acquired an international dimension, at the same time it has generated implications for the domestic political systems of the Arab world. An Iraqi doctor who suffered under Saddam Hussein told me that while he welcomed US troops into Baghdad, he could not support the bombing strikes and the subsequent manner in which the US has carried out its military occupation of Iraq.

The common suspicion is that the more the US government will impose its political model of reform into the Arab world the more likely it is that there will be further resentment toward them. Even though Arabs assert that they are capable of finding their own solutions, the evidence suggests that the status quo within their societies has been maintained rather than reformed through history. Arabs do not pretend that they are champions of democratic ideals in the sense that Europe, the United States or even Japan would argue. While Arab Bedouin societies have a concept of common consensus -- where the tribal leader's decisions are based on consensus from amongst the tribe -- its adaptation to large and populous Arab nations is highly questionable.

Wherever the concept of adult franchise has been adopted for Arab societies, the influence of tribes in the elective process has generally been a strong feature of their political landscape. Though with the more assertive political role of Islamic parties it would seem that religion is a more powerful electoral tool than tribal loyalties. However, when it comes to imposing a Western model of democracy Arabs will remain suspicious of the full intent of the US intentions in the Arab world. This is especially so in view of the fact that most members of the Arab intelligentsia are aware that elections in an emotionally charged region would bring the orthodox elements into legislatures -- and hence not necessarily help the notion of Western-style reforms in the Arab world. Historically, these societies have been steeped in the feudal and tribal systems that were an ingrained part of their society. When overlaid with religious sentiment, the emotive element of a theocracy becomes an integral aspect of any attempted democracy.

In the overall context, however, it is apparent that the experiment toward reforms and democracy in Iraq are crucial to set the benchmarks for the other Arab and Muslim countries to follow. However, we must make a distinction between the need for a democratic government on the one hand and the need for reforms on the other hand. Broad based reforms can encompass a move towards a demoractic system, however the democratic process in the current environment in some countries would delay social reform with the election of orthodox Islamic political parties, such as would be the case of say Afghanistan in the current climate.

It would seem that the traditional monarchies would be more inclined, initially at least, to bring about a reform process where a Bahrain-style monarchy with an elected parliament and an appointed government is tried out first. Other Arab countries like Egypt, who have tried their own version of "selected" elections, will face the heat in terms of reforms that their electoral process will need. It is more possible, if left on their own, Arab societies will find a more meaningful balance between a Western style democracy and a monarchy which might not be half as bad as it may sound.

In this regard it would seem that while the invasion of Iraq and the urgent need for political stability within Iraq dictates what the Americans wish to do in Iraq, elsewhere the call is strictly for reforms. The possibility of having reforms within existing political systems in the Arab countries ensures that Washington will still have political partners they can continue to deal with as they have done so in the past. Yet the scope and content of these reforms will be difficult to gauge in societies where the expectations for democracy are rising. The population expects more far reaching reforms than are available in some of the societies, especially the more populous countries like Egypt, Iran and Iraq. Thus it is not unusual to see the intelligentsia in these countries wanting full democratic reforms but being also wary that, with a large emotional appeal of the religious orthodoxy, the fruits of democratic reforms will eventually be eroded by an Islamist majority in parliament curbing freedoms rather than encouraging truly democratic traditions. This has certainly been true of countries like Pakistan where conservative governments and the religious orthodoxy have actually curbed democratic ideals rather than nurtured them.

In countries like Pakistan the problems of terrorism complicate the full flowering of democratic reforms. These problems were highlighted when India accused Pakistan of training and arming Kashmiri rebels to create volatility in the disputed Himalayan territory that both nations claim. For Pakistani leaders, the rude awakening was that the radical Islamists within their own society suddenly became strong advocates of Osama bin Laden; they saw Osama as some sort of modern day hero who confronted the might of the United States. For successive governments in Pakistan the problem of roping in militant groups was a desired political and perhaps social aim. But no government really saw them as an immediate threat. In addition, during the rule of General Zia ul Haq, the army's Inter Services Intelligence Agency became extraordinarily powerful but also displayed the same religious zeal that the militant Islamist groups had professed -- thus undermining the professionalism of the ISI and its ability to implement the political dictates of the government in power.

American officials had insisted early in the war against terrorism that assurances be given that the ISI would fully cooperate in the "hunt for terrorists rather than assist them evade the Americans." It was in the same vein that the American Deputy Secretary of State Richard Armitage is supposed to have called a Pakistan general of the ISI after 9/11 and, seeking cooperation, suggested that the US "would bomb Pakistan back to the stone age if cooperation was not forthcoming." This assertion was even made by General Pervez Musharraf in his best-selling book – which was published in 2006 – but Armitage denies having used those words. The fact remains that pressure was indeed applied not only on Pakistan but also indeed on many other countries in the region to cooperate in the fight against terrorism. Intelligence experts feel that had more subtle means and diplomatic pressure been used, perhaps the intelligence agencies of these countries would have been more cooperative as some, while having the information which might have been useful, were indeed as shocked by the scale of the problem of militancy as they were amazed at the bulldozing tactics of the US officials.

Pakistan perhaps faces the toughest challenges in terms of fighting terrorism as religion has been a very strong social ingredient which the Pakistani Taliban have exploited in the North West Frontier Province. This has led to the government making compromises with these elements in some areas thereby altering the rule of law to succumb to the rule of the gun and religious zealots who have not electoral sanction for their demands. It is this use of social aspects of society that gives terrorist elements in Pakistan their teeth and the government remains weakly cautious on how to deal with them not realizing each compromise will only allow these elements to focus on the next usurption of due political process.

The delimma that Pakistan faces is best highlighted in respect of the killing of Osama bin Laden by US forces. On the one hand the US would not trust their Pakistani counterparts to share information with them and infact conducted the operation as if it was invading a country. On the other hand, no matter how loudly Pakistan protested to its own religious orthodox Muslims that it neither knew of the raid on Osama bin Laden's hiding place and nor did it cooperate in the raid it was unlikely that they would be believed.

For Americans in general, understanding what their strategic objectives are within the Middle East seems to be a confusing exercise. Clearly the pivotal role that Israel plays in the Middle East for the US dictates a large measure of their policy-making toward the region. So long as the US can get other Arab states to partner some peace process with the Israelis, they would feel they are on track to their objectives. However, the traditional view from the Arab world has been that US interests in the region, beyond the preservation of Israel, is to protect its own economic interests, namely oil.

Saddam's invasion of Kuwait in 1990 briefly but effectively, threatened the economic interests and also raised the specter of the Iraqi threat to Israel. For many Arabs it was unthinkable that an Arab nation could launch missiles into Israel, as indeed Iraq did during the Gulf War, and in a perverse way brought home the reality that a rogue state in the Arab world could threaten both of America's main strategic objectives in the region at the same time.

This clearly became a threat to the Americans and Israelis and indeed the moderate Arab states that were large producers of oil and natural gas. The only thing wrong with the whole picture was that Saddam chose to invade an Arab nation and in the process caused a convergence of American, Israeli and Arab interests.

This convergence, interestingly, set the stage for the first time for not only bringing a rogue state into line but also brought some consensus between the Israelis and the Arabs that at some level their strategic interests were aligned in a peaceful Middle East.

It was this incipient feeling that was lost in the weeks after the First Gulf War, as ironically the Palestinians took the moral position in support of Saddam and -- in a sense -- his invasion of Kuwait, forcing an infuriated Saudi Arabia to decline to pursue the opportunity of this convergence of interests to plead with Washington to resolve the Palestinian-Israeli issues.

In an ideal political environment, US policy-makers should want to see more Arab countries to move toward peace with Israel and reduce the tensions that in the long run could create instability in the region. Washington has been successful in bringing both Egypt and Jordan to normalize relations with Israel, and American officials often point toward the continuing benefits of that policy for those countries.

However, most Arab nations cynically point out that both these countries have given up a great degree of choice in taking this path. While direct threats from Israel against both countries may have been absent, genuine peace with Israel can only be effectively seen as a comprehensive solution involving all parties, and especially the Palestinians, and not as a piecemeal effort involving establishing diplomatic ties on a bilateral basis sequentially, one country at a time. Radical Arabs will continue to argue that unless the Americans are willing to accept a balance in their relations with both Israel and the Arab nations, there cannot be any trust of the peace process that Washington wishes to sustain. They would continue to sow mistrust into any peace process, and that is something that moderate Arabs will have to deal with as a part of the system. Yet moderate Arabs will need to find a lot more than words coming out from Israel and Washington in terms of durable and lasting peace, which would imply concessions that for the moment seem short in being offered. It is wrong to assume that the Arabs do not want peace with Israel, as most Arabs realize that the emotional appeal of a "No Israel" policy is not suited in this day and age, and a slogan that is more reminiscent of the call of the radical Islamists is now widely regarded as an anathema.

At the same time, most political watchers know that the "Weapons of Mass Destruction" (WMD) issue was only created by the Bush spin doctors to find a possible pretext for the invasion of Iraq. If indeed the intent were to follow the spirit of the Security Council Resolution 687 then the creation of a nuclear-free zone in the Middle East (Article 14) would imply pressure on Israel to also disarm and abandon its WMD program.

As far as US strategists were concerned, what mattered was that in some stretch of the moral arguments to invade Iraq, Security Council Resolution 687 gave them some modicum of legitimacy. Beyond that it was -- and is -- irrelevant that the Resolution also asked member states to take measures to make the Middle East a nuclear-free zone. The Resolution served its purpose once the invasion of Iraq began and the rest of it, especially Article 14, all went into the dustbin. It is interesting that the arguments for curbing WMD's has surfaced again in the context of Iran, and the hawks around the White House have talked about taking military action, if necessary. Arabs would rather prefer diplomatic means to bring Iran into accepting curbs on its nuclear program.

Irrespective of the idealistic reasons for invading Iraq -- namely, to bring democracy to the Arab people, remove the threat of WMD and to remove the choking hand of Saddam on his own people -- the reality is that American foreign policy-makers will be hard pressed to convince the world at large that this war was also not about oil. Yet the Arab view that oil would be stolen from Iraq, is a simplification that is difficult to accept. Perhaps what Arabs mean is that the rebuilding of Iraq will be with Iraqi oil, with oil revenues used to pay mostly contractors and US multinationals? This has indeed been the case with companies like Halliburton, long-time close associates of the Bush family, and other American corporations taking the main slice of the cake.

There is scant attention to the sensitivity of the fact that the former US Vice President, Dick Cheney, is a former CEO of Halliburton, the major beneficiary of the contracts for the rebuilding of Iraq; these are not coincidences, but strong evidence that US policy in the Middle East is also largely about economic interests. The conservative elements within the Republican Party in the US are aware that America imports more than 57 percent of its annual oil needs; that an energy policy that doesn't interact with its foreign policy would be suicidal. To what extent this interface is overtly expressed in policy decisions is a matter of conjecture, but for the Arabs to ignore the pivotal role of oil in the American policy makers thinking would also be naïve.

On a broader front -- and seen from the perspective of Muslims -- the dichotomies of US policy are seen not as coincidences but as flaws in Washington's perspective of the role it should play and could play on the world stage. Countries like Iran, Pakistan and Indonesia -- all Muslim states -- have their own unique position within the context of the Muslim world and indeed enjoy a special interaction with the Arab nations. Of course, Iran's position within the periphery of the Arab nations as a non-Arab, but Muslim country (it is the only Muslim country with a Shia majority that is politically empowered) creates complicated interactions with the Arab and Muslim world. During the Shah's period, the US saw Iran as a custodian of the Straits of Hormuz, its guardian of this vital sea lane, and a bulwark against Soviet influence. The ayatollahs, and indeed the Arab states, too, see Washington as a destabilizing influence in the region. While a lot is said about Iran's influence on exporting its brand of revolution to the Arab nations, this cannot happen as most of the Arab nations have very small Shia populations that could not be influenced to undertake regime-toppling revolutions. Iran is today the only oil producer in the region that has a deep sense of being encircled. Even though it stands exhausted from the war with Iraq, it still projects religious jingoism that scares both Washington and its Arab allies.

In the current environment Iran's nuclear policy has become a major source of friction between the United States and Iran, a dispute in which Iran has become more isolated than ever before. To consider a view of the region without due consideration for the status and position of Iran would be a grave mistake. Whether Iran's quest for nuclear power is driven by legitimate needs for energy or part of a sinister plan to acquire nuclear weapons is a matter of concern to the West. Within Iran, too, opposition to the firebrand style of the current president, MahmoudAhmedinejad, has lost him support within his own conservative ranks. Only recently, the ultra-conservative Tehran newspaper Hamshahri, a newspaper he ran when he was mayor of Tehran, criticized him for creating the crisis through his aggressive speeches. This is significant because the newspaper is currently run by Hossein Entezami, a member of the Supreme

National Security Council and a part of the team of Ali Larijani that is dealing with nuclear issues within the SNSC.

For many Muslims in the region, the emotional appeal of an Iranian confrontation with the US could well be euphoric. Still, the more moderate view remains that Iran and indeed the Muslim world could ill afford a confrontation at this time. Some Shia have also claimed that the West did not object when Israel and the Sunni Muslims (Pakistan) acquired nuclear weapons -- but when it came to the Shia (Iran) Washington's fears have come to the forefront. If indeed Iran's aim is to acquire a nuclear arsenal, the strategy behind it is to increase the chances of bringing the US to the table to discuss a new security regime in the region that would include the resolution of the Palestinian issue and a more inclusive policy toward Iran. It would be interesting to see how the Obama Administration will play out their Iran policy; keeping it focused only on the nuclear issue or expaning it to cover a broader spectrum of regional political and security issues. It is this flavor that will be the guiding yardstick of what any overtures to Iran are likely to yield.

Pakistan, meanwhile, is the only Muslim country with functioning nuclear weaponry. While the developments of its nuclear weapons were a reaction to India's pursuit of nuclear weapons, there will always remain a fear within Israel and the US that should Pakistan fall out of Washington's influence it is perhaps the one country that could seriously create disruptive issues for regional and US power politics. The nightmare scenario could be a falling out between the US and the Arab oil producers, leading to their becoming even closer to a Pakistan which, if it decided to side with Arab money, could well become a formidable power broker within the context the Middle East. Such a Pakistan would be a dramatic threat to Israel. What is even more worrisome is if Pakistan's internal social and political turmoil led to a spread of radical Islamist ideas like those of the Pakistan Taliban in Swat to encompass the country as a whole. This would mean

Pakistan's nuclear arsenal would suddenly be available to the very people who profess and ideology that the US is trying to curb in Afghanistan.

It is naïve to think that Pakistan can be dealt with in the way Iraq was because, unlike Iraq, Pakistan has an indigenous nuclear weapons program that by all accounts is high-tech and well established. The concern is serious enough for Israel to be working closely with both Sri Lanka and India to have a nearby presence to monitor Pakistan's nuclear program. There have been unconfirmed reports that the Israeli Air Force has rehearsed one-way self-destruction attack simulations where the planes, after the attack on Pakistan's nuclear sites, would be ditched. It is no secret that similar arrangements exist between Turkey and Israel to cover the eventuality of Iran going nuclear resulting in surgical strikes. The only counter weight to Pakistan's nuclear program remains India, and to that extent the US and Israel would not do anything to limit the presence of nuclear weapons in South Asia.

It would seem that nuclear weapons in the South Asian context have become acceptable as a fait accompli, while in the context of the Middle East it is highly unlikely that any country other Israel will be allowed to possess nuclear weapons. The scandal involving export of nuclear technology to Iran by rogue Pakistani scientists created a furor. From a Muslim and Arab perspective there is a double standard emanating from Washington, as it was well known that Israel's nuclear program was developed through cooperation with US scientists. The fact that this has progressively happened over decades is immaterial in Muslim eyes.

It is positive sign for the way the Middle East political picture is emerging that Pakistan's preoccupations are with India and Afghanistan, and it has never seen itself as a pivotal player in the Arab fold. Arabs realize that within the context of what can happen in the region over the next few decades, their best chance is to seek political survival within the realm of American influence in the region. It is unlikely that a comprehensive Muslim bloc will ever effectively emerge, notwithstanding the ambitions of the Arab League. A common action plan just doesn't exist for Arabs and the Muslims.

Such a plan would necessitate that the Arab leadership recognize that any progress on peace with Israel has to have two elements: the cogent and coherent support of the United States, and the acceptance of the Palestinian position about self-rule and a return of the dispossessed. The pivotal role that Washington plays in the process is not lost on the Arab leadership. It knows that by walking away from that role Washington wold would almost guarantee an abandonment of peace within the region. Arabs also are aware that the mood of world politics is undergoing significant changes and states having radical positions regarding each other have fewer chances of being able to function within the context of how Washington perceives the world stage.

This point has come home to both the Palestinian leadership and the more radical states like Libya and others. The crucial misgiving that exists is a deep rooted feeling amongst Arab leaders -- and indeed the upper strata of their society -- that the United States does not see the region from their perspective as entirely as it does view Israel's position. One Arab leader once said to me that it seemed that Washington would always see the region through Israeli-made sunglasses.

The political machinery in Washington ignores that the splitting of Palestine into separate non-contiguous territories will create more instability. Indeed, if the aim is a long lasting peace within the Middle East, then surely there has to be a modicum of balance on the approach to both Palestinian and Israeli interests. It would be no surprise that should a non-contiguous Israel be proposed, there would be immediate rejection of the idea by both Tel Aviv and Washington.

It is this central position concerning Israel that Washington puts on the front burner at all times, sometimes even relegating America's own interests in the region to a secondary position. It influences the manner and content of the relations between the United States and Arab countries in the region, as they are not entirely convinced that America gives their interests much importance.

For the Arab oil producers the one possible "weapon" they have which could influence the seriousness with which they would be viewed in the eyes of Washington is their oil. The essence of US policy inevitably needs to consider the economic importance of the region in terms of its oil wealth; the preservation of this source of energy becomes vital to US interests. It is also, by the nature of these interests, imperative that US interests are represented first through governments that recognize the importance of US interests in the region. In any assessment one has to conclude that Washington will support changes in the complexion of the governments of this region, whether elected or not, in so far as the governments do nothing to upset the strategic priorities of US interests in the region. This does not mean that puppet governments will be installed or encouraged; rather, the model will be more to allow reforms and encourage development of the region within a specific context, and that context has to recognize US presence in the region. In a unipolar world, and without serious challenge from any other power, the US has a relatively easier task in achieving its objectives.

However, being the sole superpower in the world means that, in the long run, America will have to invest more on wining the hearts and minds of people than putting guns on the streets of Arab cities.

There is some truth in the fact that George W. Bush's call to wage a "war on terror" was in essence similar, in the minds of the Arabs, to the call in 1095 by Pope Urban II for all Christians to assemble a force to fight a "crusade" against the Saracens. Arabs see Bush as reviving the Crusade spirit through arguments that are freighted with American (Christian) certitudes. Bush frequently talks about protecting the "American way of life." Many of us wonder how invading Afghanistan and Iraq would ever protect the American way of life, when there were never any Americans there? The perception of Arab is that Bush is a modern-day crusader, armed with the rhetoric that is supposedly morally driven. The images that his speeches bring to the minds of the Arabs suggest a reinventing of the "clash of civilizations," and a "clash of cultures." There seems to be little compassion or understanding in the way the message is delivered.

With the counter weight of the Soviet Union gone, the Arab nations -- especially the more republic oriented states like Libya and Syria -- now feel more vulnerable to US pressures. China, the only possible counterweight to the US, has developed strong and interdependent links with the US. It is unlikely that its political interests in the Middle East will be manifested in much more than moral support for the Palestinians; a diplomatic and economic presence is all that Beijing seeks in the regionand perhaps on the world stage. There is no doubt that irrespective of how the leadership in both camps -- the American and the Arab -- see their relationships, the fact that it is an unbalanced relationship is quite obvious. American leadership, especially under George W. Bush has been insensitive to the manner in which it has dealt with the Arab leadership and indeed with the countries too.

Citing such sensitivity on the part of Washington, the militant movements that are opposed to the Arab leadership actually foresee and welcome the divide between the people and their governments that sit upon them as it sets up the seeds of dissent in support of their own militant agenda. Where the militants have gone wrong is in their own terror attacks on Arab countries themselves, thereby ruling themselves out as a political alternate to the regimes that are currently in power – except by gaining power by force. It is clear that should militant organizations choose the path of democratic change rather than militant change, then the reception they would get would have be quite different than currently felt within the Arab world. The US leadership doesn't see the dicey path that the current Arab leadership has to tread and assume that the militants will always chose the gun as opposed to the ballot paper as their main weapon. In the emerging scenario that could well develop in the Arab and Muslim world, it is more likely that eventually the radical organizations will notice that the power of the ballot is where their ability to wrest power best lies.

Yet from the perspective of the need for reforms, Arab societies feel the pressure from the West more sharply then ever before. American strategists have argued that to reduce the threat of terror to the United States there has to be reform and moderation in Muslim and Arab societies. The argument in the Western mind is that as Muslim and Arab societies reform, the promise of a better life, especially for the youth, will wean them away from militant elements within their society.

While there is marginal truth in this, the answer for a more stable environment lies in social reforms; the bigger answer lies in the establishment of economic reforms, the eradication of unemployment amongst the youth and the need for political participation within the society. As much as there is a need to look at Middle Eastern societies from within, there is also an urgent need for the US to establish a more balanced political approach toward the region on its part. Dissatisfaction within their own societies does not mean permission for Muslim youth to attack the US. But it surely creates the reasons for them to be more militant in thinking, and when they find the unbalanced approach of the US with respect to Israel and the Arabs, their natural alignment then becomes anti-US.

For Washington the question of democracy within the social fabric of its allies was not important during the Cold War days, and some may argue that such an approach was not even preferred. Social scientists then argued that pushing political reforms in countries like Indonesia, Pakistan, Iran, Iraq, and other Muslim countries ruled by dictators would have meant the possibility that communism might sneak in through the electoral vote process. Today that same anxiety must exist in the case of some countries, like Saudi Arabia, where the Islamic fundamentalists have a fair chance of winning the polls based not on their appeal but more because of the disillusionment with the system.

In general, in a number of Muslim countries the electoral process has shown that fundamentalist Islamic parties have only done well in the polls when US intervention within the region has been higher than normal. In large measure it is true to say that the population of Arabia is inclined toward modernist and moderate governments, with an emphasis more on economic reform than anything else. This is why moderate Muslims and Arabs seek a more balanced relationship with the West, one where the West manages the process of change without the intervention into their social and political fabric.

However, with the physical presence of US military forces in the region, and the occupation of Iraq and Afghanistan, the pressures on Arab states are entirely different. The American presence has moved from the possibility of intervention to actual presence, and it would be naïve to believe that the intervention is merely military in nature.

From the perspective of Arab states, such presence can be considered a serious undermining of sovereign rights. But seen in the perspective of the long term, the more directly engaged policy of the US in the region forces existing power structures to consider reforms they would not have thought of earlier. For example, Saudi Arabia, the bastion of conservative government, has announced its own reform programs; a number of other Arab countries have taken steps for broader political participation.

Arab societies and governments are more conscious then ever before that they have to embrace change. And while the pace of this change will vary from country to country, the necessity cannot be avoided anymore. Arabia's ability to deal with a unipolar world will depend on the degree and sincerity of reforms within its own countries, and these have to be political, economic and social in nature. Half measures will not simply work, and dealing with the West will be largely determined by the manner in which they understand the strategic interests of all parties.

8

LOOKING AHEAD

Back in the 1980's – when I was living and working in the oil-blessed emirate of Abu Dhabi – I would be sometimes asked if the Iran-Iraq war would engulf the whole region, and I always said, "Unlikely." While that answer is still right in the sense that all of Arabia isn't up in flames nearly three decades later, one can argue that the Iran-Iraq war was linked to the continuum of the invasion of Kuwait by Saddam Hussein in 1990, and all that followed since then.

Consider this: The fundamental problems between Kuwait and Iraq were not territorial in nature only, with Iraq staking its supposedly historic claim to Kuwait. They also related to Kuwait's demand for the return of the billions of dollars that Iraq owed Kuwait from the time that Iraq had borrowed the sums during its war with Iran. So I would argue that in that sense the Iran-Iraq war was linked to the First Gulf War – and then the Second Gulf War. In order not to miss key connections and linkages, it's essential not to isolate events. Everything in the Middle East is interconnected, dating back to the Prophet's time.

Looking Ahead

No analysis – let alone prognosis – of the Arab and Muslim worlds, and the way other countries interact with them, can be complete without also conjecturing about what the world will look like ten years from now. Having said that, let me also state the obvious: Nobody could have predicted back in 1991 that a decade later 9/11 would occur, or that both Afghanistan and Iraq would be invaded, and that Saddam's hanging would be so dramatic. While there is no doubt that since the 1960's the radicalism of Islam has been silently going on, the shape of the Middle East in terms of nation states has changed only marginally. None of the countries that existed in 1970 have changed in terms of their territorial boundaries, barring Palestine and Israel, and to a limited extent, Lebanon, because of the Israeli-sponsored security buffer zone.

However, the internal contours of these societies have changed radically as the undercurrents of discontent, frustration and, in a few cases, hopelessness have taken hold in some of the countries. In the same vein, the genre of the political leadership has also changed hands with the passing away or removal of the leadership of some of the key countries. The question remains whether the emergence of a new leadership in the region will translate into significant and sustained progress on social and economic issues for the people of the region. However that question may be answered in the coming decades, what is more evident is that the quality of the leadership will have to change. The sendentary style of the past decades will not work in a fast paced world of social, political and economic change.

In some ways the passing of Arafat, Saddam Hussein and Hafez Al-Assad would suggest that a less rigid structure – one that's less influenced from the crushing weight of their societies' particular history – will emerge. It might be too early to see if the new leadership of these countries has truly and fully embraced the change around them to be able to steer a perceptible course in these troubled times. One has to also see if this new leadership has the tools and the skills sets to deal with the demands of a complex world where globalization and interdependence has changed the very nature of social and political interaction between states.

In the case of Palestine, the issue of leadership is perhaps the most crucial to the future of not only the Palestinians and Israelis but also for the whole region, including radical Islamist groups. For the moment it would seem the tussle between the PLO and Hamas is assuming proportions that could well determine the shape of peace between Israel and the Palestinians. However, irrespective of the current political dimension within Palestinian society there is clearly a schism between the Islamist political factions and the PLO leaders, who clearly seem more moderate on issues of coexistence with Israel.

In ensuing years, the face of Arab politics and society will be determined by not only the resolution of the current crises in Palestine, Iraq and Lebanon, but also how these societies will adjust to changing times. More importantly, how will these nations deal with the new unchartered issues that may emerge in the region between states; will they be as apt to deal with another rouge state amongst their midst? More essentially, how will these societies deal with the deeper effects of radicalism of their youth and will they have the means to win this battle for the minds of the youth?

Two very powerful and important factors will be critical for such a process: the success of the radical Islamists, and how the United States and its principal allies in Arabia approach the region in the future.

A number of undercurrents have already been set in motion since 2001. They will profoundly affect the future of the region and the society. It is possible that a number of scenarios will unfold in the coming decade but it would be a serious folly not to be conscious of the repercussions of each or a combination of these scenarios. One of these scenarios concerns America, to be sure. What is tragically clear is that should the United States withdraw from the region, even abandoning its intrusive military role for a diplomatic one, it is unlikely that the radical Islamists will see this as an end to the saga of US intervention in the region. Groups loyal to Osama bin Laden will continue their war with the "far enemy" to the point tha, as one radical said to me, "they are incapable of interfering in Muslim societies."

This problem will not simply go away. Hence, a Vietnam-style withdrawal (those televised images of American troops fleeing in Chinook helicopters from the rooftops of the US embassy in Saigon in 1975 are still searing) will not necessarily be followed in this region with the radical Islamists breathing a sigh of relief and saying things are over.

To me, it is also increasingly evident that US solutions for the way forward in Iraq are muddled, confused and essentially out of sync with the available possibilities. If the aim in 1991 was not to depose Saddam Hussein in order to avoid a civil war, then the invasion of 2003 has actually done exactly that, with the essential difference being that the civil war occurs while US forces are present as an occupying force in Iraq. It is tragically clear that US strategists responsible for the Iraq drama have the least political, intellectual or societal understanding of the issues. While President Obama has brought about clarity on the issue of withdrawal there is a faint hope that the Iraqi people will finally realize the responsibility that will rest upon them to put their house in order. One can argue that the 2003 invasion has created more challenges than were necessary and it is perhaps wishful thinking that the cycle of violence will just fall away.

Change through political and military involvement seems to have been at the root of the current US policy for the region. While the political sloganeering from the US State Department and the Pentagon suggests that the US involvement in the region concerns the establishment of lasting democracy and peace in the region, the underlying driving force had been the "war on terror." It is clear that the need to bring democratic change and reforms to the region was an afterthought emerging from the limited appeal of the war on terror. It would seem that spin doctors conjured up a palatable twist that could be given to the war on terror and at least win some friends in the media by presenting a broader case for US military and political presence in the region.

The slogan for change carries noble implications and, on the surface, one could easily have embraced it from an Arab perspective, but the fact remains that US policy-makers wanted to bring about change by asking America's allies in the region to also change toward more accountable governance. Needless to say, this also means instituting Western style democracy.

This is a tall order for a leadership that has spent decades evolving from the tribal state to the modern nation-state. The approach that the US took toward Iraq clearly shows weak political intellect and understanding of US policy makers concerning the region. Thus, the American failures in Iraq become glaring examples of why change through an interventionist policy will not find much success in keeping violence to a minimum and establishing effective institutions of governance. The Pentagon and the State Department seem to believe – rather naively, in my view – that if you remove the dictators and unpleasant regimes in the region you will suddenly have democratic tradition emerge within the country. This was perhaps the expectation that arose from the implosion of the Soviet Union. But American policy-makers need to be reminded that Arabia is fundamentally

Looking Ahead

and radically different from the erstwhile Soviet Union and Eastern Europe.

Prior to the events of 9/11, the necessity of bringing change within the Middle East was seen largely against the backdrop of the Palestinian and Israeli dialogue. Indeed, Saddam Hussein was a pesky irritant behind the UN-imposed sanctions, but after the First Gulf War his ability to be a credible military threat in anyway was simply not there. The agenda for change in the Middle East never encompassed issues of political governance and democracy for the Arab nations, and the US saw its political interests shaped by both economic and geopolitical determinants. There was no real incentive for the US to change the existing political order.

My view is that as long as the war on terror continues, the need to bring fundamental change to the region's political structure will be limited. The enormous US investment in the Iraq war (said to be approaching a trillion dollars) is surely bound to sap America's will, if not strength, to continue fighting an unwinnable war. In the post-Saddam era there was an immediate opportunity to change the image of the US from occupiers to liberators. But that opportunity was lost through weak understanding of the region; it was also lost because the Americans simply had no post-war game plan for governance. (American strategists need to study how General Douglas MacArthur methodically approached the administration of post-World War II Japan.)

The result was that aluable time was frittered away. The structure of a "new Iraq" got increasingly weak and fragile. Somewhere in those crucial months, US policy planners lost the plot. An Iraqi doctor who had fled Saddam's regime told me that after he returned in 2003, he found it was "like Paul Bremer and his colleagues were playing some game of monopoly and by buying the 'Utility' space on the monopoly board they felt they would have electricity in the whole city next day." L. Paul Bremer was the US viceroy in Iraq, for his inept, even catastrophic tenure, he was given American highest civilian award, the Presidential Medal of Freedom. From the get-go the US demonstrated, as have been learned now, how little they knew of the region, with crucial decisions and policy matters approached in a naïve and simplistic manner.

For example, the creation of the Free Iraqi Freedom Fighters under Ahmed Chalabi indicated how little the US policy makers knew about Chalabi's chicanery. Defense Secretary Donald Rumsfeld and Vice President Dick Cheney lobbied hard for Ahmed Chalabi to head the new post Saddam government in Baghdad. Chalabi, a disgraced banker with legal cases for fraud against him in Amman, the capital of Jordan, was touted as the face of the new Iraq, with his Iraqi National Congress as the political front. So much so that in the days after US forces entered Iraq, Cheney and Rumsfeld overruled military commanders and had a C-130 transport plane bring in Chalabi and his INC cohorts, along with the Free Iraqi Freedom Fighters, into Nasseryiah. What followed was that Chalabi and his thugs started engaging in a series of revenge killings and lootings, and in the end they became a terrible embarrassment for the US.

Chalabi was so confident of American support extending to well beyond the end of hostilities that he was phoning Iraqi friends around the world offering them government posts before he himself had achieved any credibility within Iraq and its people. Talk about hubris.

Those initial days after Saddam was deposed demonstrated that while the US has one of the best and most efficient military machines in the world, the political sophistication needed to deal with other societies was weak. As Jay Garner – the first American proconsul -- and his team settled into a 250-room building in Baghdad while Saddam's regime was still crumbling, it quickly

Looking Ahead

became clear that while the plan for the transition seemed good on paper there was no understanding of how to take the government of a defeated nation and put it back on track. Where does one start from? Who does what? Who stays and who goes? Where does the money come for running the system? The war and earlier sanctions had completely destroyed Iraq's infrastructure; it was all the more essential to get the system up and running again fast. As one senior Iraqi said to a US representative in Baghdad weeks after the initial fighting had stopped, "We expected the Americans to do better."

From the American side there was a tremendous amount of bureaucratic overkill, with Donald Rumsfeld controlling affairs through his Department of Defense, while Paul Bremer, who headed the Coalition Provisional Authority in Baghdad, reported directly to President Bush. Some CPA officials said there was such micromanaging that if 30 things needed to be done in a day no action could be taken without Bremer personally approving each decision. This was especially surprising in view of Bremer's corporate background; surely he would never have micromanaged to such a degree in the private sector. The irony is that those who know Bremer well – distinguished people like my friend Robert L. Dilenschneider, the former CEO of Hill & Knowlton, and now chairman of an influential strategic communications company in New York – say that Bremer is not a control freak. To make matters worse, the US and Iraqi funding for the rebuilding of the country was clogged in this process. This resulted in a serious breakdown of services, and Iraq's infrastructure deteriorated further still.

There is no doubt that the vast majority of Arabs were happy with the change of the regime in Baghdad, and while few may have agreed with the means or the reasons to justify the invasion of Iraq, there is no denying that many expected the return to normalcy in Iraq would be accomplished with ease. To some it seemed logical that the organized mindset of the Americans was coming in to replace the centralized control of a dictatorship – that from the ashes of the Saddam regime a political and administrative order could be built for the good of Iraq people.

How misplaced those hopes were, how we all felt let down. The situation has gone from bad to worse. Recent US discussions about splitting Iraq into three different countries are fraught with more instability than even the current situation dictates. The suggestion of splitting Iraq itself is divorced from the reality of the region's -- and particularly Iraq's -- unique internal situation.

The scenario for change through political and military means clearly needs a major rethink. The 1950's tactic whereby friendly regimes were encouraged to bring about social and political reforms within their own countries at a pace conducive to the timetable that these governments wished, has been pretty much abandoned. We must not forget that the moving from a passive policy of change to an active policy of interventionist politics was triggered by the events of 9/11; Republican neo-conservatives felt that conditions for terrorism would continue to create more threats to the US until there was major structural change within the Arab and Muslim worlds.

When in 1958 the United States sent in its troops to Beirut to bolster a Christian president who unsuccessfully tried to change the Lebanese constitution to bring more power to the Christian groups, the resulting internecine conflict was perceived by Washington as a major threat to US interests ,and it intervened. That was America's first intervention in the region, and one that is not often mentioned in current geopolitical debates. In 1981, the United States embarked upon a limited incursion into Beirut and left soon after with the bombing of the Marines barracks in downtown Beirut. In 1991, the level of involvement increased significantly on the back of the war for the liberation of Kuwait, and was actually welcomed by all parties as it was seen by Arabs and others as being a righteous war, given that Saddam Hussein

Looking Ahead

had invaded Kuwait. The good will earned from the First Gulf War was seriously eroded in the events after 1991, and this itself shows that the understanding needed to deal with the region was largely absent. In the 12 years after the First Gulf War, nothing was thought of an alternate to the Baath Party of Saddam Hussein other than the use of sanctions.

The problem with the scenario for change occurring in a comprehensive manner is that until the situation in Iraq is not stabilized, and peace and economic prosperity returned to the Iraqi people, the clear judgment must remain that interventionist policies for change have failed. The United States cannot consider another military intervention in the region, given that it seems quite bogged down in both Afghanistan and Iraq. In the case of Afghanistan, the initial feeling was that the selection of Hamid Karzai, a former oil executive of an American company -- and for a short while a junior minister in the Taliban government -- there would be a chance for a home-grown government that would emerge from the chaos that the Taliban were leaving behind. So much so that when the early stages of the planning of the invasion of Iraq got underway, US officials in the Department of Defense were often heard saying "Find an Iraqi Hamid Karzai." However, in view of the fact that the situation in Afghanistan is far from stable it would seem in the years ahead there will further challenges to deal with in that hapless mountain country.

The reality is that change through intervention creates confrontations that cannot be easily handled. We could expect there to be far-reaching changes within the Arab world in the years ahead, and these will be crucial to shaping the region's political and societal landscape. It is more likely that change will happen in the form of limited democracy in some of the countries with better economic models for sharing the wealth of the region. It would seem that countries like the Gulf States (barring Saudi Arabia, which is a different case), Jordan and to some extent Yemen, will experience the voluntary model of change coming from within. While these may not be extensive changes that the West expects, they will be significant in terms of the region's ethos and dynamics. The United Arab Emirates and Qatar have managed to create models of social welfare that have had a very positive impact on their people, and it would be fair to say these countries have managed the aspirations of their people through benevolence and care. A second tier of countries like Egypt, Sudan, Algeria, Libya and Iran have major political adjustments that will need to be made for them to come to terms with the realities of what their people expect.

In Egypt, for instance, the need for political reform is urgent, and the one-party system has to be shed off to allow for a broader representation and the creation of a system under which government is transparent and held accountable. As Libya adjusts to the reality of a unipolar world, it is not entirely possible that it will be able to institute political or social reforms under the present rule. Iran presents itself as the most complex case for reforms to occur, and it is more likely that the internal pressures on an ever more vibrant youth of Iran will create conditions for change.

The current model for change suggests, at least theoretically, that the spread of democracy within the Arab world will reduce the risk of terrorism. This stems from the American leadership's belief that the US fighting in Iraq and Afghanistan for freedom and democracy. Ironically, from an Arab perspective the man in the street believes that American forces are in Iraq because of its interest in oil, while the more educated and the political leadership of the Arab world believes that it's about broader strategic interests, an engagement that was accelerated by the events of 9/11. As a leading Arab politician told me, "If Kuwait grew tons of potatoes instead of pumping millions of barrels of oil, it is unlikely that a single US soldier would have been sent to fight for its liberation." His comment is not far off the mark, and it would seem that the US leadership has done nothing concrete to prove its sincerity toward the Middle East and its special issues. A senior member of the PLO executive committee, who for long lived in the Gulf States, once told me that Palestinians and Arabs will only believe US policy is for their good when Washington is willing to demonstrate "What it will do for the creation of a Palestinian state." This is essentially a credibility issue insofar as it concerns the matter of change within the social, and perhaps more importantly, the political fabric of the Arab world.

Outside the scope of Iraq the pace of change, while slow, will nevertheless go on. This can be witnessed through a number of shifts in the policies of existing monarchies and rulers of the Arab world. The fact that even the conservative Saudi ruling family has talked of an agenda for change highlights that there is a desire and necessity felt by the ruling class for bringing about change. The pace of this change may not be suit the timetable that the US policymakers may wish to see. It is debatable if the agenda for change initiated by the Arab leaders themselves is because of pressures from the West or from their own realization that their own societies face unique challenges that need to be addressed in a more meaningful manner.

Most Arab leaders have been concerned about events and undercurrents that appeared within Saudi society. There may not have been serious concern for a mass revolution along the lines that Osama bin Laden has advocated. But there's definitely concern that Saudi youth are vulnerable to recruitment by radicals. The feeling that democracy will bring about the conditions that will defeat terrorism is naïve, given that the terrorist strain with Muslim societies comes from a political Islam and not a conservative Islam. It is indeed the very politicization of Islam by a group of religious leaders and their high profile followers that has created conditions of confrontation under the doctrines of the "near enemy" and the "far enemy." Religious seminaries have been the recruiting grounds for a great deal of the followers of this radicalism, but it would be wrong to assume that fundamentalist Islam nurtures terrorism.

Thus in such an environment any move toward widespread democracy will play into the hands of the radical Islamists. They are organized enough to swap the machine gun for the ballot box with equal ease. Whether they can then subsequently make the necessary political transition to be representative of the whole population is highly debatable, of course. It is more likely that parliamentary majorities will be used to enact laws that strengthen oligarchies and parliamentary dictatorships.

I don't mean to imply that Muslims and Arabs are not ready for democracy. But without broad-based education, an independent judiciary and a free press, experiments with democracy for the sake of simply trying them would be a disaster. Change can come only gradually. What role can the US and its partners play in this process? Perhaps the most important role they can play is to gradually nurture the process and encourage Arab solutions for Arab problems rather than imposing a set of conditions that are perhaps going to be alien to the region and the people. America has to be patient with the Arab world, and it has to take measures that do not exclude Arab society from the process of integrating into the process of peace and tolerance.

Most importantly, for the process of change to work it is essential that the US work with both Arabs and Israelis to find a lasting solution to the issue of Palestine. This is where the US suffers most today in terms of credibility. If terrorism is to be fought then the battlefield is, in Arab eyes, on the negotiating table of the peace process between Israel and the Palestinians, and not on the battlefields of Iraq and Afghanistan. Not only would change within Arab society be more attainable, such a move would out-maneuver Al Qaeda and other radical groups, and take away the emotional appeal that they exploit on the issue of Palestine.

Looking Ahead

It would seem for the near future, given the few options that the US has in terms of its policy in both Iraq and Afghanistan, the confrontation between radical Islamists, and the US and its partners will get worse. In addition, the very forces that the US went to destroy in both countries have been damaged only on the exterior. There have been signs in both countries of an emerging nationalism which runs the risk of bringing to the fore the very old forces of the Taliban (in Afghanistan) and Saddam's Fedayeen (in Iraq) under new names and new battlegrounds.

Al Qaeda has been rebuilding its network with a new leadership at the grassroots level. When US forces secured a seemingly quick victory over the Taliban, veteran observers noticed that the very structure and composition of the Taliban was such that it dissolved back into society. The Taliban would surely re-surface when it found an opportune time to take the battle against America to a new phase. The failure of Hamid Karzai's government to make a real difference in the provinces of Afghanistan has meant that while economic life may have improved marginally, the promised dividend from removing the Taliban does not seem to have been procured for everyday Afghans.

Iraq presents a trickier scenario because the competing strains of ethnic animosity have come to the forefront with a majority Shia population flexing its political and militant muscle; the Sunni population for the first time seems to be under siege. As Shia politicians try and work their place into the government of a New Iraq their militias are settling old scores with the Sunni clans who were the principal supporters of the ancien regime. There is a very real danger, too, that the Kurds, who feel the Americans for helping in the war against Saddam promised them a larger measure of autonomy, may decide to go it alone. Assuming that there were outside forces determining the outcome of the communal violence within Iraq, it is unlikely that the violence will stop even if Iran, Saudi Arabia, Syria and the

Americans all decide not to take sides in the internal turmoil in Iraq. While Saudi Arabia and Syria would be concerned about any Sunni slaughter by the Shias, so too would Iran be concerned if the Shia were cornered. But Iran and others realize that it is not in their interests to let Iraq implode. The consequences of a fractured Iraq are too grave for the region and it is clear no one will benefit. However, if this is the case then what supports the violence?

Iraqi internal violence primarily emerges from three sources; with a fourth element causing what may be called "opportunistic terror." The first source of the violence within Iraq is clearly communal, with the Shia and Sunni elements slugging it out in the post-Saddam scenario. The radical Shia had many scores to settle with the Sunni minority that had long ruled Iraq. However, we have to make a distinction between the political Shia as opposed to the radical Shia groups in this regard. While initially it would seem the Mahdi Army of Moqtadar Sadr, while on its collusion course with the US forces, became the target for what it saw as American attacks. It then saw it best to broaden the scope of its own action to include Sunni and even moderate Shia elements as legitimate targets.

Only when Ayatollah Ali Al Sistani issued a call to Moqtadar Sadr and his Mahdi Army to accept a truce in the battle in August 2004 at the Iman Ali Mosque, did the role of the Sadr forces change. But well trained force like the Mahdi Army will always pose a threat to a central order; others may suggest it has acted as a natural counter force to the Sunni militias that have emerged after Saddam's fall. Sistani's role as perhaps the most important Shia cleric in Iraq is enormous and his edicts (fatwas) have been instrumental in allowing the political process to advance. His order that Iraqi women should vote in the elections and that Shia must not resort to violence against the Sunni or indeed all forces bringing order to Iraq, were critical to the process of nationa building. This has made Sistani a target for some of the radical Shia groups, as is seen by the recent plot of the Jund-al-Samaa (Soldiers of Heaven) to assassinate Sistani in January 2007. The group was previously unknown, but its very emergence points to the determination of small groups that seek to destabilize the country's fragile communal situation even further.

A second element of the violence is the former Fedayeen of Saddam's Baath party. They were deeply loyal to him and had a huge vested stake in the continuation of Saddam's regime. The Fedayeen who were set up in 1995, thrived on the economic benefits of the Baath regime and infiltrated every segment of Iraqi society during the Saddam era. It is believed that the American de-Baathification policy, which removed thousands of government officials and teachers and professionals from the work force, was done in fear of the underlying presence of the Fedayeen.

While the large majority of Fedayeen were from the Sunni population, there was loyal Shia too. They now portray themselves as nationalists, pointing to the current communal turmoil as evidence that only a Fedayeen-inspired Iraq has a future. However, lacking any political platform and zealous about their allegiance to Saddam and the Baath principles, they are the most likely source of violence against the Americans and the new Iraqi forces. While the Shia-Sunni communal violence is undertaken for revenge or power positions, the Fedayeen faction operates under the radar and seemingly has never claimed responsibility for any attacks.

The argument for this segment existing is very simple: prior to and during the invasion of Iraq, a number of these Fedayeen carried out hit and run operations and were by design beefed up prior to the war to carry out Vietnam-style operations against any invading force. With the botched hanging of Saddam Hussein, their vengeance will come to the fore as indeed they do not really care about a political agenda anymore and would be the most willing to make it tough for the Americans and any successor system in Iraq. It was estimated that at one point prior to the invasion of Iraq there were close to 40,000 members of the Fedayeen. While a number of Fedayeen leaders seem to have been arrested, it is plausible that many of the 2,000-odd attacks a day in Iraq are carried out by such elements.

A third source of violence is the disbanded Iraqi army, which, in post-Saddam Iraq, was suddenly sent home, some without pay. This has caused a tremendous dislocation in a society where service in the armed forces was considered a stable and secure element of social economic sustenance. A large number of these elements have joined various militant factions and represent a mercenary element within the Iraqi insurgency. Recognizing their political loyalties does not necessarily reveal their current allegiance. These former Iraqi forces have not been absorbed into the new Iraqi social fabric, and their unsettled state allows them not only access to hidden caches of arms but also to adapt their fighting skills to a new form of urban guerilla warfare where the militarily superior American forces have an distinct disadvantage.

While the Fedayeen might have linked with these former soldiers, many of the Fedayeen consider these former Iraqi soldiers to be weak-bellied and open to compromise with the "enemy." Nevertheless, the style and depth of the insurgency has caused many analysts to believe this cannot be simply planning done by radical communal elements of Iraqi society; the weapons and attack patterns are too "military-like."

A fourth element, which the US has made a great fuss about, is the international wing of Al Qaeda. It is usually accused of fomenting the insurgency in Iraq. There is no denying that elements of Al Qaeda would have infiltrated into Iraqi society given the fragile situation, but their presence is not considered to be numerous enough to be considered a military problem. However, their tactics and methods are extremely violent and perhaps present the greater threat to the image of what is happening there. The death of Abu Musa Zarqawi, a Jordanian national, who was the figurehead of Al Qaeda in Iraq, while having dented the movement, hasn't necessarily finished it off.

The ranks of such Al Qaeda forces are drawn from as far as the US and Canada to Arabs from the region, all fired with the zeal to settle scores with the "far enemy." While their initial tactics seemed to be focused on sensational kidnappings and beheadings – with the entire gruesome beheadings being recorded – now it would seem with the loss of Zarqawi the focus seems to be more on fanning the flames of communal violence between the Shia and the Sunnis. Some intelligence reports even suggest that Al Qaeda wants to bring the Iranians into the Iraqi civil war. This makes sense as, from a Taliban-Al Qaeda perspective, they have the experience of the Afghan civil war through the chaos of which emerged the conditions in which the Taliban rose to power.

The strategy and hope of the Al Qaeda in Iraq would be the same – which is to say, to create the conditions for chaos from which they feel an Islamic movement of unity would emerge. For the Americans, the battle against Al Qaeda is supremely critical. This is a battle that has no defined battlefields, and thus the enemy for the US remains highly elusive. Al Qaeda's tactics seem to have changed in the face of some major reversals in Iraq, Saudi Arabia and Pakistan. Another battle is being waged by Al Qaeda elements with other traditionalist Islamic parties, who are well entrenched in the Muslim world. A case in point would be the Muslim Brotherhood in Egypt, from whose midst a number of the soldiers of Islam emerged to fight for Osama bin Laden in Afghanistan against the Russians, and later in Bosnia and Chechnya and more recently against the Americans. However, it would seem that Dr. Ayman Al-Zawahiri, being frustrated with the lack of open or tacit support for Osama bin Laden in a number of countries, has embarked on infiltrating Islamist political organizations in various places.

The emergence of Mohammed al Hukayma in the Muslim Brotherhood in Egypt as a young leader who is openly questioning the old guard of the Brotherhood and openly professing support for Osama bin Laden, suggests that this new tactic is being employed by Al-Zawahiri to gain a wider following in the Muslim world. While the Muslim Brotherhood was providing recruits to Osama's cause, its religious leadership never really endorsed his tactics or strategy.

This does not mean that Osama bin Laden does not have an emotional appeal in the streets of Cairo, Karachi or Jakarta; all it means is that the emotional support for him does not mean much in the scheme of the battle that is being waged between the US and Al Qaeda.

It would seem that the Al Qaeda strategy is to widen the battle with the Americans, and they need a new theater of operations, preferably away from both Iraq and Afghanistan, to ensure that American forces are spread more thinly. It would seem that the next battle between Al Qaeda and the Americans will be waged in Egypt, after having failed to bring the Al Qaeda into Iraq with any meaningful results other than sensational kidnappings and killings. Al Qaeda's following in Iraq during Saddam's time was absent largely because the Sunni population, from whom Al Qaeda could have garnered support, was already well placed as a minority in the power echelons for some 30-odd years. In contrast, the Shia opposition in Iraq, apart from being repressed by Saddam Hussein, were ideologically divorced and strained from the mainstream of Sunni-inspired Al Qaeda. While in the post-Saddam Iraq the political voice and weight of the Shia groups will be more conspicuous than ever before, it is not going to be

Looking Ahead

an easy process for them to get into national governance in the tradition of the Sunnis.

The three main Shia political groups that have emerged after the changes in Iraq are the Sadrists (followers of Moqtadar Sadr); the Islamic Dawa Party (led by Ibrahim al Jafiri); and the Supreme Council for the Islamic Revolution (led by Ayatollah Mohammed Baqir al Hakim, whose brother is Abdul al Hakim who leads the party and the Iraqi government). All these factions have a large following in the Shia community but it is not yet certain if they have the means or the political will to control the large number of armed Shia irregular militias within Iraq. While Moqtadar al Sadr has strong control over his Mahdi Army, and has been the subject of run- ins with both the American forces and the Iraqi police, the
political strength of the party is based on its firebrand style of leadership and confrontational politics.

A fractured Middle East with military confrontations extending from Afghanistan through Iran to Iraq, and the tension between Israel and Palestine, will all create conditions which Al Qaeda will exploit to the maximum. In addition one has to remember that there are a number of more radical Islamist groups in the region who would be the first to also take advantage of the situation. Groups like the Palestinian Islamic Jihad, the Hezbollah, Hamas and even some of the marginal groups within the Arab and Muslim world, will consider this an opportunity to hurt both the "near enemy" and the interests of the "far enemy."

One cannot be sure that such a broad confrontation can be managed by the US. It has always been the professed policy of the Al Qaeda to encourage social and political disorder into which their recipe of social and religious reform would find more followers. This would allow a new Islamic order to emerge from the chaos in the region. The radical elements would benefit from the chaos as they would want the unsettled state to affect those more affluent Arab countries where a social welfare system has not created the right conditions for them to exploit and bring about instability in the region. US policy-makers have not quite understood this aspect of the face of radical Islamist movements who have always done better with the masses during social and political chaos.

One of the more likely situations in the Middle East will be the continuation of the present conditions with the odd escalation in the situation. The situation in Iraq might well reach a stalemate in which US presence, while essential, might have to be scaled down due to domestic pressures from within the country – particularly in a presidential year. While the risk of a total US pullout of Iraq in the present state of the country would most certainly spell disaster for it and the region, there is a greater chance that a reduced presence of US troops backed by a bolstering of Iraqi forces may be the only solution to move forward.

The execution of Saddam Hussein has created a bigger divide between the Shia and the Sunni within Iraq, making the task of reconciliation all the more difficult. It is unlikely that Saddam Hussein's execution will rally the Iraqi nation considering his rule alienated more people than ever before, and yet if the situation within Iraq continues to deteriorate people cannot help but compare it with the situation during Saddam's rule, some suggesting repressive peace is better than anarchic democracy.

The continuation of the status quo does not imply things will not change; all it means is that all parties to the region and its conflicts will not do anything radically different that the continuation, as far possible of their current policies. This implies that Iran or the US will not adopt a conciliatory path with each other. This implies there will be no improvement in the situation between the Palestinians and Israel. And this implies that the situation in Iraq and Afghanistan will linger on at the same pace with internal strife and the lack of progress on the political front.

Looking Ahead

In the case of Iraq, there will likely be a further breakdown of the state machinery. The government's inability to control the country will lead to a worsening of the civil war. For the Gulf States, the continuation of the current status quo is not a bad thing given that anything that would add to the turmoil in the region is not good for them. Their economic prosperity and development would be at serious risk if the entire region were to suffer any setback in terms of an expansion of the confrontation between the US and other parties in the region.

Having said that an analysis of the war situation in the region shows that through the Iraq-Iran war, and the two Gulf Wars the Gulf states actually benefited because their economies got a boost from the situation as they became conduits for the supply and support system.

Prior to the invasion of Iraq, there was a period during the Hashemi Rafsanjani era in Iran where a rapprochement with Saudi Arabia was developing and King Abdullah, then the Crown Prince, had also warmed up to the realities of the solutions for peace in the region. The situation in Iraq has complicated the scene in that Iran has had to seek a position of asking for non-intervention in the region by America while the Saudi, by overt alignment with the United States, have had to accept that the solution of the problems in Iraq have, for the moment, to be seen through Washington's perspective. Herein lies the problem for the future as it would seem the longer the situation in Iraq lingers on, the role of regional players will always be colored by the United States position on the region. Indeed the election of Mahmoud Ahmadinejad brings to the forefront a firebrand president who has so far shown a nationalist streak and developed a confrontationist policy on a wider front that Iran has followed for some years.

Central to the dispute he has brought up is the pursuit of the Iranian nuclear program, which he claims is peaceful. But Iran has not really completely complied with the requests for proper inspections and controls to ensure it does not have a military angle to the program. The issue is more complicated considering that Dr. A Q Khan, a Pakistani scientist, and considered the brains behind Pakistan nuclear weapons program, was allegedly trying to sell designs of centrifuge chambers to Iran. These chambers are used in the enrichment of uranium to weapons-grade uranium. While small traces of highly enriched uranium have been found in some nuclear waste from Iran's existing atomic facilities, it is not enough to conclude that Iran has enriched uranium to the point of weapons grade -- given that even those traces that were enriched were significantly below weapons-grade quality.

Iran's position on the issue of nuclear energy is a complex matter, given that the media is more excited by the ensuing confrontation and might well be ignoring some key aspects of Iran's position. One has to understand that the Iranian leadership does not like being dictated to, and hence they do come across as being extremely nervous and sensitive about the nuclear issue. Iran's position is that it needs nuclear power for energy, given the eventual depletion of their oil and gas reserves and the growing demands from their economy for sustainable energy growth. Successive Iranian governments have maintained their position on the development of nuclear power for peaceful uses and feel that the European offer of August 6, 2005 offering a proliferation-free technology for nuclear energy and enriched uranium from European sources was rejected as it continued to make "Iran dependent on third parties for its energy needs."

Seeing this confrontation developing, the Supreme Leader Ayatollah Ali Khamenei on August 9, 2005 issued a fatwa (a religious decree) that forbids Iran from acquiring nuclear weapons as they are forbidden in Islam and hence unethical. Interestingly, this position was reportedly contradicted on February 21, 2006 by a statement from Hojatoleslam Mohsen Gharavian, an important cleric from the Qom faction of Iran's clergy whereby he allegedly said that should the country be threatened by a nuclear power, (such as the US) then the injunction forbidding an Islamic country to build nuclear weapons can be overturned. The same evening of his remarks being quoted in a newspaper, Gharavian emphatically stated that he has been misquoted and all he said was that Iran could take that position of revering the religious edict but certainly would not consider that option as the edict of Ayatollah Ali Khamenei was binding on the people of Iran. Arm twisting in the same newscycle?

The US position on Iran's nuclear program is governed by political considerations and suspicions, and it is believed that the CIA has reported privately to the President that there is currently no conclusive evidence of Iran having embarked on the route of building nuclear weapons. However, it would seem that the current US administration's position remains one of caution given that some of Iran's leadership states that Israel has no right to exist as a nation. The Bush administration clearly fears that should Iran develop a nuclear weapons, its purpose would be to use it against Israel. In essence, the US position is more for creating a deterrent to any possible designs of the Iranian leader to sneak a nuclear weapon on the world.

While the US will adhere to a compliance mechanism that the IAEA and the European Union agrees to in respect of inspections of Iran, it will put its weight behind making them very stringent.

The fact that US intelligence and political policy on the issue of "Weapons of Mass Destruction" in Iraq were way off the mark suggests that US intelligence and political policy makers cannot be entirely trusted on the matter of Iran. This might explain the reason the international community might be a bit hesitant to back the more radical solutions that the United States might be suggesting on Iran's nuclear program and its containment. While Iran has done everything in its power to portray its policy to be clandestine, the US intelligence community has more conjecture than hard evidence to support a case against Iran. Indeed the international community is also aware that US political motives under the previous Administration were directing the approach rather than the pragmatic and conclusive evidence as to Iran's real intentions.

There are concerns amongst United State's allies within the region, especially Saudi Arabia, that any military action against Iran will destabilize the region significantly more than the invasion of Iraq did. While Washington's undisputed military position could well encourage it to take some military action, it is more likely that such military action would be a series of surgical air strikes against possible Iranian nuclear sites, in the same way as Israel did against Iraq.

It is also likely that the US,will come under tremendous pressure from Israel to do something about the Iranian nuclear program. A failure on the part of the US to deal with it might mean that Israel will be forced to take action of its own. This is a prospect that would doom the Middle East as the situation in this decade is radically different than 25 years back when Israeli action against Iraq was only met with condemnation from the Arabs. One also has to consider that an attack by Israel on Iranian nuclear facilities will prompt Pakistan to feel wary of the situation and perhaps take action of its own or assist other Arab states in the wake of this attack to acquire nuclear weapons.

The face of the Arab and Muslim world will change in the years ahead but the factors that will influence this process are a combination of domestic and international events. While the regional situation might well center around Iraq, Iran and the Palestinian statehood, the domestic situation will be more a battle for the mind of the youth of the Muslim world.

Al Qaeda will also try and extend its influence into the Muslim world to the point of bringing internal conflicts and turmoil in most of the Arab and Muslim countries. There is no denying that the cat and mouse game between Al Qaeda and the US will continue in various theatres of the world. The crux of that battle will be fought in the mind of the youth of the Arab cities and slums. This is where the battle will intensify as an elusive group like Al Qaeda will battle the US and its interests in different forms but its successes in the minds of the youth will go unnoticed.

The only way that battle can be won is to take away the tools of exploitation that can be used by the radical Islamists in such a battle -- the tools of poverty, the non-settlement of the Palestinian statehood issue, the social and economic reform of the region and, most of all, a shift in American policy bringing more balance in US policy objectives concerning the Arabs and the Israelis.

There also has to be a major rethinking of US policy in the region and the role that it wishes to play with the Arab and Muslim world. Important in such rethinking will be a reassessment of the manner in which that US has been dealing with these countries, especially in the post 9/11 environment. Issues like the Patriot Act and the Homeland Security regime that the US has brought about have created deep resentment and concern in the moderate Muslim world. It would seem the dictum is that all Muslims are "bad" unless they prove they are good Muslims has resulted in marginalizing a large population of the Muslim world who would perhaps have been the best allies for the war on terrorism.

It would seem that the neo-con elements in the US administration were bent on imposing their view of the world on all others and there was little to reason with them as they seem to live in the belief that it is the only way to protect the United States. The election of President Barrack Obama brought new a whole new approach of reconciliation toward Arabs and Muslims. In a sense the Arabs and Muslims have thus far been impressed with the statesman like qualities of President Obama and his call for a new understanding of the issues has echoed well in the Muslim world. His recent stance of a two state solution for Palestine has been seen as a key element of his new approach to issues that remain central to the political psyche of the Muslims and Arabs.

There is no denying that the Middle East, and particularly both Iraq and Iran, will be the focus of attention in the West; there is much speculation about how US policy and actions will be shaped in both countries. The realization has been for long that the US has got seriously bogged down in Iraq, failing to form the transition toward "freedom and democracy." As the violence has escalated, military solutions continue to be sought in what is essentially a political problem. The feeling that should Iran and Saudi Arabia, along with perhaps Syria, take the step forward to support a reducing of tensions within Iraq, there is a vague possibility that the security situation in Iraq can be improved.

This might theoretically sound a perfect scenario, but there is little appreciation within the West that Iraqi Shia and especially the Iraqi leadership such as Ayatollah Sistani do not wish to be seen as subservient to Tehran. On the contrary, they would not accept any diktat on Iraq's internal situation from the Tehran leadership, be it political or religious. While there is religious reverence and mutual respect for the clergy and especially Ali Khamenei, the Iranian Shia spiritual leader, it does not in any way imply that they would be accepting orders from Iran. There is no doubt that with the hanging of Saddam Hussein and some of his former leadership, the Sunni militants will feel a greater need for revenge. Many Saddam supporters felt that it was the Mahdi army that was in control of the proceedings of the hanging. These Sunnis will also feel a greater threat from the Shia majority who now have political control within Iraq.

Looking Ahead

There is a greater danger that there is no indigenous leadership within Iraq that can bring a sense of unity to the war-torn country. The lack of any political unity between the forces that politically opposed Saddam Hussein during his long reign suggests that the mechanism for political forces to work with each other has been absent on the Iraqi political landscape. It was believed that with the Americans controlling Iraq after its invasion in 2003 they would act as the political binding force that would bring the different groups to one political platform.

This will always be the subject of deep debate for years to come in trying to understand how the American administration lost the initiative in Iraq. Its early attempts to bring a political leadership seemed sloppy. Imposing leaders like Ahmed Chalabi on the political scene were seen as dictates from Washington aimed at preventing the Shia leadership to have their say. While through most of the past three decades it would seem that the Americans had a better working relationship with the minority Kurds in the north, they too are feeling intensely insecure and disillusioned with the manner in which the political events within the country have taken shape.

While the current prime minister Nouri al Maliki of the Dawa Party is certainly portrayed as neither a US appointee nor as an Iranian lackey, his remit of authority has to be centered around the level of security that can be brought into play to bring some semblance of law and order in the country.

Iraq's stability is therefore vital in many respects as a barometer to gauge the intent of US policy in the region. It is not unreasonable to assume that if the aim of getting rid of Saddam Hussein was to show the Arab world that there are stable alternatives to dictatorships, then a failure of Iraq as we know it will be a terrible blow to those intentions. In the face of the growing internal tensions within Iraq a new view has emerged of a three-nation state concept, which was briefly touted, but nevertheless has a dangerous connotation were it to be considered.

The alternate that is quietly being flouted is a loose confederation between the Kurds, Sunni and the Shia within Iraq, allowing a great degree of autonomy to the three confederating regions under the banner of a united Iraq. While theoretically the idea seems very plausible, one has to see it within the context of the political maturity within Iraq -- and this suggests rather unique problems.

Tensions between regions drawn along ethnic and religious lines in Iraq against the backdrop of what are essentially civil war conditions cannot be contained; and it is more likely that such an arrangement in the long term will break Iraq with more serious consequences. In addition, the unease that both Iran and Turkey would have over regional autonomous regions being given powers of quasi-statehood on the basis of religious and ethnic considerations causes enormous pressures over the issues of their ethnic minorities.

The matter of grave concern for the region is naturally going to be the manner in which the United States deals with countries like Iran; the current theme seems to be one of confrontation between these countries. While the hawks in Washington would like to consider some sort of action, even short of an invasion of Iran, the reality is that America cannot afford such a move even if the political will existed. The fact that President Obama has made it a policy objective to engage in a dialogue with the Iranian leadership is a step in the right direction and the key will be how Tehran reacts to this.

It is more likely that the hawks would consider any move from Iran to actually acquire nuclear weapons capability to be reason enough for a surgical strike against Iran along the lines of the Israeli strike in 1981 of Iraqi nuclear facilities. It is not inconceivable that Israel would be encouraged to carry out the strike rather than US planes participating in such a strike. On the other hand, the more moderate voices will suggest that any strike against Iran will actually create conditions for an upsurge in Iranian nationalism and more importantly prolong the current regime in power.

In a more regional perspective such an action will be seen as reckless not only by regional countries but also by the Russians and the Europeans. The Russian leadership has been suggesting for sometime now that the United States has been acting irresponsibly in its conduct of foreign policy in the region. It would seem that some of the European countries and the Russians will be working behind the scenes for the Iranians to come clean on the nuclear issue. Coupled with the efforts that Saudi Arabia has been making with the Iranians, there is a better chance that diplomacy may work in this case.

Saudi Arabia has realized the enormous regional influence it can have, and hence has been more active on the diplomatic front with both its overtures to Iran and the negotiation of peace talks between the PLO and Hamas. The interesting aspect of the Saudi position is that they seem to prepare the groundwork behind the scenes and their diplomacy is usually below the radar. It is no secret that while they have been concerned over the safety of the Sunni population in Iraq, they have worked hard, both directly and through Syria, to keep those elements of the moderate faction of the Sunni political leadership engaged in the political dialogue within Iraq.

In time it would seem through political measures and indeed the economic muscle that Saudi Arabia has, that it can bring about conditions within the region that might be conducive to resolving the issues of security. But this has to also be balanced by the United States understanding and complimenting these efforts. The Saudi position on even Israel has been quite clear and it would seem that should the Israeli side be brought to accepting a Palestinian state and allows it formalization, Saudi Arabia would lead the process of the recognition of Israel. This is fundamentally a very different position from that of years ago. Moderate voices in Israel and the United States should consider that there are opportunities for peace in the region but these could well be squandered if not heeded.

It is also essential that the Arab governments and leadership understand that if they do not change, the pressures within their own societies will force changes on them which will not be comfortable. It is important for these leaders to understand that the world around them is changing rapidly, and there is a need to face the issues of reforms within their society. It is to this effect that the educational, economic and judicial systems in these countries need to be overhauled.

While secular-style governments may not be that easy to encourage in the present state of the Islamic world, it is more likely that modern thinking governments will be more the rule than professed secular governments.

There has to also be a major effort exerted by all sides to bring a better understanding on the issues of faith, and to forge a better understanding on matters of coexistence. We do live in a dangerous world today and it would seem that a failure to change the face of the Middle East in a meaningful way will bring more misery and pain to the people of the region. In this endeavor ,all sides have to play the part. Failure to do so will mean the consequences will be too great for not only the region but the emerging world order too.

EPILOGUE: ONE WORLD OR MORE?

Western friends who know that I have lived and worked in the Middle East for nearly three decades, often ask me, "What will the region be like in 10 or 20 years?"

As one can expect, this isn't an easy question to tackle. It's actually a terrifying question because – especially with the uncertainties in Iraq and within the extended region of the Middle East – one can't even say with any certainty what Arabia, and the World of Islam, will be like a year from now. When I attempt to ask Arabs – particularly members of the elite – that same question, it's impossible not to get the sense that the history of the region will surely affect its future, perhaps far more acutely than the history of other regions does for their prospects.

Not long ago, for example, I was chatting with a well traveled member of the Bahrain royal family about the prospects for the future. We were sitting in a posh restaurant in Dubai, out on a pier with the late-afternoon breeze of winter in our faces, and he leaned forward, looking around him to make sure no one was close enough to hear, and said:

"You know, if a relationship breaks up, for every year together it takes a year plus one month to heal."

He then smiled and said if the Americans remain in Iraq for 10 years it will take 11 years to simply heal.

"And when will nation building start?" I said.

"Not all relationship completely heal after they have been fractured," the Bahraini said.

This Bahraini royal is perhaps different from the larger group of the rich elite of the Arab world. While they may have a degree of positiveness about the future for the region, there is little doubt that their conduct, overseas assets and lifestyle, suggests that a number of them are as apprehensive of the future as the teenagers in the streets of Gaza or Baghdad. While the current prognosis for change for this elite is to create a broader based economy and spur social development through economic progress, the task is more complex than what socio-eonomic modeling would suggest as a solution. While the rich Arabs want to and see their economic and social future wedded to their own societies they have little political presence to bring about the change needed and hence cooperation with existing government is the only model for political change.

However, as interdependence and globalization is becoming more pronounced the manner in which the region shapes its future is being driven by powers and factors that are also external to the people of the Arab world. While their governments have sketchy track records in handling their domestic challenges, now the task of managing the geopolitical interests of the United States and others makes the conduct of domestic governments all the more sensitive. Countries like the United Arab Emirates and Qatar are following a model for economic well being to bring prosperity to their populations, with considerable success, while

Epilogue

others like Saudi Arabia having the same resources are still handicapped through their recent history and track record in understanding the issues within their own society.

Is the Middle East going to end up being a nasty relationship between Arabs and Americans that is not amenable to repair, let alone healing?

Will there have to be more chaos and bloodshed before people realize that conflict is not inherent in their region and can be cast aside? Are the Arabs and Muslims going to admit that not all their problems begin at the Israeli or American doorstep? Will the Israelis finally acknowledge that their state was grafted onto a region and that they need to also extend a hand of peace to the other side? Will the United States realize that all that is expected of it is something very simple – to be fair? Will the Arab leadership ever stand up and realize that in general they have failed in truly leading their people?

These are long questions for which there cannot be short answers, and certainly not facile ones. For the Arabs and the Muslims, the issues that have become important are radically and fundamentally urgent for them to resolve. They have to consider the issues of accountability and progress in their broadest sense and more importantly sooner or later have to address the huge expectations of their own people for a better life. They cannot, as a society and even as a religion, continue to postpone some decisions they have to make about the complexion of their own societies. In the wave of the social discontent amongst their youth and the appeal of radical means for change the urgency for positive change become all the more imperative. This is where sensing the mood, needs and aspirations of the next generation become all the more important for the leadership of the region.

Crucial to this vision of the future for the Arabs and Muslims has to be the economic vision for their people. While the Arab countries are divided into distinctly two different camps of the rich on the one hand, and the poor on the other, the rich happen to be rich beyond the wildest of imaginations and the poor continue to spiral down into worse squalor. While the rich GCC States have provided aid to a number of Arab countries, and in some cases even assisted in direct social rehabilitation projects, the impact has been nominal in most cases. This is perhaps because the basic infrastructure in a number of the recipient countries is weak and in a number of cases fraught with corruption or a tribal system that does not want to see change (Yemen is a good example of this case).

There cannot be a doubt that the youth of the Arab world face a challenging and even perhaps a bleak future in the absence of proper housing, education and job opportunities. While the economies of the region are expanding, perhaps more into the services sector, there are question marks on the pace of the integration of this young generation of skilled people into the work force in a timely manner. A large part of the disgruntled youth in Saudi Arabia were the unemployed 'graduates' of Saudi Arabia's countless universities who could not get a job. They are the segment that are easily led astray into the model of radicalism and in some cases even militancy. My precise argument has been that the war being fought now is not about territory or influence, but it is a war for the minds of this youth of the Arabian and Muslim world. It is here that the battleground will be the most intensely fought over between those who want reform and change with a progressive mind, and those who want to bring out a radical but conservative outlook for society.

They also need to make extremely important decisions on the form of governance within their political systems, and more importantly, on the degree of accountability that will prevail. It is not important, in my view that they necessarily have to choose a Western-style democracy. It is far more important that they institute greater accountability, transparency, and public choice as important foundations of a genuinely strong society. The model for governance has to fall within the possibilities of what is functionally possible rather than a just transplanting a foreign system into their societies. Yet the acknowledgement of a system based on adult franchise, with a one-person one vote, system has to be basis of governance and nomination, the exact system needs to be carefully architectured so it is acceptable and takes cognizance of the realities of each country and each society.

There has to be a new approach toward education, and this implies reforms that also encompass the legal and social framework. To what extent these societies are willing to accept such reforms is still open to question. Other critical issues such as women's rights, the role of gender in governance, and the role of people from non-Islamic religions need to be addressed with straightforward conviction and fairness. Secular thought within an Islamic framework has to be developed which allows predominantly Muslim societies to deal with the concept of a modern society that can remain Muslim in character and yet broad-ranging – and therefore broad-minded – in essence. The history of Islam in countries like Spain and elsewhere shows that it has long had the tradition of dealing with non Muslim sections of its population with a remarkable amount of tolerance considering the context of history in which such governance occurred. It the is failure to address these hard issues in a timely manner within Muslim societies that actually plays into the hands of the radical Islamists who will not accept a divergent view about society and culture.

Such adjustments within any society are likely to create pressures, some of which will be hard to contend with. Because these societies do not necessarily debate the changes they make it is more likely that the pressures of acceptance and adjustment will, at times, be expressed in a violent language. Some of these pressures may take the direction of social reform sideways, or even backward, as there is a tendency to mix religion into all aspects of society and governance. However, there is no denying that unless there is more empowerment injected into the system, a process that takes decision-making away from the select few to a broader and more responsible section of society, the benefits of economic and social reform will not accrue to the people. This empowerment has to be accompanied by more accountability and more public oversight of the process of government, which would imply, as a first step, the strengthening of a free press and media.

I believe that the Arab and Muslim leadership have come to the crossroads where they need to address the question of communal tensions through the prism of religion. Progress has to be balanced against public sentiment; it has become more and more obvious that in the years ahead Arabia will be increasingly subject to external pressures inherent in the vicissitudes of international politics. Pakistan, Iraq and Lebanon are all examples of societies where religious schisms within Islam have flared into open conflicts and sectarian strife on a number of occasions. The civil war of Lebanon, the Shia-Sunni divide in Iraq and the underlying war between the Sunni clergy and the Shia minority in Pakistan are just some examples that it is wrong to see the Muslim Ummah as an indivisible monolithic bloc of society.

Whether it is the lack of education or the social tension drawn through society by the religious elements who are not tolerant is not clear. However, societies such as Iraq, Pakistan and Lebanon face the prospects of prolonged civil strife on the back of religious tensions between their own communities. This highlights

Epilogue

the inability of the nation building to have matured enough to create the bond of nationalism strong enough to over come the religious divisions within the same country. There is little evidence that there are natural processes in place to overcome these divisions. In the case of Pakistan and Iraq the whole fabric of social interaction remains divided between the Shia and Sunni communities, each with their own mosques, communities centers, schools and even political parties. Thus the emphasis remains of division rather than cohesive nation building, and into this schism comes the political agenda of each faction or sect to the point where the potency of the social fabric is based on hatred rather than cooperation. This is the most aspect of these societies that will determine the health of these societies in the years ahead.

I have viewed this region and its remarkable journey toward modernity with my own particular passion, and with the compulsions that seek progressive, egalitarian change. Yet I have also felt the emotional distance the region wants to impose on those who wish to help it most.

I was once visiting an English development-aid worker who was married to a Palestinian. She had lived through the turmoil of Gaza, and shared the anguish of the Palestinian people. Her husband and she were talking about the Palestinian "problem" in my company. The Englishwoman suggested that Palestinians had to learn help themselves rather than wait for the world to save them.

Her husband became furious.

Oblivious to my presence, he said "But that is what they are doing. Why do you think they blow up Israeli buses? They want to make the world listen to their helplessness"

His wife raised her voice, attracting the attention of the people in the café that we were in, and said, "You think blowing up people is a solution?"

"Yes, it perhaps the only solution -- and how would you understand? You are an outsider," the husband said. As he spoke, I thought, "These two have only been married for 20 years, and she is still an outsider in the eyes of her own husband?"

The husband's attitude, of course reflected the sad and troubled weight of the region's past -- that someone who spoke the Arabic language, suffered the same indignities in Palestine that Arabs did, rescued the children through raging gunfire, and now after 20 years of trying her best to assimilate was still an outsider! I'm pleased to report that their marriage survived that episode, but it has remained for me a poignant reminder that no matter how close we – the "outsiders" – are allowed to come toward the looking glass, we are still people looking in from the outside. You can convert to Islam and become a Muslim, but if you aren't born an Arab, well, you'll never be an Arab. Only through birthright can you claim citizenship of the world of Arabia.

The questions of which world do we live in is crucial to humanity as a whole. As with the rest of us, Arabs and Muslims have the option to see the world through our own perspectives, or to develop a wider view. I have always argued that it is no more a question of one world, two worlds or many more worlds, but, more crucially, we have to retroactively examine the notion of what survival should mean to an American, an Iraqi in uniform, a Palestinian child or an Israeli settler. The imperative is for the world, and more so for Arabia, has to be creating a stable and sustainable world order. Just as Americans have to learn that their vision of the world has to encompass the better world for all people so too have the Arabs to embrace the notion of a world where there is peace and posperity for all nations. Turmoil in their own backyard or in a land further away cannot be good for anyone in a highly interdependent world.

Dick Cheney's horror scenario of mushroom clouds of nuclear explosions and sleeper terrorist cells within the US, summons for many Arab leaders the prospects of a long-term presence of US troops imposing their brand of democracy on a people who, as one top American official put it, "really don't know what this animal called 'democracy' is all about." Such assumptions for the region are never questioned and in general seep into the framework for foreign policy formation based on fears that have never really been addressed through balanced enquiry and dialogue.

There is no denying that the era of George W Bush as President of the United States of America has altered the way Americans see the Middle East and more importantly eroded what little trust existed of US policy intentions in the region. While there was a modicum of hope in Bill Clinton and earlier US Presidents public stance on seeking peace in the Middle East; George W Bush will be held singularly responsible for the total break down of any trust that was possible between Arabs and the US. His policies, aided by hawks like Dick Cheney and others, were myopic, totally self centered and a major destabilizing factor in the conduct of world relations. This has meant that in the ultimate analysis there is unlikely to be a return to the realm of trust from even the moderate element within Arab and Muslims societies. I have so often heard modern thinking Muslims, who seek positive change, refer to the George W Bush era as perhaps the most damaging era of US policy for the region.

The presidency of Barrack Obama is seen as being full of expectations of change in foreign policy of the United States and a more equitable view of the world. While this burden of expectations may seek quick changes in US policy there is always the danger that the longer President Obama procrastinates on policy change the more difficult will be the task of winning acceptance within the Arab mind. His announcement to withdraw US troops from Iraq by the mid of 2010 has been greeted with positiveness even if the applaud has not been too public the intent for change has been felt. For the Obama administration the difficultly of handling the worst economic crisis in history and the worst foreign policy standing at the same time will be most challeneging. The Arabs nations do not expect miracles from the Obama Administration but they do feel that the intent and sincerity of change has to be carried through.

What remains surprising through this episode of history, over the past eight odd years, is that the media seemed to stand on the sidelines and let the executive branch of government rule the roost with abandon; feeding on the very fear of terrorism that it was unwilling to understand the roots of this anger. Americans will look back at this period of their history decades from now and wonder why the oversight of public opinion and independent thought never marshaled in the hawks who felt that Washington's best answer to world strife was in using military means. Indeed in the case of the invasion of Iraq even the most hawkish political pundit would struggle to be convinced that the invasion was a 'liberation' of Iraq. While Saddam Hussein was no popular hero many within Iraq knew that his removal had to be followed by the establishment of law and order and not necessarily democracy.

In my discussions with Arabs the one thing that comes out clearly and consistently is that the sense of imposition from the outside is what seems to undermine their confidence in the Americans. There is the crushing weight of 500 years of failure in the Arab world, something that historians do not let them forget. And now once again Arabia stands at a crossroads where its successes in promoting tolerance and openness in Spain, and the glory of the Islamic era of the Ottomans and Mughals, seem to be consigned to the detritus of history. While the past three odd decades have given some of the Arab countries the economic power and means to change their own life beyond their own imagination. While this has created a segment of Arabs who are the 'haves' the larger majority have remained the 'have nots',

Arabs and Muslims need to once again reclaim their historical greatness, ridding their societies once and for all of the damning condemnation that they cannot accept other faiths in their midst. They need to bring to the fore a more – much more compassionate face of Islam. It would seem over the transitions of the colonial era of the European powers, the demise of the Ottoman Empire and the brith of the modern concept of nation-state, Muslim and Arab societies have continued to battle with the progress and in a sense have not felt the impact they could create, in a positive way, on the world scene. While the glory of bygone years seems hard to repeat there seems to the struggle to modernize and in a sense seek their own revivalist movment weighing heavy of their own societies. Have the colonial years and the earlier rule by Ottoman's drained the will of the Arab people to define their own destiny? Is there a recognition within their own realm that being assertive in the modern world will need a whole set of new skill sets and resources for which a deep inward though process is necessary?

Some of my friends in Arabia argue that this face of Islam does indeed exist, that the majority of Muslims and Arabs actually shun violence and the ways of nihilists such as Al Qaeda. As a leading government figure from Dubai told a visiting international journalist in my presence recently, "Look at Dubai -- we have 180 nationalities and a person from every faith living here. I challenge you to show me one instance of intolerance."

One could argue that Dubai is an unusual model of racial and religious tolerance, but it need not be the only one in Arabia. A senior cabinet minister from a Gulf country told me, "We need to let the West know that violence is as much our problem as it is that of America."

Is this not the "one world" of shared experiences and development goals that we all seek, the minister said? And then he added, "Perhaps for the Americans the aim of removing Saddam was important and having done it they could have installed another dictator and left." But they chose to stay, and look how besieged Arabia has become.

Perhaps the truth is that America's escapade in Iraq was planned and carried out on the fly, and hence long-term plans were not fashioned, successor governments were not sought, and programs to create a safe and secure society were never quite on Washington's radar. The effect of an ill planned political solution, if there indeed could be one imposed from the outside, has been a total break down of the political direction of the Arab world. The Arab leadership has become overtly conscious of the power and influence the US government can and has shown to have in the backyard of Middle Eastern politics and thus even if they exerted a latitude of indpendence in their political goals, the chances are where and when these goals will be divergent to what is perceived by the US as their owns strategic interests then Arab leadership will have to adjust to the realities set in Washington and not in their own capitals. I am not implying that Arab leadership is impotent in the face of US pressure but merely that the face of real politik has changed on the world scene to the extent that the question of 'one world' or 'two worlds'

It is difficult to see anything but a fractured future for the region – a future where the existing power structures will be altered in a

Epilogue

more profound way than the collapse of Soviet Union. As I write this, it is difficult to see much beyond a gathering state of anarchy, one in which Arabia may be dragged into a long period of chaos and confusion. I told an American friend the other day, "A failure to stabilize Arabia now will make us re-live the 15-year civil war in Lebanon -- only the scale and battlefield will be much larger."

I wasn't saying this out of some exaggerated assumption of being the "Oracle of Dubai," and I wasn't saying this because I wish Arabia ill. On the contrary anyone who has lived in the region is deeply touched by its history and traditions, and by the reflexive warmth and hospitality of its people. But Arabia is besieged, and there is no end in sight to the region's tragedies. The mentality of this siege is actually very subtle, at times Arab's themselves will assert that such a siege does not exist, and perhaps during short periods of their history they may well be right. However, the fact that there is a deep vested interest in the region cannot be denied. Threats to worlds oil production and supply cannot be tolerated by the United States and some of its allies, irrespective of where the threat may emerge from. However, in a uni-polar world it has become more obvious to the US policy makers that the threats to internal security and intra regional threats, whether they may be from Saddam's Iraq or Iran, cannot be tolerated. As much as this is a battlefield filled with gunfire and missiles there is a bigger battlefield emerging where the battle is for the mind of the people. It is here that the biggest hopes and the saddest tragedies of the Arab people will be born from. While the battle field may be contained today, the reality is that the boundaries of this battle are getting more blurred and more of the youth are engaging in a battle for a different world and a different set of expectations.

I certainly hope the battlefield doesn't widen, that those tragedies don't deepen. As someone who was born a Muslim and who prides himself on being a secular humanist, I certainly hope that I am wrong when I say that Arabia's future looks grim and embattled. But I don't think so. If the battle is without violence then the reality of the new world will perhaps be more conducive and positive for the next generations. However, if the battle will be violent and bloody then the repercussions of such a scenario will be terrible not only for the next generation of Arabs and Muslims but also for all those who will interact with them.

I am not sure that the people of the region understand the urgency with which these issues need to be resolved within their own mind. In equal measure I am not sure that the worlds predominant leadership, i.e. the US, appreciates, accepts and understands the compelling demands that are placed on it to lead with fairness. The world is fractured at this moment in time and its healing will be difficult if the only solution we have is violence.

ABOUT THE AUTHOR

Born in Quetta, Pakistan in 1955, Anwer Sher, was brought up in a military family where his father Brigadier Abdul Qayum Sher, served with distinction. His mother, Amita Sher, was an educationist, writer, social worker and a strong advocate for women's rights. Anwer was writing from an early age and went on to do his Master of Science from Islamabad and after a brief stint in a strategic think tank, joined banking. The career brought him to Abu Dhabi where he went on to being a CEO of the bank and retiring to then continue his private business interests. An avid photographer and horse lover, he also continued his prolific writings which covered a vast spectrum of topics, from banking and finance, to social commentaries and political commentaries. He has written for Gulf News, Khaleej Times, PostGlobal (Washington Posts' online opinion site) Al Arabyia and many others.

Anwer Sher is married to Eileen Verdieck and they share their love for horses. He has two sons from a previous marriage.

ENDNOTES.

[i] The term "Middle East" may have originated in the 1850s in the British India Office, and became more widely known when American naval strategist Alfred Thayer Mahan used the term. During this time the British and Russian empires were vying for influence in Central Asia, a rivalry which would become known as "The Great Game." Mahan realized not only the strategic importance of the region, but also of its center, the Persian Gulf (which Arabs prefer to call the Arabian Gulf). He labeled the area surrounding the Persian Gulf as the Middle East, and said that after the Suez Canal, it was the most important passage for Britain to control in order to keep the Russians from advancing toward India. Mahan first used the term in his article "The Persian Gulf and International Relations," published in September 1902 in a British journal, The National Review.

One widely used definition of the "Middle East" is that of the airline industry, maintained by the standards organization, the International Air Transport Association (IATA). This definition — as of early 2007 — includes Bahrain, Egypt, Iran, Iraq, Israel, Jordan, Kuwait, Lebanon, the Palestinian territories, Oman, Qatar, Saudi Arabia, Somalia, Sudan, Syria, United Arab Emirates, Pakistan and Yemen. This definition is used in world-wide airfare and tax calculations for passengers and cargo.

With the disappearance of the Ottoman Turkish Empire in 1918, the previously used tern "Near East" largely fell out of common use in English, while "Middle East" came to be applied to the re-emerging countries of the Islamic world. At the United Nations, the Middle East is referred to as "West Asia."

[ii] I would recommend the enduring classic, "The Seven Pillars of Wisdom," by T. E. Lawrence.

[iii] Please see Stanley Wolpert's biography of Jinnah.

[iv] On September 13, 1993, Israel and the Palestine Liberation Organization agreed to the "Declaration of Principles On Interim Self-Government Arrangements," a document also known as the "Oslo Accords." The document was signed at a Washington ceremony hosted by US President Bill Clinton on the lawns of the White House, during which Palestinian leader Yasser Arafat and Israeli Prime Minister Yitzhak Rabin ended decades as sworn enemies with an uneasy handshake. This agreement was the fruit of secret negotiations between Israel and the Palestinians, represented by the PLO, following the Madrid Conference in 1991.

The Oslo Accords contain a set of mutually agreed-upon general principles regarding a five year interim period of Palestinian self-rule. So-called "permanent status issues" are deferred to later negotiations, to begin no later than the third year of the interim period. The permanent status negotiations were intended to lead to an agreement that would be implemented to take effect at the end of the interim period.

[v] According to the popular Web site PalestineFacts.Org: "Israel needs a strategic deterrence capability because it is surrounded by much larger neighbors that are hostile to its very existence. Arab nations have repeatedly gone to war against Israel. In the Gulf War, Iraq launched Scud missiles against Israeli cities and has threatened attacks

with gas or biological agents. Syria, Iran and Iraq have threatened the use of weapons of mass destruction. Terrorists constantly attack Israel to undermine its stability and will to resist. In this environment, Israel has to maintain the ultimate deterrent to forestall even more aggressive acts by its enemies.

The United States has recognized this requirement and has supported Israel's refusal to bind itself to the NNP treaty so long as Israel remains ambiguous about its capability, a diplomatic nuance. Even though the US has lobbied against other small nations that desire to acquire nuclear weapons, the US has recognized that Israel's case is unique. It is easy for nations that have superior military strength, peace, and secure borders to rationalize the need to give up nuclear weapons. It is quite a different strategic calculus for Israel who is facing huge, oil-rich Arab states that have sworn to destroy her, states that have attacked her with large invading armies, that have openly supported campaigns of terrorism against her, and that continue to assert the intention to reduce or destroy the Jewish state. In this environment, why should Israel give up her most effective deterrent weapon?

Israel supports, in principle, preventing the spread of nuclear weapons, even though international support of the concept has been ineffective in curtailing Iranian and Iraqi weapons production. Israel is willing to consider eliminating nuclear weapons from the Middle East when its enemies have credibly renounced them and after a sustained period of peace that will give Israel confidence in its own security."

[vi] Many Americans in the early 1800s believed that it was the destiny of America to control all of the North American continent. This belief was called "Manifest Destiny." The term originated from a New York newspaper editorial of December 27, 1845, which declared that the nation's manifest destiny was "to over spread and to possess" the whole continent, to develop

liberty and self-government to all. In the eyes of the Americans, it meant that it was God's will that Americans expand their territory from coast to coast.

This idea of Manifest Destiny strongly influenced the attitudes of the people and the policies of the U.S. government. Americans believed that they were bringing God, technology and civilization to the lands in the west. What they brought, in fact, was death, disease and wars to the Native Americans and Mexicans who occupied these lands. Americans used the idea of Manifest Destiny to justify their dishonest, cruel, and racist treatment of the Indians and Mexicans who already occupied these lands. Americans looked upon Native Americans as dumb savages and upon Mexicans as inferior people who were lazy and ignorant.

The idea of Manifest Destiny did not begin in the 1800s, but began back when Puritans were first settling the Atlantic coast.

In 1803 Thomas Jefferson was President of the United States and the Mississippi River was thought of as the western border of the United States. Napoleon Bonaparte was the ruler of France which controlled a huge piece of land west of the Mississippi River. This land stretched from the Mississippi River all the way to the Rocky Mountains and was called the Louisiana Territory. Napoleon was on the verge of a war with Great Britain and needed money to finance the war. President Jefferson took advantage of this situation and offered to buy New Orleans from France. Napoleon Bonaparte offered to sell the entire Louisiana Territory for $15 million. President Jefferson agreed and purchased 830,000 square mile of land west of the Mississippi.

[vii] According to Herman J. Cohen, a Washington-based scholar: "The arrival of the film 'Blackhawk Down' in cinemas in the United States and around the world reminded Americans that Somalia has never been far from the center of Washington's national security concerns. This vivid memory of the tragedy that

befell American soldiers and Mogadishu fighters on October 3, 1993, comes at a time when Somalia is drawing worldwide attention as a potential hiding place for Al-Qaeda terrorists seeking to escape from U.S. forces in Afghanistan.

Starting as far back as the Second World War (1939-1945), the United States paid particular attention to Somalia in its Africa policy. Since Italy was an enemy nation, allied with Nazi Germany and the Axis powers in the Second World War, Italian-controlled Somalia, Eritrea and Ethiopia were early military targets of the United Nations powers. Thanks to British forces based in Kenya, these territories were among the first to be liberated from Axis control in 1942. This was important to the United States because Mogadishu, Asmara and Djibouti were relay stations for U.S. forces operating in the Middle East.

Even before the end of the Second World War, the problem of Somali irredentism caused some friction between the United States and Britain. In August 1944, the British proposed to consolidate all Somali peoples into one nation, including the Ogaden, Italian Somaliland and French Somaliland, which became Djibouti. (Of course, they conveniently omitted the Somalis living in northeast Kenya, a key British colony..)

The United States objected to the inclusion of the Ogaden in Somaliland because Ethiopia had entered the war as an independent state and as an ally of the United Nations powers. For the same reason, the U.S. acquiesced in the amalgamation of the Italian colony of Eritrea with Ethiopia, without consulting the people of Eritrea.

After the merger of the Italian and British Somalilands into one independent nation in 1960, the United States regarded Mogadishu as an important African country given its strategic location next to the Red Sea and Persian Gulf. Following the military takeover led by Mohammed Siad Barre in October 1969, and his adoption of "scientific socialism" as Somali state policy, Somalia became a pawn in the Cold War between Washington and

Moscow. The country's strategic location made the U.S.-Soviet competition all the more intense.

The essence of Siad Barre's foreign policy was Somali nationalism and irredentism, with a focus on uniting all Somali people under one flag. This policy constituted a major threat to Ethiopia's Ogaden region, where the vast majority of the inhabitants are Somalis. The policy also provided an opening for the Soviets, who had no inhibitions about pouring arms into Somalia in order to menace Ethiopia, America's main ally in the Horn Africa. As part of this process, the Soviets developed an air and naval facility in the port city of Berbera on Somalia's northwest coast.

[viii] I offer herewith a very cogent history and analysis of Wahhabism prepared by The Federal Research Division of the Library of Congress (http://lcweb2.loc.gov/frd/cs/satoc.html)

The political and cultural environment of contemporary Saudi Arabia has been influenced by a religious movement that began in central Arabia in the mid-eighteenth century. This movement, commonly known as the Wahhabi movement, grew out of the scholarship and preaching of Muhammad ibn Abd al Wahhab, a scholar of Islamic jurisprudence who had studied in Mesopotamia and the Hijaz before returning to his native Najd to preach his message of Islamic reform.

Muhammad ibn Abd al Wahhab was concerned with the way the people of Najd engaged in practices he considered polytheistic, such as praying to saints; making pilgrimages to tombs and special mosques; venerating trees, caves, and stones; and using votive and sacrificial offerings. He was also concerned by what he viewed as a laxity in adhering to Islamic law and in performing religious devotions, such as indifference to the plight of widows and orphans, adultery, lack of attention to obligatory prayers, and failure to allocate shares of inheritance fairly to women.

When Muhammad ibn Abd al Wahhab began to preach against

these breaches of Islamic laws, he characterized customary practices as *jahiliya*, the same term used to describe the ignorance of Arabians before the Prophet. Initially, his preaching encountered opposition, but he eventually came under the protection of a local chieftain named Muhammad ibn Saud, with whom he formed an alliance. The endurance of the Wahhabi movement's influence may be attributed to the close association between the founder of the movement and the politically powerful Al Saud in southern Najd (see The Saud Family and Wahhabi Islam, 1500-1818, ch. 1).

This association between the Al Saud and the Al ash Shaykh, as Muhammad ibn Abd al Wahhab and his descendants came to be known, effectively converted political loyalty into a religious obligation. According to Muhammad ibn Abd al Wahhab's teachings, a Muslim must present a *bayah*, or oath of allegiance, to a Muslim ruler during his lifetime to ensure his redemption after death. The ruler, conversely, is owed unquestioned allegiance from his people so long as he leads the community according to the laws of God. The whole purpose of the Muslim community is to become the living embodiment of God's laws, and it is the responsibility of the legitimate ruler to ensure that people know God's laws and live in conformity to them.

Muhammad ibn Saud turned his capital, Ad Diriyah, into a center for the study of religion under the guidance of Muhammad ibn Abd al Wahhab and sent missionaries to teach the reformed religion throughout the peninsula, the gulf, and into Syria and Mesopotamia. Together they began a jihad against the backsliding Muslims of the peninsula. Under the banner of religion and preaching the unity of God and obedience to the just Muslim ruler, the Al Saud by 1803 had expanded their dominion across the peninsula from Mecca to Bahrain, installing teachers, schools, and the apparatus of state power. So successful was the alliance between the Al ash Shaykh and the Al Saud that even after the Ottoman sultan had crushed Wahhabi political authority and had destroyed the Wahhabi capital of Ad Diriyah in 1818, the reformed religion remained firmly planted in the settled districts of southern Najd and of Jabal Shammar in the north. It would become the unifying ideology in the peninsula when the Al Saud rose to power again in the next century.

Central to Muhammad ibn Abd al Wahhab's message was the essential oneness of God (*tawhid*). The movement is therefore known by its adherents as *ad dawa lil tawhid* (the call to unity), and those who follow the call are known as *ahl at tawhid* (the people of unity) or *muwahhidun* (unitarians). The word *Wahhabi* was originally used derogatorily by opponents, but has today become commonplace and is even used by some Najdi scholars of the movement.

Muhammad ibn Abd al Wahhab's emphasis on the oneness of God was asserted in contradistinction to *shirk*, or polytheism, defined as the act of associating any person or object with powers that should be attributed only to God. He condemned specific acts that he viewed as leading to *shirk*, such as votive offerings, praying at saints' tombs and at graves, and any prayer ritual in which the supplicant appeals to a third party for intercession with God. Particularly objectionable were certain religious festivals, including celebrations of the Prophet's birthday, Shia mourning ceremonies, and Sufi mysticism. Consequently, the Wahhabis forbid grave markers or tombs in burial sites and the building of any shrines that could become a locus of *shirk*.

The extensive condemnation of *shirk* is seen in the movement's iconoclasm, which persisted into the twentieth century, most notably with the conquest of At Taif in the Hijaz. A century earlier, in 1802, Wahhabi fighters raided and damaged one of the most sacred Shia shrines, the tomb of Husayn, the son of Imam Ali and grandson of the Prophet, at Karbala in Iraq. In 1804 the Wahhabis destroyed tombs in the cemetery of the holy men in Medina, which was a locus for votive offerings and prayers to the saints.

Following the legal school of Ahmad ibn Hanbal, Wahhabi ulama accept the authority only of the Quran and sunna. The

Wahhabi ulama reject reinterpretation of Quran and sunna in regard to issues clearly settled by the early jurists. By rejecting the validity of reinterpretation, Wahhabi doctrine is at odds with the Muslim reformation movement of the late nineteenth and twentieth centuries. This movement seeks to reinterpret parts of the Quran and sunna to conform with standards set by the West, most notably standards relating to gender relations, family law, and participatory democracy. However, ample scope for reinterpretation remains for Wahhabi jurists in areas not decided by the early jurists. King Fahd ibn Abd al Aziz Al Saud has repeatedly called for scholars to engage in *ijtihad* to deal with new situations confronting the modernizing kingdom.

The Wahhabi movement in Najd was unique in two respects: first, the ulama of Najd interpreted the Quran and sunna very literally and often with a view toward reinforcing parochial Najdi practices; second, the political and religious leadership exercised its collective political will to enforce conformity in behavior. Muhammad ibn Abd al Wahhab asserted that there were three objectives for Islamic government and society; these objectives have been reaffirmed over the succeeding two centuries in missionary literature, sermons, *fatwa* (see Glossary) rulings, and in Wahhabi explications of religious doctrine. According to Muhammad ibn Abd al Wahhab the objectives were "to believe in Allah, enjoin good behavior, and forbid wrongdoing."

Under Al Saud rule, governments, especially during the Wahhabi revival in the 1920s, have shown their capacity and readiness to enforce compliance with Islamic laws and interpretations of Islamic values on themselves and others. The literal interpretations of what constitutes right behavior according to the Quran and hadith have given the Wahhabis the sobriquet of "Muslim Calvinists." To the Wahhabis, for example, performance of prayer that is punctual, ritually correct, and communally performed not only is urged but publicly required of men. Consumption of wine is forbidden to the believer because wine is literally forbidden in the Quran. Under the Wahhabis, however, the ban extended to all intoxicating drinks and other stimulants, including tobacco. Modest dress is prescribed for both men and women in accordance with the Quran, but the Wahhabis specify the type of clothing that should be worn, especially by women, and forbid the wearing of silk and gold, although the latter ban has been enforced only sporadically. Music and dancing have also been forbidden by the Wahhabis at times, as have loud laughter and demonstrative weeping, particularly at funerals.

The Wahhabi emphasis on conformity makes of external appearance and behavior a visible expression of inward faith. Therefore, whether one conforms in dress, in prayer, or in a host of other activities becomes a public statement of whether one is a true Muslim. Because adherence to the true faith is demonstrable in tangible ways, the Muslim community can visibly judge the quality of a person's faith by observing that person's actions. In this sense, public opinion becomes a regulator of individual behavior. Therefore, within the Wahhabi community, which is striving to be the collective embodiment of God's laws, it is the responsibility of each Muslim to look after the behavior of his neighbor and to admonish him if he goes astray.

To ensure that the community of the faithful will "enjoin what is right and forbid what is wrong," morals enforcers known as *mutawwiin* (literally, "those who volunteer or obey") have been integral to the Wahhabi movement since its inception. *Mutawwiin* have served as missionaries, as enforcers of public morals, and as "public ministers of the religion" who preach in the Friday mosque. Pursuing their duties in Jiddah in 1806, the *mutawwiin* were observed to be "constables for the punctuality of prayers . . . with an enormous staff in their hand, [who] were ordered to shout, to scold and to drag people by the shoulders to force them to take part in public prayers, five times a day." In addition to enforcing male attendance at public prayer, the *mutawwiin* also have been responsible for supervising the closing of shops at prayer time, for looking out for infractions of public morality such as playing music, smoking, drinking alcohol, having hair that is too long (men) or uncovered (women), and dressing immodestly.

In the first quarter of the century, promoting Wahhabism was an asset to Abd al Aziz in forging cohesion among the tribal peoples and districts of the peninsula. By reviving the notion of a community of believers, united by their submission to God, Wahhabism helped to forge a sense of common identity that was to supersede parochial loyalties. By abolishing the tribute paid by inferior tribes to militarily superior tribes, Abd al Aziz undercut traditional hierarchies of power and made devotion to Islam and to himself as the rightly guided Islamic ruler the glue that would hold his kingdom together. In the early 1990s, unity in Islam of the Muslim *umma* (community) under Al Saud leadership was the basis for the legitimacy of the Saudi state.

The promotion of Islam as embracing every aspect of life accounted in large measure for the success of Wahhabi ideology in inspiring the zealotry of the Ikhwan movement. Beginning in 1912, agricultural communities called *hujra* (collective pl.) were settled by beduin who came to believe that in settling on the land they were fulfilling the prerequisite for leading Muslim lives; they were making a *hijra*, "the journey from the land of unbelief to the land of belief." It is still unclear whether the Ikhwan settlements were initiated by Abd al Aziz or whether he co-opted the movement once it had begun, but the settlements became military cantonments in the service of Abd al Aziz's consolidation of power. Although the Ikhwan had very limited success in agriculture, they could rely on a variety of subsidies derived from raids under the aegis of Abd al Aziz and provisions disbursed directly from his storehouses in Riyadh.

As newly converted Wahhabi Muslims, the Ikhwan were fanatical in imposing their zealotry for correct behavior on others. They enforced rigid separation of the sexes in their villages, for example, and strict attention to prayers, and used violence in attempting to impose Wahhabi restrictions on others. Their fanaticism forged them into a formidable fighting force, and with Ikhwan assistance, Abd al Aziz extended the borders of his kingdom into the Eastern Province, Hail, and the Hijaz. Ultimately, the fanaticism of the Ikhwan undermined their usefulness, and they had to be reckoned with; the Ikhwan Rebellion (1928-30) marked their eclipse.

In the 1990s, Saudi leadership did not emphasize its identity as inheritor of the Wahhabi legacy as such, nor did the descendants of Muhammad ibn Abd al Wahhab, the Al ash Shaykh, continue to hold the highest posts in the religious bureaucracy. Wahhabi influence in Saudi Arabia, however, remained tangible in the physical conformity in dress, in public deportment, and in public prayer. Most significantly, the Wahhabi legacy was manifest in the social ethos that presumed government responsibility for the collective moral ordering of society, from the behavior of individuals, to institutions, to businesses, to the government itself.

[ix] Toby Craig Jones, writing in "Strategic Journal" of the Naval Postgraduate School, Monterrey, California, says: The *sahwa* or "awakening sheikhs," [is] a group of former dissidents who have come to support the regime—at least for now. Of particular interest are two of the *sahwa*'s most prominent and remarked upon members, Salman al-Awdah and Safar al-Hawali, both of whom enjoy considerable noteriety for being hard-line and for allegedly continuing to support al Qaeda. That they have provided inspiration for radicals in the past is unquestionable, although their present role in providing spiritual comfort to militants is less certain.

[x] The U.S. Department of Defense has estimated the cost of the Gulf War at $61 billion; however, other sources say that number could be as high as $71 billion. The operation was financed by more than $53 billion pledged by countries around the world, most of which came from Kuwait, Saudi Arabia and other Gulf States ($36 billion) and Germany and Japan ($16 billion). Some of the money pledged by countries such as Saudi Arabia was delivered in the form of in-kind services to troops, such as transportation and food.

[xi] According to Wikipedia, the emergence of a Saudi state began in central Arabia in 1744, however the region which the country stands in today has an ancient history. Regional ruler, Muhammad bin Saud, joined forces with a cleric, Muhammad ibn Abd-al-Wahhab, to create a new political entity. This alliance formed in the 18th Century remains the basis of Saudi Arabian dynastic rule today. Over the next 150 years, the fortunes of the Saud family rose and fell several times as Saudi rulers contended with Egypt, the Ottoman Empire, and other Arabian families for control on the peninsula. The Saudi state was founded by the late King Abdul Aziz Al-Saud (known internationally as *Abdul Aziz bin Saud*).

In 1902 at the age of only 22, Abdul Aziz Ibn Saud re-captured Riyadh, the Al-Saud dynasty's ancestral capital, from the rival Al Rashid, Al Qatif, the rest of Nejd, and Hejaz between 1913 and 1926. On 8 January 1926 Abdul Aziz bin Saud became the King of Hejaz. On 29 January 1927 he took the title King of Nejd (his previous Nejdi title was Sultan). By the Treaty of Jeddah signed on 20 May 1927, the United Kingdom recognized the independence of Abdul Aziz's realm, then known as the Kingdom of Nejd and Hejaz. In 1932 the principle regions of Al-Hasa, Qatif, Nejd and Hejaz were unified to form the Kingdom of Saudi Arabia.

Abdul Aziz's military and political successes were not mirrored economically until vast reserves of oil 1938 in 1939, began in earnest in 1946 and by 1949 production was in full swing. Oil has provided Saudi Arabia with economic prosperity and a great deal of leverage in the international community.
Internationally Abdul Aziz initially chose to follow an isolationist policy. He refused to allow Saudi Arabia to join the League of Nations, and he chose to leave his kingdom on only three occasions from 1916 until his death in 1953. One of which was the meeting with President Roosevelt pictured above. Eventually however Abdul Aziz acceded to the realities of world politics and in 1945 Saudi Arabia became a founding member of the e and joined the United Nations.

Prior to his death in 1953 Abdul Aziz, aware of the difficulties facing other regional absolute rulers reliant on extended family networks, attempted to regulate the succession. He took steps to provide that his eldest living son, Saud, would become king but that he would be required to work closely with his more financially and diplomatically astute brother, Faisal.
e

Intra-family rivalry was one of the factors that led to the assassination of Faisal by his nephew, Prince Faisal bin Musa'id, in 1975. King Khalid succeeded him until 1982 and then by e. When Fahd died in 2005, his half-brother Abdullah ascended to the throne.

[xii] According to the CIA Factbook, Saudi Arabia is the birthplace of Islam and home to Islam's two holiest shrines in Mecca and Medina. The king's official title is the Custodian of the Two Holy Mosques. The modern Saudi state was founded in 1932 by ABD AL-AZIZ bin Abd al-Rahman AL SAUD (Ibn Saud) after a 30-year campaign to unify most of the Arabian Peninsula. A male descendent of Ibn Saud, his son ABDALLAH bin Abd al-Aziz, rules the country today as required by the country's 1992 Basic Law. Following Iraq's invasion of Kuwait in 1990, Saudi Arabia accepted the Kuwaiti royal family and 400,000 refugees while allowing Western and Arab troops to deploy on its soil for the liberation of Kuwait the following year.

The continuing presence of foreign troops on Saudi soil after the liberation of Kuwait became a source of tension between the royal family and the public until all operational US troops left the country in 2003. Major terrorist attacks in May and November 2003 spurred a strong on-going campaign against domestic terrorism and extremism. King ABDALLAH has continued the cautious reform program begun when he was crown prince. To promote increased political participation, the government held elections nationwide from February through April 2005 for half the members of 179 municipal councils.

E

Saudi Arabia has an oil-based economy with strong government controls over major economic activities. It possesses 25% of the world's proven petroleum reserves, ranks as the largest exporter of petroleum, and plays a leading role in OPEC. The petroleum sector accounts for roughly 75% of budget revenues, 45% of GDP, and 90% of export earnings. About 40% of GDP comes from the private sector. Roughly 5.5 million foreign workers play an important role in the Saudi economy, particularly in the oil and service sectors. The government is encouraging private sector growth to lessen the kingdom's dependence on oil and to increase employment opportunities for the swelling Saudi population. The government is promoting private sector and foreign participation in the power generation, telecom, natural gas, and petrochemical industries. As part of its effort to attract foreign investment and diversify the economy, Saudi Arabia acceded to the WTO in December 2005 after many years of negotiations. With high oil revenues enabling the government to post large budget surpluses, Riyadh has substantially boosted spending on job training and education, infrastructure development, and government salaries. The government has announced plans to establish six "economic cities" in different regions of the country to promote development and diversification.

[xiii] According to a report prepared by the United Nations Security Council, for the last quarter of a century, Afghanistan has been embroiled in conflict. The Soviet invasion of Afghanistan in 1979 was followed by a decade of clashes between Soviet troops and Afghan fighters, the mujahedin. After the withdrawal of the Soviet army in 1988, and the collapse of the Soviet Union in 1991, factional fighting among the mujahedin forces continued until 1996, when the capital, Kabul, was taken by the Taliban. The Taliban never completely controlled Afghan territory, and continued to clash with mujahedin factions in the north

of the country. The US-led invasion following the attacks in the US on 11 September 2001 toppled the Taliban, but US and NATO troops have yet to bring peace to the whole country. Afghanistan has made some strides towards stability, but is still considered to be a fragile state.

Afghanistan, a country of multiple ethnic communities—Pashtuns in the south and east, Tajiks and Uzbeks in the north, Hazaras in the central regions—joined the United Nations in 1946, as one of its earliest members. The country benefited from a range of bilateral and multilateral development initiatives between the 1950s and the 1970s, but by the late 1970s Afghanistan was a major front in the Cold War. After three coups in the 1970s that toppled a monarchy and two communist governments, the Soviet Union invaded Afghanistan. In December 1979, Soviet forces deposed President Hafizullah Amin, who had risen to power after leading a revolt against communist President Nur Mohammed Taraki.

After the Soviet invasion, Islamic groups and ethnic forces began to clash with the Afghan communist leaders and the Soviets, whose presence reached more than 100,000 troops. By 1980 the opposition forces, known as the mujahedin, were fighting Soviet forces with arms and money supplied by the United States, Pakistan, China, Iran and Saudi Arabia, all countries that either opposed Soviet rule or had wanted to stem the flow of over three million refugees out of Afghanistan. The mujahedin were joined by thousands of Muslim radicals from the Middle East and Africa, eager to fight the Soviet Union in the name of Islam. Among them was Usama bin Laden, who first came to Pakistan and Afghanistan in the early 1980s for a period, and built training facilities for foreign recruits.

During the Soviet occupation, and the ensuing war with the mujahedin, both sides of the conflict committed serious human rights abuses, attacking civilians, and destroying civilian infrastructure. The Afghan government working alongside the Soviet forces committed grievous state-sponsored acts of violence against its own people. Villages and refugee camps were bombed and shelled, landmines were used indiscriminately, and civilians were forcibly evacuated, arrested and imprisoned or killed. The indiscriminate attacks on civilians, especially in the countryside, and the repression in the cities eventually caused up to 5 million Afghans to flee Afghanistan for the relative safety of Iran and Pakistan by 1987-88. With up to 3 million refugees, Pakistan became the logistical base for the mujahedin resistance, and began to suffer direct attacks from Afghanistan.

In 1986 the Babrak Karmal government, installed by the Soviet forces, was replaced by one headed by Dr. Najibullah, a communist, who had been forced into exile for his political activities, but returned in 1979 after the Soviet invasion. Before becoming the president of Afghanistan in 1986, Najibullah had headed up the notorious and brutal secret police.

The war in Afghanistan placed a considerable strain on the Soviet Union, both economically and politically. In the second half of the 1980s, the Soviet Union became increasingly amenable to finding a solution which would allow its troop withdrawal in a face-saving manner. Negotiations to find such a solution took place in Geneva, facilitated by the UN. After almost a decade of brutal conflict, in April 1988 the Soviets agreed to a peace agreement, known as the Geneva Accords, and withdrew their troops. As part of the agreement, Afghanistan and Pakistan, who had been engaged in a low-level cross-border conflict, also signed an agreement on non-intervention. Significantly, the mujahedin were not a party to the Accords, and subsequently refused to accept its terms, leading to renewed conflict.

Following the withdrawal of the Soviet troops, the ethnic, clan, religious and personality differences among the mujahedin and other militias resurfaced, and the civil war continued. In 1992 mujahedin troops took Kabul forcing President Najibullah to take refuge in the UN compound, where he remained until his violent death four years later. The mujahedin factions installed Sebghatullah Mojadiddi as president, succeeded several months later by Burhannudin Rabbani.

The Taliban, a group of Islamic fundamentalists and the product of a network of religious schools in Pakistan (madrasas), which had been sources of recruitment for mujahedin during the war against the Soviet Union, became the main opposition to the Rabbani government in 1994. Mostly Pashtuns that were children of mujahedin soldiers who grew up in exile, the Taliban criticised the country's Uzbek and Tajik leaders for allowing corruption and called for stricter adherence to Islamic law. The Taliban favoured laws based on strict tribal code, its version of Islamic law, which included such punishments as stoning for adultery and amputation for burglary. The Taliban and its leader, Mullah Omar, with assistance from Pakistan, overthrew Rabbani, and took Kabul on 26 September 1996. Rabbani fled to the relative safety of the north. During the takeover, former president Najibullah was dragged from the UN compound and executed. Images of the execution and of the dead bodies of Najibullah and his brother hanging in central Kabul set the tone for the people of Kabul of what could be expected from the Taliban regime. Usama bin Laden, exiled from his native Saudi Arabia, returned to Afghanistan in 1996 after his refuge in Sudan was cut short by the Sudanese government, and developed a close relationship with Mullah Omar. He set up a base of operations in

Kandahar where he trained fighters to fight alongside the Taliban, and began setting up the extensive network of communications and financing between related groups and individuals, which was to become Al-Qaida.

During the period of Taliban control, from 1996 to 2001, fighting continued with separate groups and factions, particularly in the north of the country, which the Taliban never successfully controlled. Parts of the territory under the Taliban control, such as Kandahar, for example, were more peaceful than in the preceding years, in part because the Taliban directed most of their energies into the war effort and maintaining security. However, the human rights and humanitarian situation for Afghan people worsened considerably. Human rights abuses under the Taliban were horrific. They included indiscriminate bombing, the targeting of civilians, torture, restrictions on the freedom of association, expression, the rights of women and rampant religious intolerance. At the time, there was no applicable constitution and no national judicial system.

The Taliban imposed severe restrictions on the population, particularly women. The restrictions required that women be fully veiled, forbid them most education and employment and imposed strict limitations on their access to public services, including health care. The Taliban have also required men to grow full, untrimmed beards, cut their hair short and attend mosque. They forbid any social mingling or communication among men and women outside the family.

The opposition within the country was led by the Northern Alliance, a coalition of different groups based in the north-eastern part of the country. The coalition of separate groups together called themselves the United National Islamic Front for the Salvation of Afghanistan, or the United Front. The United Front included Rabbani and consisted of four groups of ethnic minorities. They received support from both Russia and Iran.

During this period, international humanitarian aid and development assistance was curtailed due to the ongoing hostilities and the insecure environment; the humanitarian crisis worsened. Both the Taliban and certain United Front forces routinely engaged in human rights abuses, targeting civilians, women and ethnic minorities. There was widespread use of rape, forcible displacement and abduction of women as means of war.

The Northern Alliance was dealt a serious blow when their charismatic military leader, Ahmed Shah Massoud, was killed by two suicide assassins posing as journalists on 9 September 2001, in a final effort to undermine resistance to the Taliban. The killing of Massoud was followed by the attacks on the United States two days later, on 11 September 2001, when suicide bombers used hijacked airplanes to attack targets in New York and Washington DC The next day, the Security Council, in resolution 1368, "unequivocally condemned in the strongest terms the horrifying attacks." On 28 September 2001, acting under Chapter VII, the Council adopted resolution 1373, deciding that all states should prevent and suppress financing of terrorist attacks and called on all states to cooperate to prevent and suppress such attacks, and to deny safe haven to those who finance, plan or support terrorist acts. Attention had focused by this time on Usama bin Laden, and the protection offered to his organisation, Al-Qaida, by the Taliban in Afghanistan.

On 7 October 2001, after the Taliban refused American demands to extradite Usama bin Laden, a US-led international coalition attacked Afghanistan.

The operation was named Operation Enduring Freedom (OEF). Northern Alliance forces, with support from the coalition, took Kabul on 13 November 2001. By late November the Taliban were effectively removed from power. Coalition forces, most of them now under NATO command, have continued to fight pockets of Taliban and Al-Qaida resistance. During 2006, Taliban resistance grew in strength. As of November 2006 much of southern and eastern Afghanistan is relatively insecure.

[xiv] Between December 25th, 1979 and February 15th 1989 a total of 620,000 soldiers served with the forces in Afghanistan (though there were only 80,000-104,000 force at one time in Afghanistan). 525,000 in the Army, 90,000 with border troops and other KGB sub-units, 5,000 in independent formations of MVD Internal Troops and police. A further 21,000 personnel were with the Soviet troop contingent over the same period doing various white collar or manual jobs.

The total irrecoverable personnel losses of the Soviet Armed Forces, frontier and internal security troops came to 14,453. Soviet Army formations, units and HQ elements lost 13,833, KGB sub units lost 572, MVD formations lost 28 and other ministries and departments lost 20 men. During this period 417 servicemen were missing in action or taken prisoner; 119 of these were later freed, of whom 97 returned to the USSR and 22 went to other countries.

There were 469,685 sick and wounded, of whom 53,753 or 11.44%, were wounded, injured or sustained concussion and 415,932 (88.56%) fell sick. A high proportion of casualties were those who fell ill. This was because of local climatic and sanitary conditions, which were such that acute infections spread rapidly among the troops. There were 115,308 cases of infectious, 31,080 of typhoid fever and 140,665 of other diseases. Of the 11,654 who were discharged from the army after being wounded, maimed or contracting serious diseases, 92%, or 10,751 men were left disabled.

[xv] For excellent account of the role played by the British in the Arab-Turk conflicts, I would suggest "Lawrence of Arabia: Mirage of a Desert War," by Adrian Greaves (London: Weidenfeld & Nicolson, 2007).